PACKARD: the complete story

MICHAEL G. H. SCOTT

TAB BOOKS Inc.
Blue Ridge Summit, PA 17214

FIRST EDITION

SECOND PRINTING

Printed in the United States of America

Reproduction or publication of the content in any manner, without express permission of the publisher, is prohibited. No liability is assumed with respect to the use of the information herein.

Copyright © 1985 by TAB BOOKS Inc.

Library of Congress Cataloging in Publication Data

Scott, Michael G.H.
Packard: the complete story.

Includes index.
1. Packard Motor Car Company—History. 2. Packard automobile—History. 3. Automobile industry and trade—United States—History. I. Title.
HD9710.U54P38   1985   338.7′6292222   84-24009
ISBN 0-8306-2108-3 (pbk.)

Front cover: The Edward Benson Family's 1940 One Twenty (photograph by Susan Scott). Back cover: 1941 One Twenty Club Coupe owned by Steve Messenger.

Ask the Man Who Owns One

Contents

Dedication		ii
Acknowledgments		v
Introduction		vi
1	The Early Years	1
2	Refinements	7
3	Pioneers	10
4	Remembrances	19
5	New Designs	22
6	The Liberty	32
7	Quality and Competition	36
8	Lineage	39
9	Glimpsing the Past	42
10	Boom and Bad Years	69
11	Weathering the Depression	82
12	Enduring Identity	102
13	Changes	108
14	Dutch Darrin's Designs	121
15	The Super-8 Arrives	125
16	Wartime	142
17	The Clipper	146
18	Nothing New	154
19	A Seller's Market	158
20	Against All Odds	166
21	Conner Avenue	173
22	Gothics	177
23	Original Aura	180
24	Rebuilding Tips	182
25	Sources	186
	Epilogue	193
	Further Reading	195
	Index	199

to: Katharine
          Elizabeth
            Joan
            Ann
          Dorothy
    ladies and scholars all

Ask the Man Who Owns One

Acknowledgments

So many fine people aided me that a roll call seems more a slight than thanks. William H. Friedrich—founder in 1953 of the Packard Club and a thoroughly gracious gentleman who has owned 56 Packards through the years—generously loaned many of the rare photographs seen on these pages. Another longtime aficionado, Ross M. Lee, furnished most of the ads and many more photographs gathered over the years. John A. Conde, formerly with American Motors, supplied a number of factory photographs. My beautiful and talented sister, Susan K. Scott, worked tirelessly both behind the camera and in the darkroom to provide still more photographs. And thanks to John H. Jacobson for indomitable spirit.

My father, DeWitt H. Scott, with three books of his own out or in the works, gave invaluable support. My thanks go to Sheridan W. Hale, gentleman, renaissance man, unparalleled technician, and Tom Gates, recently retired history specialist for the Contra Costa Library System, working out of the Pleasant Hill, California central branch, for unflagging pursuit of accuracy.

Richard M. Langworth, editor of the *Packard Cormorant Magazine,* many excellent automotive books, and *Finest Hour,* quarterly of the International Churchill Society, gave encouragement and helped keep things in perspective.

Thanks also go to Steve Bolt of TAB BOOKS, and TAB's Dorothy Greenberg, who remind me that it is the high quality of people I've encountered that has been the real boon in this automotive dabbling.

Introduction

Packard is as much a twentieth-century icon as *The New York Times* masthead, the CBS eye, or the MGM lion. Packard is ingrained on our memory through historic occasion and movie alike. To say that Packard built the world's finest production automobile is not explanation enough.

Aside from a look at Packard from its beginnings through its end nearly 60 years later, I've also stopped to consider the eras through which Packard rolled. My aunt supplies us with recollections of the years before the first world war that are as fresh as last week.

Since Packard has often been called "the American Rolls-Royce," even as knowledgeable Britons themselves deferred to the Detroit product, I've compared and contrasted these two independents. And after decades of myth, there is a look at prewar performance.

To aid those refurbishing a Packard, I've included a list of suppliers of parts and services. There are also a few rebuilding and maintenance tips to help new owners enjoy the reliability and performance Packard intended.

Ask the Man Who Owns One

Ask the Man Who Owns One

1

The Early Years

The first of the Packard family came to the New World from England in 1638. James Ward Packard's grandfather sired nine children. Leaving Lordstown, Ohio during the 1849 Gold Rush, never to return to California, he lost contact with his family until four of his grown sons traced him to a mountain cabin in 1874. He died three years later, a judge in Kernville County, never finding gold.

One of his sons certainly found wealth. Warren Packard was a self-made man (if there is such a thing). He worked in an iron goods store, rising to ownership of what today could only be called a diversified chain. He owned iron and hardware stores, a rolling mill, and lumber interests, which furnished half the lumber for what was to become the Erie Railroad, as well as three million feet of planking for the "oil rush" Titusville and Pithole Plank Road. Packard bought property and vacationed at Lake Chautauqua, New York, long a cultural resort and still a setting of handsome summer homes and concerts. There he established the town of Lakewood, where James Ward Packard and his wife would retire.

James Ward Packard's family had been prominent in Warren, Ohio business for several generations. Warren is five miles north of Lordstown, the current site of a General Motors assembly plant. This nearly brings things to a full cycle because Packard's original electrical business remained in Warren (only the new automobile venture moved to Detroit) and still echoes from the past—stamped on the ignition wires of millions of new GM cars and trucks.

James Ward had an older brother, William Doud, who developed into as apt a businessman as James Ward did an engineer. James Ward graduated from Lehigh University, at age 20, with a mechanical engineering degree. One of his first five cars, his Model As, is currently on display in Lehigh's James Ward Packard Engineering Building. Packard had rigged his dorm so that electric motors operated from his bed opened and closed the door and windows. In 1928, Packard died at age 65. Unfortunately that was too early to see the Electromatic clutch in his 1941 namesake, a device the college student in him would no doubt have loved.

Packard took out many patents; his earliest was for a magnetic circuit and a light bulb later sold to Westinghouse. After an internship at a New York light bulb manufacturer (which later became part of Westinghouse), Packard returned to Warren where he and his brother William founded Packard Electric Company in 1890. Their company originally made light bulbs: "The Packard High Grade Incandescent Lamp; Lamps of all Candle Power and Voltage to Fit any Socket." They also made transformers and specially contracted electrical devices. The Packard Electric Company grew from 10 employees in 1890 to 13,000 today (joining General Motors in the early 1930s). For tax and business reasons, the Packard brothers created the New York and Ohio Company in 1891.

James Packard bought a 25-foot, 4-horsepower naptha (gasoline) motor launch in 1892, tinkering with it at the family's Lake Chautauqua property. In 1893, Packard Electric and General Electric fought over some of the Edison patents. While James was in court, William became interested in some foreign autos—including a Daimler and a Benz at the World's Columbian Exposition in Chicago.

A trip to Europe in 1895 led to the brothers ordering a De Dion-Bouton gasoline tricycle. It was a primitive and miserable thing, but Packard played with it. In 1896, he put an employee—who, in 1878, had masterminded a 7-ton, steam-powered road wagon—to work as a draftsman and patternmaker on his own idea of a gasoline vehicle. The idea didn't become reality until 1899; it was then that Packard's first of five Model As rolled onto the Warren streets.

Packard's first car was clearly not just an engineer's hobby. Even before he "had

Lehigh University President Martin Whitaker, left, and his successor, Dr. Harvey Newville, seated in the Packard Model A on permanent display at the Packard Engineering Building on the Lehigh campus. Photo John A. Conde Collection.

it out" with Alexander Winton after the $1,000 Winton Packard bought proved troublesome, Packard had sounded out a couple of Winton employees on their joining an automotive venture with him.

The Model A had an automatic spark advance, something not found on other cars—including Winton's—until years later, an "H" gearshift pattern (patented by Packard), a foot pedal to control engine speed, and a float-fed carburetor. Its single cylinder displaced 142.6 cubic inches, 5 1/2 × 6, with "automatic" or suction intake valve, and mechanical exhaust valve, churning out 9 honest horsepower at 800 rpm. The ignition was jump spark, lubrication was by drip oilers on the main piston and pin bearings, with a grease cup on the connecting rod. The cooling system held 4 gallons, with a recirculating pump and radiator.

The planetary transmission had four forward speeds and two reverse gears. Given the road conditions in those pro-horse, anti-horseless days, all the gears were needed. There were no idle gears once cruising along in high range. Not until the model C did Packard use a three-speed sliding gear transmission.

The frame was 2-inch channel iron, from which the wire, bicyclelike 34-×-3-inch wheels were suspended by two back-to-back transverse semielliptic leaf springs in front. In the back, as in more modern autos, there were two lengthwise, parallel, full-elliptic leaf springs. The car steered by a direct-action tiller—boats were still the steerable popular mode of travel—and the driver had two methods of halting progress short of running into hay bales: a hand lever acting on the transmission, and a modern foot pedal to the brake band on the center of the rear axle. The wheelbase was 71 1/2 inches (a sub-compact by today's standards).

The body was all wood and varnished black (there would be no production lacquer until 1926). Upholstery was flawlessly fitted quality leather. Standard equipment included a chime foot bell (which we should have today; it would make for a less frenetic rush hour), oiler, tools (which you had better learn to use), and a lamp. The only instrumentation was a double-throw ignition switch.

Even with 34-inch wheels, 9 horsepower at 800 rpm meant cruising at a realistic 20 miles an hour. An early press release claimed a top speed of 30 (which sounds reasonable), and a 35-mile range.

All of the above specifications apply to the 49 Model Bs produced in 1900. Exceptions included, at 76 inches, a 4 1/2-inch increase in wheelbase, a bulb horn on the steering tiller (the chime foot bell remained), and the customer's choice of varnish color. All five Model As and 49 Model Bs were bodied by a local buggymaker; Morgan and Williams, located five blocks from the corner of the New York and Ohio Company. The company had been named Packard & Weiss (after one of the pilfered Winton employees, George Weiss), but it was soon to grow into the Ohio Automobile Company.

The first Packards not only had higher quality than the Winton that had irked James Ward, they had a higher-quality price. At $1200, the base single-seat roadster was $200 more than the often horsedrawn Winton. A rear seat ran another $50, and a top over them both cost another $75.

Packard was in the car business. Packard, like Rolls-Royce, originally built electrical equipment. Ironically, all that's left of James Ward Packard's original business is the Packard Wire and Cable Division of General Motors.

It's telling that both Packard and Rolls-Royce—the two firms most typifying, respectively, engineering and craftsmanship during the first half of the twentieth century—should have their roots in electrical equipment. Discounting such recent developments as celluloid photo film (1887), the Kodak camera (1888), the photoelectric cell (1895), and the Curies' discovery of radium (1898), electrical equipment was "high tech." The very nature of electrical machinery demands close tolerances and precision workmanship; both would be found in the automobiles of James Packard and Henry Royce.

Although the 1890s produced changes in American life, the electric light and the telephone were among the new devices giving fewer Americans than we like to think a life otherwise unaltered since the rapid spread of railroads in the 1850s.

In these days when our automobile companies are run by bland, unimaginative back-slappers of the sort Brock Yates calls "the Detroit Mind" in his *The Decline and Fall of the American Automobile Industry*, it is important to remember that, in the 1890s, the horseless carriage attracted the sort of minds today drawn to solar, geothermal, breeder-reactor energy or to California's Silicon Valley. There is little in fossil-fueled, rolling-appliance building to attract today's best and brightest.

The automobile we've known for 80 years is dying. Most authorities predict that, at present consumption, the last known major petroleum reserves in Saudia Arabia will dry up around 2030. Either personal transport becomes powered by other than petroleum (renewable methane, for example) or we're faced with nuclear holocaust in the "cradle of civilization" in less than 50 years (about the length of time Packard reigned as the most prodigious maker of first-class automobiles in the world).

Packard is interesting not only because, during the years of inexpensive gasoline, it consistently produced the finest quality production cars in the world, but also because it is itself a microcosm of the rise and fall of the American auto industry.

Coal-stoked reciprocating steam was the power of the nineteenth century. During the early years of our century, automakers considered 15 to 20 miles per hour fast enough for any sensible motorist. Yet the New York Central's Empire State Express was clocked at 112.5 miles per hour in 1893. Also in 1893, the Duryea brothers became the first Americans to operate an American automobile on an American road. And in 1905, the Pennsylvania Flyer thundered over 3 miles of rails in 85 seconds (127 miles an hour).

A petroleum by-product, gasoline—only a few years earlier discarded in rivers

The 1905 Gray Wolf. Photo John A. Conde Collection.

A 1907 Model 30 landaulet. Photo John A. Conde Collection.

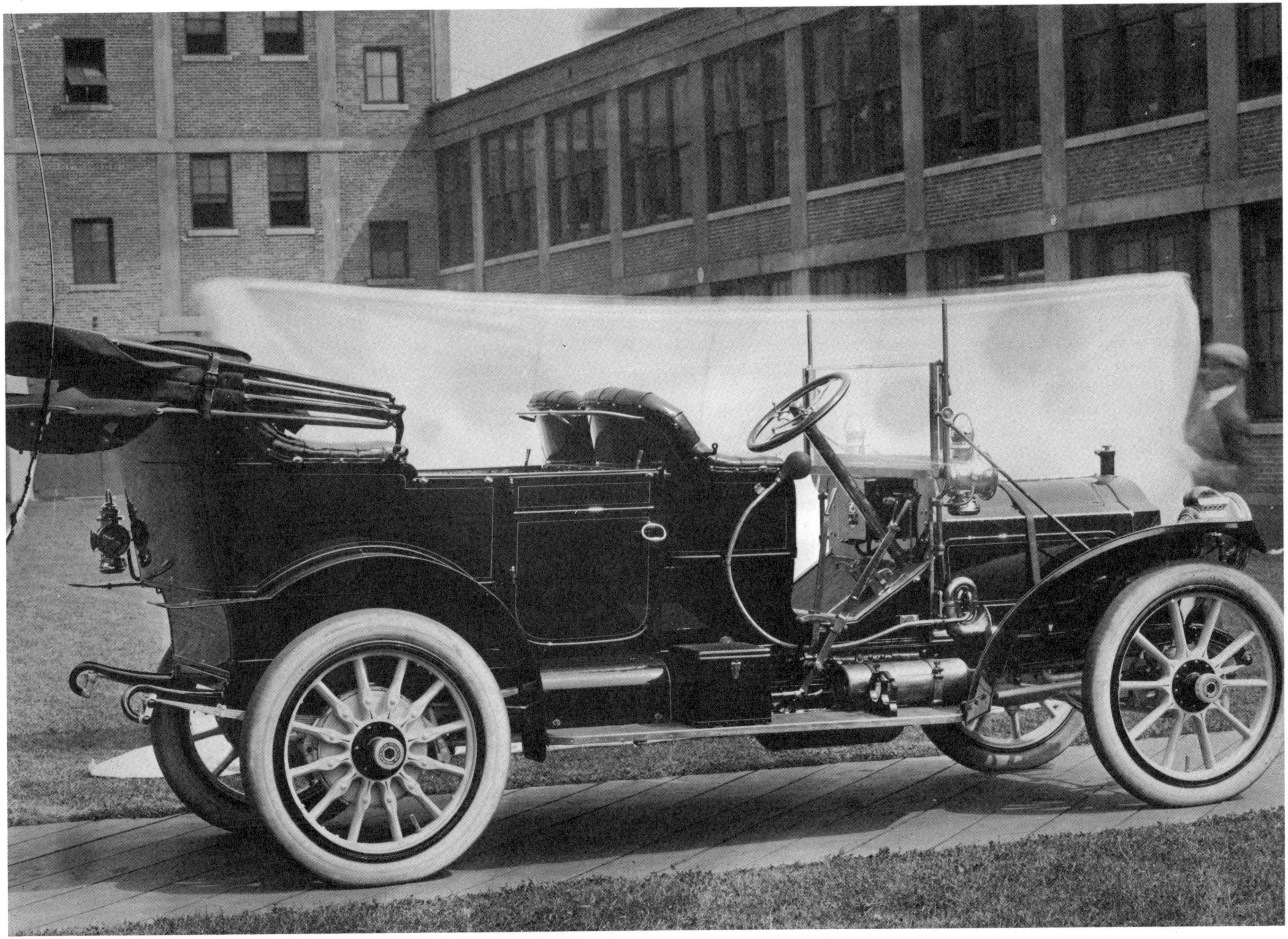

A 1909 Model 30, seven-passenger touring car. Photo John A. Conde Collection.

and streams—freed those affording a horseless carriage from railroad timetables and streets laden with disease-hosting horse manure. Bicycles had grown from a fad to a useful conveyance by the 1890s, but the staying power of the cyclist's leg muscles still measured a trip's length.

Early inventors and investors were naturally drawn to the idea of personal motorized transportation. At the turn of the century, 40 percent of all automobiles were quiet steam, 38 percent were noiseless electric, and only 22 percent were noxious internal combustion. Now that fossil-fueled internal combustion vehicles have run their course, and that the decades of first naturally inexpensive, then artificially inexpensive (inflationary price-controlled) gasoline are over, it's gladdening to see the other methods of powering personal transport drawing attention. Electric cars are still, unfortunately, burdened with range and speed limitations—as they were 80 years ago.

But steam cars do hold development promise. William Lear (Lear Jet and Gates Learjet) was working on steam cars before his death. Steam automobiles need no complex electrical system, can run on nearly any combustible, and—producing torque from rest—can smoothly and quickly accelerate without the assistance of complicated transmissions. And they're fast.

In 1906, the year after the Pennsylvania Flyer clocked 127 miles an hour, Fred Marriot matched the speed in a Stanley Steamer on Florida's Ormond Beach. The following year, due to a lack of aerodynamic knowledge, the car became airborne after hitting a bump in the sand. Marriot (miraculously unscathed) claimed 190 miles an hour on the speedometer.

Two years before the Stanley Steamer's official 127 mph, in 1904, on the same Ormond Beach, Packard engineer Charles Schmidt set an American record of 77.58 mph for the mile (only .4 seconds off the unlimited international record) in the Packard Gray Wolf. Not until 1910 would an internal combustion automobile—Barney Oldfield in a Benz—beat the steam car: 131.724 mph. Next year another Benz would raise the 1-mile record another 10 miles an hour (141.732), which would stand until 1919 when Ralph DePalma, driving the Packard "905" (for cubic inches), reached 149.875 mph.

As popular as steam cars had been, their smooth, fast, quiet going had been undone by the time necessary to get underway. Of course, when the electric starter appeared on gasoline automobiles, the resulting convenience killed steam's promise. Later models of Doble Steamers eliminated the early steamers' problems. The Doble had no pilot lights, no Bunsen-type main burners, no great thirst for water, no need for a dual kerosene-gasoline fuel system, and no long wait to build steam pressure.

Given the level of electro-motive potential against the flexibility and promise of the new gasoline engines, it's not surprising that James Packard pursued internal combustion. The same decision was being made by a number of pioneers. When we consider the fouled air, carcinogenic filth, and the inflation eight decades of gasoline automobiles have given us, we wish James Packard, Henry Royce, and the others had developed electric—if not steam—cars.

Some 20 years ago, an article in *Harper's* first brought to national attention a study showing that children living near highways and busy streets tested lower in reading and mathematical ability than those living in quieter locales. Steam and electric cars will solve this and other problems the gasoline automobile has brought us.

So whether we toy with a Model T Ford, or a gleaming example of the consistently finest production automobile in the world, we have much, very much about which to be humble.

2
Refinements

Ask the Man Who Owns One

Approaching a century of American production automobiles, it amuses us to think that another 3 horsepower qualified the 12-horse Model C as an automobile "for high speed," according to its makers. A Packard patent was obtained for the round copper cooling jacket encircling the Model C's cylinder, now displaying 183.8 cubic inches (6 × 6 1/2). As in the two earlier Packard models, the Model C's final drive ratio was a chain-driven 7:1. With the larger displacement, single-cylinder engine pumping out its 12 horsepower at a feverish 850 rpm, the Model C would do well over 30 miles an hour. James Packard streaked 136 miles in five hours in two Model Cs (a 27.5 mph, rutted and muddy-road average).

The first record of a Packard driver arrested for speeding was driving a Model C; the driver was cited for going 35 to 40! Countering claims that his Model C was more powerful than routinely required, Packard (or Ward Packard, as he often signed correspondence) claimed there was "a growing demand for such a machine from experts." The *Motor Vehicle Review of Cleveland* called it "the new racing machine."

Packard's automobiles only reflected the primitive, by French standards, American roads. The Warren, Ohio area was uncommonly hilly as well. No doubt the increased speed and power spurred many owners to venture nocturnal trips. The earlier single, self-generating gas solar light was replaced by a pair of Dietz oil auto lamps. The 12 30-inch-long, half-inch-diameter radiator tubes—placed under and forward of the floorboards—meant, in Packard's words, "(water) does not have to be renewed oftener than once a day."

Another periodic check, at 150 to 200 miles, was required of the engine bearing oil cups. The oil supply was cut when the engine was shut off; a valve then releasing pressure in the cylinder. The valve closed again when the engine was restarted. As long as the driver kept the oil tank filled, it was impossible to run the engine on dry bearings. In addition, there was no fear of oil flooding the engine. Variable displacement engines are nothing new. The Model C had an adjustment on the connecting rod so that it could be either shortened or lengthened for less or more compression. This was no doubt a great boon to motorists faced with not just a difficult time finding gasoline, but gas of reasonable quality and octane.

Having shown Alexander Winton that he knew how to build a proper automobile, Packard would now rival the best French efforts. This went beyond any post-De Dion-Bouton trauma. The French, with relatively sophisticated makes like Panhard et Levessor and Mors, were still the last word in automotive refinement.

I rode in the same displacement Model F once. The horseless carriage will always have deeper meaning because of the experience. You sit high, with your head at least 7 feet above the ground. Thanks to a large muffler the great explosions in the 183-cubic-inch cylinder (over two-and-a-half times the displacement of a four-cylinder Toyota Corolla, and the same number of cubic inches as the first Duesenberg straight-eight Indianapolis cars) seem no louder than a sneezing subterranean gopher.

At 15 miles an hour, you begin to see why speeds over 30 were daredevil feats. As the piston flies back from its power stroke, the car seems to lurch forward the slightest trace beyond its otherwise steady speed maintained by a tremendous flywheel that looks for all the world like a pilfered manhole cover. You sit high, surveying all you see, as the mechanism does its quiet best beneath the floorboards. It is an apt precursor to later velvet-smooth straight-eights and V-12s.

The machine seems almost a living thing as if iron, steel, copper, wood, and rubber can hold and call forth the spirits of the men who stamped and shaped those materials into a self-propelled creation in those enthusiastic and innocent days. The gopher sneezes and a nanosecond later you scoot ahead at perhaps 15 1/2 miles an hour, only to sneeze again as the speed falls back to 15. Under fair road conditions, these early one-lung Packards would get gasoline mileage in the 20s. The single-seat models were comfortable for two people, but four or five could travel if the owner ordered the two-seat surrey or roadster with rear-facing seat.

The only problem I recall was keeping an eye open for "low" branches overhanging the street.

Packard was encountering an interesting problem, and one that can be traced to a certain type of owner even to this day.

"Strange as it may seem," said James Ward Packard, "we have had more trouble with the carriages that found their way into the hands of mechanical men—and there were several that did—than those belonging to men who made no pretense of knowing anything about mechanical matters. The trouble with the mechanical men is that they know too much—or think they do. They are not content to follow the rules that we laid down for the operation of the carriages with implicit confidence, while the more ignorant, mechanically, are. The result has been that most of the repairs and changes that we have been obliged to make were in carriages that were owned by mechanical men. Having been through this experience, we have much more confidence in the ability of the average citizen to run a motor vehicle without trouble than we had at first. We are now preparing to go ahead with the manufacture of our carriages on a larger scale and by next spring will be able to supply a considerable demand."

Actually, Packard's observations do not seem strange today. I've often thought that complex mechanisms in the hands of intelligent neophytes content to trust the manufacturer's engineering pride, follow the suggested maintenance schedule, and drive sensibly, provide as much, if not far better performance than those owned by compulsive tinkerers and adjusters. But then James Ward Packard was the sort of customer he lamented.

Packard sold an increasing number of his French-quality automobiles to "mechanical men" and "average citizens" (if anyone with $1500 to $2000 to spend on a horseless carriage of any quality was considered average in those days). There were 81 Model Cs sold in 1901.

Besides the now universal "H" shift pattern and his many other innovations, Packard's Model C debuted one of automobilia's most famous—if not *the* most famous—development, which he immediately patented: the steering wheel. The nautical aspect of automobiles in the tiller era cannot be overemphasized. Reports in period papers called speeding horselesses "flying road cruisers" and the like. The Packard Model C's steering wheel actually "swung away" long before Ford Thunderbirds of the 1960s. William Rockefeller, brother of John D. Rockefeller, bought two Model Cs. One was a surrey, and it was no doubt appreciated because of the ease of entry and egress the moveable steering column allowed.

Packard defended his steering wheel, "that foreign thing," as visitors at the first New York Automobile Show in Madison Square Garden called it. "In machines that are designed to travel in excess of 20 miles an hour, a steering wheel was necessary said Packard, "although levers are perfectly satisfactory below this speed."

Because Packard automobiles were certainly now among the most refined and advanced in the world—a remarkable bit of progress for a company so young—it is not surprising that a Bostonian named Honeywell, whose name would later become associated with high tech, should also buy a Model C right off the automobile show's floor.

Packard made a logical decision by attending that first New York show in 1900. Automobiles were still truly the playthings of the rich. At this time, autos were still too new and unproven to attract a general market even if Packard, or any other early maker, had beaten Ransom E. Olds and Henry Ford to mass production and pricing.

Because quality still meant high cost, Packard followed the sun to the nation's hot bed of wealth—New York. Doctors and enthusiasts aside, most automobiles were still being bought by the cliquish wealthy. Once someone in the circle was drawing attention with his new horseless, all his friends had to have one as well. Los Angeles was still little more than a desert town, Hollywood wouldn't blossom for over another two decades, and Chicago was seen as a booming slaughterhouse whose highest social set was little more than new-moneyed rustics.

So off to New York where the socially prominent would fall in love with the idea of rolling along country lanes on their Long Island estates "as fast as a bird can fly" in their smart new Packards adorned with delicate French curves. Unlike the French offerings, which were designed for long-established paved boulevards, the Packard Model Bs and Cs, with their higher ground clearance and numerous ball joints, were designed for "as fast as a bird can fly" on the crude American roads that could turn from merely treacherous to mayhem in a few moment's notice.

The first accident recorded involving a Packard was with a Model B; its tiller whipped back when one of the front wheels slammed into a particularly bad rut. The driver and passenger were only shaken and bruised, and the Model B was returned to the factory for repair. Early customers, still word-of-mouth in those days, would be told the advantages of the new (to Americans) steering wheel.

As time passed and other automobiles approached the refinement of a handful of French and American makes, increasing numbers of wealthy folk abandoned their landaus, barouches, broughams, and gigs for one of the new automobiles. Packard was already conscious of design. He insisted that his product not appear "as a carriage in want of a horse."

After September, 1900, Packards could be bought somewhere else besides the Ohio Automobile Company factory. George Blackmore, a Painesville men's haberdasher who had sold the trendy high-wheeled bicycles since the 1880s, became Packard's first agent. Only two months before, Packard's automobiles had been offered only from "Packard-Weiss" of the New York and Ohio Company.

And in October of the following year, there was the first appearance of that best and simplest slogan in a *Motor Age* advertisement:

PACKARDS

Are built for combined reliability and speed over any roads. Ask the man who owns one. Our machines can and do prove their efficiency in every detail. Descriptive catalog free.

We shall exhibit at the New York show.
OHIO AUTOMOBILE Co.
Warren, Ohio

That slogan has never been surpassed, for all the brainstorming and millions squandered on Madison Avenue and media and market surveys ever since. The exact occurrence and date of this resounding utterance is still conjecture, though it was certainly James Ward Packard's busy reply for information of some sort. We can only wish more automakers, and manufacturers in general, today spent most of their time—as Packard did in those early years—on improving and refining a product, not glibness.

Packard's partner, former Winton associate George Weiss, handled the booth at the first New York Automobile Show, in 1900, and gave reporters and would-be customers a simple, straight spiel. No doubt the approach was refreshing in those days of ridiculous and grandiose claims from makers whose products were hard pressed to start, let alone run, for any length of time. Reading Weiss' appeal, and recalling the great slogan that was to come a year later, it's not difficult to see why these men were partners:

"We have no million-dollar factory" said Weiss, "but we are turning out thoroughly practical road vehicles for delivery, which is more than many who are making bigger claims are doing. Our desire in bringing out a gasoline motor vehicle has not been an endeavor to make anything radically new or especially light and cheap, but has had in mind the attainment of perfect service under ordinary American roads." Presumably Weiss meant *over* ordinary roads.

The Packard Models B (some fitted with steering wheels) and C made such an impression at the New York show that several days later the Ohio Automobile Company opened its eastern headquarters on what was already becoming New York's auto row—lower Broadway. From there, other enthusiasts fell for the simple Packard design, and the beginning of one of the most successful and cohesive automotive dealer networks of the twentieth century was underway.

The first production Model C was sold to another early visionary—Yonkers' Charles C. Otis—whose elevators would soon remove another stumbling block to the new tall buildings structural steel was making possible. Like other cities throughout the world, New York would soon exhibit tremendous growth. Packard, soon to become the icon of our automotive industry, grew with them.

Ask the Man Who Owns One

3
Pioneers

In 1895, no more than four automobiles making successful runs were built in the entire nation. By 1899, when the five Packard Model As appeared, over 2500 cars were built. In 1902, about 9000 automobiles were produced in America. Between 1895 and the close of 1902, 128 automobile concerns built 25,629 cars, while 107 of these pioneer firms began during 1900, 1901, and 1902.

Not only was the auto row concept already established in Manhattan, but throughout the nation there were "trade ins." Horses, wagons, carriages, and even harness and saddle were taken in trade. A fellow who sold cars beginning in 1924 told me that it was not, even at that late date, uncommon to see Dobbin and his accounterments traded in for both new and used cars in various price ranges.

Competition was especially tough during the opening years of our century as the many automakers were competing for a limited, if growing, crop of customers. Pioneer automakers were struggling, for the most part, without the aid of money men because most bankers and investors were still following the lead of tycoons like Harriman, Vanderbilt, and Jim Hill. They put their dollars into railroads and other proven, if not formerly spurious, ventures.

For those who learned from history—and specifically the lessons of the early plank roads, railroads, and canals—the budding automakers would prove to be a terrific investment; assuming they chose a sound company. The investors who watched, and then aided, the Ohio Automobile Company did very well.

The son of a wealthy investor in the Michigan Central and the Chicago, Burlington & Quincy railroads was a three-fold visionary. Henry Bourne Joy saw promise in the inevitable growth of the infant automobile industry, and the sound, even-keeled Packard, as well as the promise of Detroit—which served a ranging supply of both raw materials and finished components by land, river, and lake.

Not only was Detroit served by railroads, water, and nearby abundant hardwood forests, but the Midwest in general was already the center of carriage and wagon manufacture. Many early automakers had already settled in Detroit. Ransom E. Olds had mass produced thousands of his one-cylinder, curved-dashed Oldsmobile and offered it for under half the price of the one-lung Packard. Henry M. Leland turned the remnants of Henry Ford's Detroit Automobile company into Cadillac, even as Ford began his namesake company. William Crapo Durant later combined Olds, Cadillac, David Dunbar Buick's company and that of Louis Chevrolet into General Motors. Henry Joy thought a rapidly expanding Packard should also be in Detroit.

Henry Joy bought several Packards and was, like most owners, impressed. Before October, 1902, when Joy's name first appeared in Packard minutes and the firm's name was changed from the Ohio Automobile Company to the Packard Motor Car Company, this enthusiastic and heaviest investor had been involved with the business. Joy even urged James Packard to hire certain engineers.

The 66.4-acre former cow pasture Henry Joy paid $19,434 for in 1903 would be served by the Michigan Central. The investors Joy brought to Packard agreed that James Packard's tack of building both the simplest and best automobiles possible would not be changed. Of course, such cars would be built in a modern plant rather than one of the makeshift and hazardous affairs abounding.

The new Packard plant would be well-ventilated and feature much skylighting. The first eight buildings architect Albert Kahn erected were conventional wood-beam and brick mills. But this construction didn't allow the expanse of open floor space needed for efficient automobile production. In 1905, Albert Kahn enlisted his brother, Julius, who had perfected a new form of construction using concrete reinforced with steel rods. The next Packard building built by the Kahns changed the face of in-

A 1906 Model 24 (or S) touring car with victoria top. Photo John A. Conde Collection.

dustrial architecture. Among early automakers, Hudson, Chalmers, Ford, the Dodge Brothers, and GM would also use this form of construction. And so there was another Packard first; it was the first industrial building made of reinforced concrete in the nation.

The Packard plant just outside Detroit (the young city had not yet expanded its boundaries to include it) was the most modern automobile factory in the world. A ventilating system changed the air every half hour. Compared with the usual crowded, poorly lit, and stuffy firetraps most automobile factories were, the brightly painted, clean, and well-lighted Packard plant contributed to its products' quality by providing the workers with safe and pleasant surroundings.

Albert Kahn went on to serve as Ford's architect for over 30 years. His efforts included the Highland Park plant on Woodward Avenue where the Model T was mass produced in 1913. In Hamtramck, Kahn designed the Dodge Brothers factory, "Dodge Main," that was dismantled in the early 1980s to make way for a new Cadillac plant.

For nearly 20 years, Kahn was also Chrysler's architect. Kahn designed 150 plants for General Motors, including the then-largest office structure in the world—the $20 million General Motors Building in 1919-20. The Fisher Building is another of Albert Kahn's creations. In 1942, when Kahn died at 73, he was still designing buildings for Packard, and $2 billion worth of his structures covered the world's industrial landscapes.

While the new Detroit plant was going up, new models were introduced in Warren, Ohio. The Model F was much the same as the highly successful Model C. It used the C's engine, but larger fenders and a longer 84-inch wheelbase were the major changes. The Model F cost $2250 as a two-seat roadster, without the detachable rear tonneau. With the detachable rear tonneau, it was a five-seater priced at $2500. This was the first Packard to be advertised in the *Saturday Evening Post* (April 25, 1903), starting a Packard tradition, continued through 1956. The ad pictured the Model K rear-entrance tonneau and beneath it the words:

PACKARD The machine ahead. It is one of the easy things in this business to make up a car with an attractive exterior. The painter can do wonderful things with his brush. It is easier still to make a host of glittering promises about what the car will do.

Your first task should be to find out what its past record is and what it is doing every day.

We don't expect you to believe us when we tell you that, with the same care and attention, the Packard Motor Car will give you better satisfaction than any other automobile made, but we do want you to "ASK THE MAN WHO OWNS ONE" because *he knows* and you will believe *him*.

Seats five people.   Price $2500.00

Letter designations were often set aside for models in the works or models expected to be introduced. There never was a Model D, and the pair of Model Es were experimental factory cars.

Although the Model F wasn't built on an assembly line, each stage of production took place in that particular shop.

The Model G was the longest-wheelbase Packard yet at 91 inches. Like the Model F, the Model G was available with a detachable tonneau. A surrey version offered a fixed rear seat. The Model G rode on the largest tires as well (4 1/2 × 36 inches). The engine was also the largest Packard motor yet, and in another break with the past it was a horizontally opposed two-cylinder engine with 24 horsepower (although still placed under the body). The crankshaft was parallel with the axles, and the cylinders were to the left of the center line of the car with the flywheel to the right. Each cylinder had its own carburetor. Ignition was by jump spark, with two coils and a battery. Lubrication was by a mechanical oil pump, cooling by a rotary pump sending 8 gallons of water through a 24-tube radiator.

Although the fenders were of aluminum, the eight-passenger rear entrance tonneau weighed 3950 pounds. That made it by far the heaviest Packard yet. Scorned as a "leviathan" by one of the motoring magazines, a Model G nevertheless won one of two President's Cups for the highest number of points possible for the Automobile Club of America's New York to Boston Reliability Trial. A Packard Model F won the other cup, and the gold medal.

The Model K was the first four-cylinder Packard, with the engine now under the hood. This French practice was a departure from James Packard's single-cylinder preference. Yet as early as 1903, multicylinders were used. The Model K also emulated French practice with its sloping Renault-like hood. At $7500, the Packard Model K was about the most expensive car in the country. It was also complicated and unreliable. The Model K was to cause much unhappiness. Truman Newberry, Henry Joy's brother-in-law and one of the original investors and board members, wrote a strong letter to James Packard after Newberry experienced trouble with his Model K.

James Ward Packard withdrew from the Packard Motor Car Company because of the letter; he may have wanted out anyway. Packard was an engineer and Joy, Newberry, and company were primarily money men (if enamored of quality). The automobile industry was moving quickly now, and a certain callousness would be necessary to stay on top. James and William Doud had supported the move to a larger plant in an industrial city, but they never had plans to move with it. The Packard Electric Company was flourishing as the producer of waterproof wiring for the entire automotive industry, and the New York & Ohio Company was selling all the light bulbs it could produce. William Doud was—at the time of the move by the automobile business to Detroit—negotiating the sale of the New York & Ohio Company to the National Electric Lamp Company (which was to become part of General Electric). The Packard brothers had enough to concern them in Warren.

In 1902, Charles Schmidt was one of the engineers Henry Joy recommended

A 1908 Model 30 touring car on the Glidden Tour of that year. Photo John A. Conde Collection.

A 1910 Model 18 limousine. Photo John A. Conde Collection.

to James Packard. A Frenchman with over eight years design experience in his native country, Schmidt served the Mors works both as plant superintendent and part-time racing driver. Schmidt didn't share James Packard's distaste for cylinders plural; the current Mors was an opposed twin.

The first successful four-cylinder Packard, the Model L, was Schmidt's design and its lines reflected the Mors; especially the front end. The tombstone radiator and matching hood shape that was to say Packard to millions the world over, even until the company's end, were first seen on the Model L. Although the first Model L was built in Warren, the model is generally called the first Detroit Packard.

The Model L was (in basic mechanics) much the same as the famous Packard Gray Wolf, itself based on one of the unsuccessful Model Ks and called the K Special racing car. The K Special, or Gray Wolf, was seen as needed publicity and it would help revive spirits dampened by the troublesome K. Multicylinder luxury cars—both foreign and domestic—were giving Packard's single-cylinder Model F, though an excellent car, a good run in the marketplace.

The Model L would remedy all this. Charles Schmidt's Gray Wolf campaign had been enormously successful. The 1310-pound, aluminum-bodied racing car, with its full belly pan and copper cooling tubes running nearly the length of its 92-inch wheelbase had terrorized (with its mere 25 horsepower), all the day's racing juggernauts. The 90-hp Fiats, 60-hp and 90-hp Mercedes, 75-hp Simplexes, 90-hp Panhards, 60-hp Decauvilles, and 40-hp Darracqs and Wintons would trail the light and nimble Gray Wolf. The Gray Wolf garnered considerable publicity by setting national and international records.

The one-cylinder Model F had given a good account of itself. A Vermont doctor

A 1911 Model 30 phaeton. Photo John A. Conde Collection.

A 1912 Model 48 limousine. Photo John A. Conde Collection.

and his mechanic had driven a used two-cyclinder Winton from San Francisco to New York in 63 days. That the product of James Packard's old antagonist had first crossed the continent might have spurred the company to send Warren employee Tom Fetch on a similar trek. Fetch managed to cross the country in only 53 days. In doing so, he racked up a great deal of publicity. Fetch's "Old Pacific" suffered a broken front spring in Colorado, in Iowa Fetch had to grind the exhaust valve, and in Lyon, New York, the drive chain broke. Repairs were made on the road, and Old Pacific reached New York with one of its original tires. That was quite a feat considering the mere 150 miles of paved roads in the entire nation at the turn of the century.

No matter how much publicity the Gray Wolf and Old Pacific brought, the company needed a successful four-cylinder model in the marketplace. It had one in the Model L, which weighed only 1900 pounds, and was halfway between the lightweight Gray Wolf and the production Model K. The three-speed sliding gear transmission gave speeds of 10, 25, and over 40 mph. High gear was supposedly good from 4 to over 40 miles an hour. At $3000, the Model L was three times the cost of a Cadillac, but half the price of a Peerless. The engine was an L-head four—3 7/8 × 5 1/8 inches bore × stroke, 241 cubic inches, and 22 horsepower at 900 rpm—with the crankshaft turning on three main bearings. Ignition was by jump spark, battery, and coil. A float-fed carburetor, force-fed lubrication system, and 6-gallon cooling system served the dependable power plant. The tonneau body style came on a 94-inch wheelbase.

On August 6th to 8th, at the Grosse Point track, Charles Schmidt and two other

Packard employees took turns at the wheel of a stripped-down Model L. The car ran 1000 miles without a single motor stop at a sustained speed of over 33 1/2 miles an hour. "Another proof of Packard perfection" heralded period ads.

The Model L did well for Packard in 1904, and so did the Model N the following year. The Model N offered a foot-longer wheelbase, 28 horsepower at 900 rpm (4 1/16 × 5 1/8, 265.7 cubic inches), and entrance to the rear seat by doors in the side of the body. That the body could now be ordered pinstriped was an industry first pioneered on the Model L.

A new and larger model, the S or 24 (for horsepower), was introduced in September of 1905. The Packard 24 showed the rapid evolution of the automobile. Front springs were now in the lengthwise position (semielliptics extending well past the frame). The 24 was capable of a mile a minute off the showroom floor. Such a speed previously was reserved only for racing cars like the Gray Wolf.

While the 24 horsepower figure was reached at a mere 650 rpm, there were independent reports of 40-50 hp at higher speeds. Seven body styles were offered on the 24's 119-inch wheelbase. These included a touring car, a limousine, and a landaulette. A runabout was offered on a shorter 108-inch chassis.

With a 37-degree rake of its steering column, the engine and radiator sat behind the front axle, and with its long fenders the 24 runabout anticipated the later "speed" models from Mercer and Simplex. The 24 engine displaced 350 cubic inches (a T-head four with bore × stroke of 4 1/2 × 5 1/2). The price range was $4000 to $5225.

Determined ever since the troublesome Model K not to release a new model "before its time," Packard was to continue its policy of rigorously testing each new car. Between engineering and sales, the Packard Thirty prototype built over the winter of 1905-06 logged over 50,000 miles. The Model "T" designation had been given to the Packard truck of 1905, and the Model U designation was never used in Packard Thirty advertising.

As was popular in the industry, the name designated horsepower, though it actually developed 55-60 brake horsepower from its 432 cubic inches (bore × stroke 5 × 5 1/2) at 650 rpm. A T-head four propelled touring cars, limousines, and landaulettes on a 122-inch wheelbase (or a runabout on a 108-inch wheelbase). Prices ranged from $4200 to $5600.

The Packard Thirty was immensely popular, and responsible for Packard's inclusion with the other two of the "Three Ps": Packard, Peerless, and Pierce-Arrow. A Packard Thirty served as patrol car on the new Glidden Tour, each day covering over twice the mileage of the contestants, and while carrying from five to eight passengers.

The Packard Thirty was offered for five years. Developments such as shock absorbers and the dry plate clutch (in place of expanding flywheel clutch) were added over the model run, as were new body styles called the phaeton, coupe, and brougham.

In 1908, Jacob Murdoch, a businessman who wintered in Pasadena, California, became the first motorist to drive his family across the continent. With daughters ages 14 and 18, a 10-year-old son, and 1200 pounds of supplies, Murdoch reached New York in 25 days. Packard printed a 32-page illustrated booklet, *A Family Tour from Ocean to Ocean,* to publicize what was to become an annual event for the Murdoch family.

In 1907, Packard sales trailed only those of Ford, Buick, Reo, Maxwell, Rambler, Cadillac, and Franklin; all of these were far lower in price.

In the summer of 1908, the "18" was introduced. Smaller and lighter than the Thirty, although otherwise of identical design construction, the 18 was meant for city and suburban driving. With a wheelbase of 112 inches (runabout 102 inches), body styles were the same as offered on the longer and heavier 30. Prices ranged from $3200 for the short-wheelbased runabout to $4400 for the landaulette. The 18 engine displaced 326 cubic inches (4 1/16 × 5 1/8) and produced, as its name suggested, 18 horsepower at 650 rpm.

New people were entering the Packard fold. In 1910, Packard directors heard of the general manager of Burroughs Adding Machine Company, Alvan Macauley—earlier with the National Cash Register Company—who had exhibited formidable management talent as well as a flair for new marketing methods and manufacturing skill. Macauley not only understood mechanical development work but production and distribution as well. That year he came to Packard as general manager.

In 1916, Macauley became president of Packard. Believing that the United States would be drawn into war, Macauley insisted Packard be ready with a powerful aircraft motor that became the basis for the Liberty engine. Macauley's steady, conservative leadership came to typify Packard. He served as president until April of 1939, and then as chairman of the board until April of 1948. Macauley also served as president of the Automobile Manufacturers Association from 1928 through 1945. As Packard's president through both the Roaring '20s and the Depression, Macauley was often referred to as "the only gentleman in the automobile business."

In 1905, Earle C. Anthony, at age 25, became the Los Angeles Packard dealer. He began another Packard tradition by photographing members of the growing movie colony alongside Packards. Doubtlessly Anthony contributed to the proliferation of Packards on the silver screen through the years. Anthony claimed to have opened the world's first gas station (which he might or might not have done). He was responsible for first using the new neon light for advertising. During the '20s, Anthony anticipated the rise of radio, and he built the powerful Los Angeles station KFI, over which he advertised Packards.

Packard had another brash distributor in Alvan Fuller, in Boston, who went on to become governor of Massachusetts. Fuller took on Packards in 1903, sold 18 cars the following year, and sold nearly 400 autos in 1910. Fuller also sold Cadillacs that at the time were upper-medium-priced products and not competitive. By 1927, Fuller—pressured by Packard Motor Car Company—appeared to sell out his Cadillac interests. Actually his son took over the franchise in a building down the street. The street was Commonwealth Avenue, and it became Boston's automobile row after Fuller's new dealership—featuring extensive plate glass windows, relatively new to the retail motor trade—was built there in 1910. Alvan T. Fuller is most remembered, however, as the Massachusetts governor who let Sacco and Vanzetti go to the electric chair in August of 1927.

Packard did well to listen to successful distributors like Anthony in California and Fuller in Boston. They suggested bright and innovative color schemes and body variations. The company might have done well to listen to its men in the field in later years as well.

4
Remembrances

No tome encompassing early automobilia would be complete without some first-hand remembrances. My beloved and gracious aunt, Mrs. Lawrence N. Scott, has supplied me with such impressions. Only one of the cars mentioned in this chapter is a Packard, but most of the others are certainly quality machines. Aunt Dorothy's automotive recollections hail from Marietta, Ohio. This college town is about 120 miles south of the Packard motor car's birthplace of Warren, Ohio.

Most of us are unable to recall a time when horses worked alongside automobiles. Nearly all such autos, in those Theodore Roosevelt/William Taft/Woodrow Wilson days, were open affairs traveling largely on dirt roads. Certainly there were no white-gowned service writers, national consumer complaint agencies, or any real government monitoring of either manufacturers or repairers.

Not only were there not gas stations on every corner, but gasoline was often sold by the druggist and at the general store. And much maintenance and repair was handled by blacksmiths. The newest Scott Joplin rag sold for a dime at the neighborhood sheet-music store. The automobile, the electric light, and the telephone were the only major technological changes in most people's lives since Abraham Lincoln's presidency.

As you read Aunt Dorothy's reminiscences, keep in mind a world without radio broadcasts, neighborhood movie theaters, and suburbs. Rather, a world of slow-paced rural life, interrupted only by the slightly brisker pace of small towns and cities. Trolleys and interurbans were the mass transit, and passenger trains carried longer-distance travelers now served by airlines and interstate highways.

Either you attended a concert, the theater, or a vaudeville show or you made your own entertainment. Letter writing, and written communications in general, were more important than they are today, which was reflected in the quality of education from elementary level through the universities. Fast food was a watermelon chilled by block ice and served on an August evening. Mrs. Scott remembers:

My parents always had Peerless cars, one Packard, too, in the teens. In those days, the top cars were referred to as the Three P's: Peerless, Packard, and Pierce-Arrow. And that was true, and not just because we had them. Anyway, good friends of my folks drove a gorgeous White steamer. It really *was* white with lovely red leather upholstery. I used to go very often to ride with them, and my father offered to pay me to tell him every time the steamer caught fire, which was quite often. We always carried a bucket of water. I was very loyal to the Bartletts, and it was some time before I claimed my father's bribe. Mr. Bartlett got wind of my treachery, and agreed to give me a dime *more* not to report the fires.

I would be sent to the barn to tell the chauffeur, Dan, to "Fire her up," and about 20 minutes later we were all set to take off. I can hear that boiler purring now. The Bartletts' son was afterward governor of Oklahoma, and still later U.S. senator, but that was many years later.

In those days few families in town had cars, and we knew everyone we met, their car, and license number. Many of us had chauffeurs dressed accordingly. Ours served as gardener and as butler, on the very rare occasions when we thought we needed one (I never did). He was one of my very dearest friends; we used to visit homes while my mother shopped. They played the piano, and we all sang. To this day I can't hear those old songs without thinking tenderly of those times. Mert would say, "We have to go now, your mother will be through shopping, and ready to go home." And I'd say, "Let her wait." *Now* I can see why he almost forcibly tore me away from "Moonlight Bay" and my other favorites.

You asked what year and model our cars were. I have no idea about the models.

In the early years I, at least, never heard models referred to—it was the make, horsepower, and wheelbase (if unusually large). Our Packard was supposedly given to my father in very late 1909, and may have been a used one (likely a Packard 24 or 30).

Our first Peerless, a small five-passenger, was a 1910. The next, a seven-passenger, very fancy for that day, beautiful woodwork, name panels on the doors, etc., was 1912. The first Chevrolet, known affectionately as The Whoopy, was a 1911. The big Peerless had the first self-starter and an electric tire pump. All were left-hand drives, and had bulb horns on the seat beside the driver. The big Peerless had a klaxon operated by pushing a button in the end of the upholstery beside the driver. All 'til the Chevrolet had Prestolite lights. And the Chevy may have had a right-hand drive. The rest I know didn't.

The (Packard's Prestolite) headlights were lit with matches, and had to be adjusted each time they were used. "Turn them up a little. No, that's too bright. Down a bit." The tank of Prestolite for their fuel was carried on the side of the car along with the spare tire. It was a right-hand drive, no doors in front. The gas tank was reached under the passenger seat (front), so he had to get out each time the gas tank was filled. In those early days, the only gas pumps were inside garages; not all garages, comparatively few—and also way in the back where they kept the cars which were for sale. The tool box was a rather small half-circle box on the floor of the back seat compartment, and really a part of the back of the front seat. Its top was upholstered with tufted leather, as was the rest of the car, and served as an extra, extremely uncomfortable seat. It was often my fate to ride on this thing, always backward of course.

The Packard finally became demoted to our second car, and my father became a Peerless fan. Our first Peerless added a few modern touches—a half door on each side of the front, and a trunk in back. Our next (the *big*) Peerless bought in 1911, had folding seats to make it a seven-passenger, but it was a real hassle to get them from their place at the side of the back seat to their sitting position between the front and back seats. And they were not comfortable. We sold the Packard, and bought a little Peerless for our second car. It was the first we ever had with a self-starter, but it came with a crank—just in case, which was pretty often. It also had battery-powered headlights, a left-hand drive, and had full doors front and back.

(This) little Peerless we called Trilby. Trilby my folks gave to one of my brothers who used it as a taxi in San Diego until a streetcar hit and demolished it in 1915. Doctors had advised his going there in hopes the climate would benefit his health. It didn't.

Then the first world war came along. No more cars 'till a 1920 Buick, an open sedan for which we later purchased one of the new California winter tops—the Devil's own invention.

(It) was a lot to a car as enclosing a sun porch is to a house. It left much to be desired, but was better than the old-fashioned side curtains which had always been the order of the day before. Now there was when some strong language came in handy—trying to get those confounded side curtains on when rain suddenly descended. They were kept always under the back seat, which necessitated much inconvenience. They were made of cloth and isinglass, and were labeled Front, Left; Back, Right; etc. but seldom meant what they said. And the screws which held them in place were numerous and rarely functioned. All this time ran was pouring down and in. And the roads were getting muddier and muddier, as there were few pavements in those days. So then you probably had to get under the back seat again to bring out the chains so you could negotiate the mud—you *hoped*. Those were the pioneering days, but we didn't know any better, and thought they were wonderful.

In 1923 I bought a Willys-Knight three-door, but it was too frustrating to get someone to drive satisfactorily and take proper care of it; so I sold it. No more cars then 'til Uncle Lawrence bought the used Caddy, which had been a luxurious thing, and gave us splendid service 'till we got our first new Chevy. Lawrence believed in trading every two years, so we had about three more Chevrolets, two Pontiacs, three Oldsmobiles, and three Buicks—Skylarks, Wildcats, and Impalas (much later).

Saturday mornings I listen faithfully and with much interest (heaven knows why) to a radio program presented by a car mechanic who goes into detail about fixing and preventing auto problems. Why do I like it? Perhaps because I heard so much of such when I was young and at home. We had a huge old barn, later dignified with the title of garage. There many cars were repaired, as repair shops were rare. Often the Peerless folks sent a man from their plant in Cleveland (author's note: today only Carling Black Label beer comes from the old Peerless plant).

There was a grease pit in the floor, a series of lights, our own air pump (electric, patronized by kids for miles around for their bicycle tires), and a buried gas tank filled monthly by the National Refining Company's big truck. It was one of my chores to run down from the house to take them the key for the padlock which protected the top of our underground tank. There was a brick-paved area which the cars could be run out on when the pit was not required for working.

I think too of how we used to buy, from a local chemical company, denatured alcohol which we put into the car radiators to prevent freezing. As I recall, sometimes it didn't. And "a little ginger" was the remedy for a leaky radiator.

Evening rides were made more pleasant (sometimes) by "opening the windshield." To do a good job, two front-seat occupants were needed—one to loosen screws on each side. The glass was divided into two sections, upper and lower, and each could be slanted to let the breeze in. The trouble was the bugs came in with the breeze, and few were the evenings the driver didn't get a bug in his eye. Often it was necessary to stop, and have the passengers take turns at probing from the animal with a clean handkerchief (no one ever heard of a Kleenex in those days). Often folks on porches came down to help the patient whose car had stopped in front of their house.

I've been reading and hearing about the "new" idea of having gasoline storage tanks in backyards. New, fiddlesticks. (Here) we had one at home when I was young, very young. It was one of my important (to me) tasks to be trusted with the key to be given only to a very select group—particularly the man who delivered the gas in his big truck—White Rose gas it was, made by Enarco, whoever they were. My father would have no other kind in his cars.

We had a brick platform built as an extension to our garage on which to run the old Peerlesses and Packard out to the pump. My brother Sprigg said (the old tank) held a hundred gallons, and then it cost no more than eight cents a gallon.

This look at an early Packard-owning family is especially fascinating when it is revealed that my Aunt Dorothy has been nearly blind since age four.

Ask the Man Who Owns One

5

New Designs

As the single-cylinder design, no matter how refined, was pushed aside by the rush to multicylinders, Packard could see now that it was time to move from four to six cylinders. The new Packard Six was introduced in the spring of 1911 on wheelbases of 139 inches (standard), 133 inches (close-coupled), and 121 1/2 inches (runabout). Touring, Phaeton, runabout, and close-coupled bodies were $5000 a copy, a touring car with leather victoria top was $5250, a phaeton so equipped was $35 less, a touring car with a full glass canopy ran $5445, a limousine $6250, landaulette $6350, Imperial limousine $6450, Imperial landaulette $6550, brougham $6300, and coupe $5700.

Packard combined the transmission and final drive in the rear axle housing. It was claimed that this reduced the load on the front wheels that were already loaded with the increased weight of the six-cylinder engine. This construction offered less torque reaction in lower gears, and less noise transmitted to the passenger compartment. The Six displaced 525 cubic inches (4 1/2 × 5 1/2 bore × stroke), a T-head producing 82 horsepower at 1720 rpm. Association of Licensed Automobile Manufacturers (ALAM) rated horsepower was 48, and in 1913 the Six was called the 48.

The 48 was advertised as reaching 60 miles an hour in 30 seconds from a standing start. The 1913 48 abandoned gas lighting for electric headlights, and moved the battery from the runningboard to under the driver's seat. Prices of the 1913 48 were reduced as much as $600 in keeping with Henry Joy's and Alvan Macauley's tack of offering as much automobile as possible but at a competitive price.

The 30 and 18 had continued to sell so the new smaller six was not introduced until the summer of 1912. It was called the 38 because of its ALAM horsepower; actual power was 60 brake horsepower. While the larger 48's crankshaft ran on four main bearings, the 38's ran on seven. Also, the 38 was an L-head engine (not a T-head like its big brother). As was common then, the block was cast in three blocks of two cylinders (as was the 48's). Standard equipment was Packard's first starter; it was a unit combined with the generator. The 38 also featured left-hand drive, as all Packards would (except export models) ever after.

Set in 1909, the steady running record, held by a sleeve-valve Knight engine, was 132 hours. In May of 1913, Packard announced, to the Automobile Club of America in New York City, a 200-hour steady run of the 38 power plant. A 38 touring car was driven from the Cleveland agency to New York. The throttle was wired open to 1200 rpm (maximum 60 hp was produced at 1720 rpm) with the timing advanced. Engineers calculated that it ran the equivalent of 888 miles a day. After eight days, the 38 ticked over the 200-hour mark.

Because all was well, it was decided to let it run until 300 hours. Four-and-a-half days later, the 38 engine was shut off, though it was still running cheerfully. Through 12 1/2 days it had turned over 21.7 million times, and used 1438 gallons of gas to run an equivalent of 11,000 miles.

The modern motor car had certainly arrived. If there was any doubt, in 1913 Packard introduced another first—spiral-bevel differential gears for long life and quiet running. This made the winner of the quality car competition a still better product. New England's 1912 registrations of the Three P's showed 943 for Peerless, 1610 for Pierce-Arrow, and 3396 for Packard.

Although Packard had virtually given up racing by now—its cars no longer needed bolstering by such publicity—it was probably just as well. Packard had never pushed "performance cars." The company viewed performance as part of the complete motoring experience, as were smooth and quiet running, long life, comfort, and dependability. Nevertheless, a standard 5-48 (1915 edition) touring car would

A 1913 Model 48 phaeton runabout. Photo John A. Conde Collection.

A 1914 Model 235, seven-passenger imperial limousine. Photo John A. Conde Collection.

A 1913 2-38, seven-passenger touring car. Photo John A. Conde Collection.

A 1916 Twin Six touring car. Photo courtesy William H. Friedrich.

readily see 70 miles an hour, something a Mercer could match only with its special Raceabout model.

In the years before the Great War, Packard steadily improved its 38 and 48. In August, 1914 the company sold its 25,000 car. The 38 and 48 were the biggest, and perhaps best-built, of all Packards. Their engines were the last word in poppet-valved inline sixes. These tremendous, yet lazy engines turned 37-inch wheels through final drives as tall as 3.11. These cars had wheelbases as long as 144 inches and carried plush bodies with ample seating for as many as eight. They were truly the "Boss of the Road," as the advertisements claimed.

Appropriately enough during these boom times, another alumnus of the adding machine school joined Packard. Jesse Vincent had dazzled the business machine world with his mechanical development work at Burroughs Corporation. At the same time, he was running the Burroughs Garage, servicing the officials' cars. At once Burroughs Superintendent of Inventions and its garage foreman, Vincent was earning enough to buy nearly any automobile he wanted. The only trouble was that none of them were fast enough for his lead foot.

Vincent left Burroughs at the end of 1910 (Macauley had left in April of that year to join Packard) to become Hudson's chief engineer. As general manager of Packard, in July of 1912, Macauley recruited his old adding-machine company associate. Jesse Vincent—with a grammar school education and only correspondence-school engineering courses— remained with Packard for 40 years. A Society of Automotive Engineers' poll at the opening of the 1980s listed Jesse Vincent among the 30 most influential automobile men in history.

The new Packard that Vincent designed was arguably the finest internal combustion engine the world had yet seen. While the inline six configuration has natural balance, Packard built that type of engine as large as passenger car practicalities permitted. For more power and flexibility, more pistons were in order. A V-8, or what Vincent called a "Twin Four" was discussed, but the drawbacks would be increased vibration at high speeds, less accessible water pump, generator, and starter. Therefore it would have less accessible valves, and the need for a wider frame, which meant a wider turning radius.

Vincent reasoned that if a six was smooth, why not a "Twin Six?" In 1915, even as W.O. Bentley was hard-pressed to convince the peers of British military aviation that cast-iron pistons had no place in fighter aircraft, Vincent's breakthrough Twin Six was introduced with aluminum pistons.

The L-head Twin Six's narrow 60-degree angle left both engine components and valves accessible. Another drawback of an increased six would have been an inordinately long and unwieldy crankshaft. The Twin Six's relatively small pistons precluded this. Its short and light crank turned in three main bearings fed by oil pressure ranging from 20 to 30 psi, depending on engine speed. The Twin Six displaced 424 cubic inches (3 × 5 bore × stroke) and developed 85 horsepower at 3000 rpm. There were no rockers; the valves ran off their own cams. The new engine Vincent would liken to a steam-powered engine weighed 400 pounds less than the Six.

Spiral bevel gears were naturally enough used in the Twin Six rear axle. The transmission, however, was now up front behind the motor where it would stay in all subsequent Packard cars. Because the Twin-Six engine was lighter than the six it replaced, rear mounting of the transmission was no longer seen as necessary for good weight distribution. In another nod to the future, the cooling system encompassed a thermostat.

The Twin Six was Packard's greatest achievement, and the buying public knew it. Police had to control throngs at showrooms. Reflecting Packard's increasing use of machine rather than hand methods were the Twin Six's low prices (lower even than the 38). Again, Packard practiced its policy of the most automobile for the most competitive price.

Packard's Detroit property was now 100 acres. New buildings were constantly erected to better accommodate (as of 1915) 10,886 workers—a 50-percent increase over 1914. Twin Sixes were offered on a 125-inch or a 135-inch wheelbase. All body styles were offered on the sixes. Prices posted in 1915 for the first Twin Sixes (1916 models) were from $2750 for the 1-25, seven-passenger touring car—the designation referred to the first year model and the last two digits of the wheelbase—to $4800 for the 1-35, seven-passenger Imperial limousine.

British road testers readily admitted that the Twin Six bested the Rolls-Royce. Although smoothness—not brute strength—was the goal for the Twin Six, any model would eclipse 70 miles an hour. The Twin Six could accelerate to that speed from walking pace in high gear smoothly and without fuss.

On the heels of the Twin Six would come Vincent's and Packard's next project: the Liberty aircraft engine.

Advertisement courtesy Ross M. Lee Collection.

Wanderlust! Already the days are long—and winter-weary folk have begun to respond to the call of tantalizing Spring

Green magic of the open! Is it yours—now that the young year's exhilarating wine fires the blood with craving for new, wide horizons?

A better car this season—a car that will give the utmost, demand the least, and leave more freedom for the stimulating joys of the road! Why not?

All the miles you can crowd into the day—all the speed the highway will permit—all the power any road condition can demand—and the confidence that you ride in the best of form *without excessive cost*—are yours if you drive a Twin-six.

A Packard exactly to your liking—now! You'll want the particular design you want—this Spring.

The days are long—and the time for action is short.

Ask the man who owns one

Twenty distinctive styles of Twin-six motor carriages. Prices, open cars, $3050 and $3500, at Detroit. Packard dealers in all important cities
Packard Motor Car Company—Detroit

Packard TWIN-6

Advertisement courtesy Ross M. Lee Collection.

Economy! Cheapest power is that which makes best use of Nature's resources. With the gliding drive of a full-rigged ship—plus a speed no craft ever had—the twelve agile and powerful cylinders of the Packard motor will carry you anywhere in greatest security and comfort—at least possible cost. The economical use of gasoline is one of the major advantages of the Twin-six. ❦ There are twenty and more Packard styles. Prices, open cars, three thousand fifty and thirty-five hundred dollars, at Detroit. ❦ ❦ Packard Motor Car Company.

Ask the man who owns one

Packard TWIN-6

Advertisement courtesy Ross M. Lee Collection.

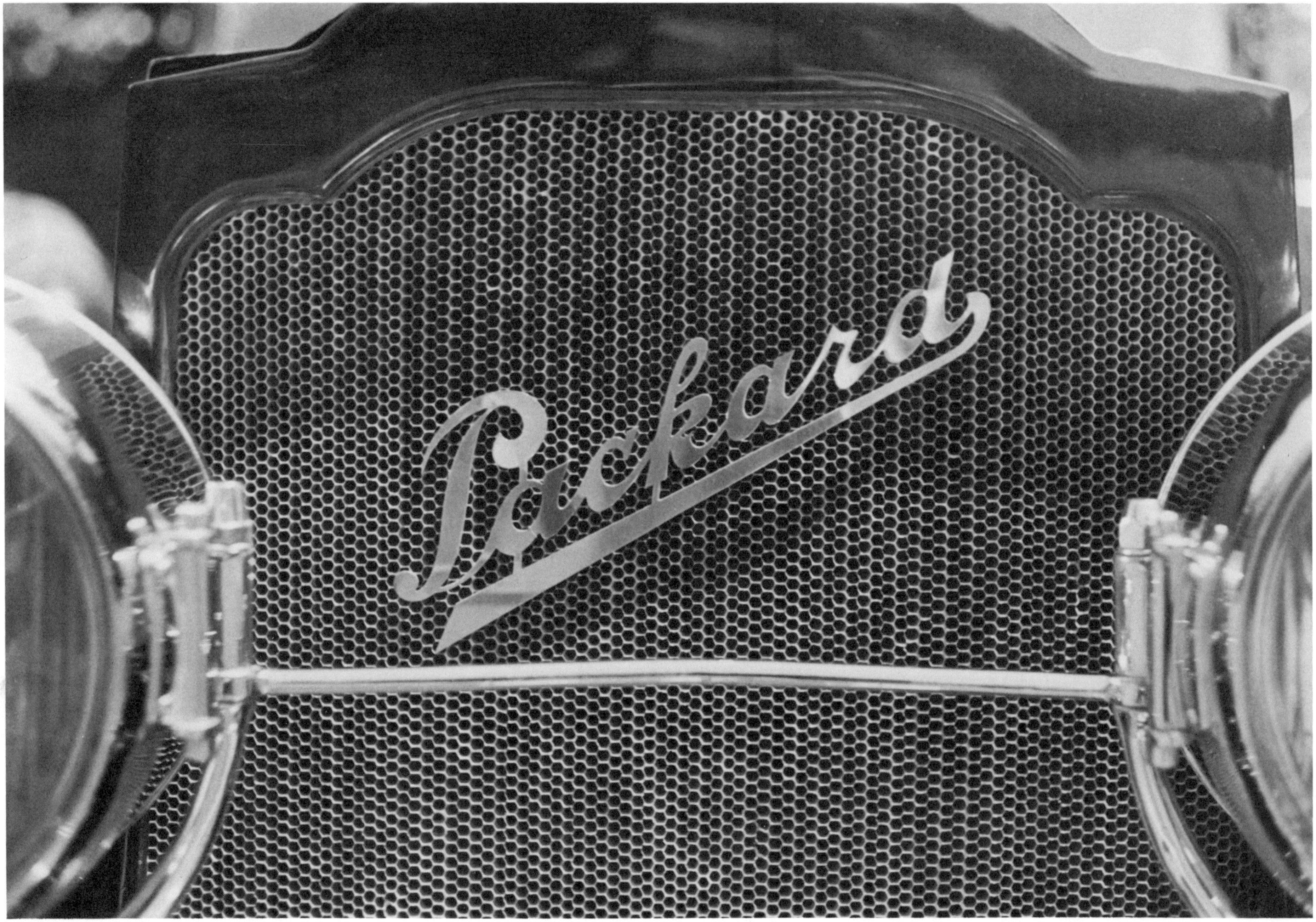

A 1920 Twin Six. Photo by Susan Scott.

A 1920 Twin Six fully collapsible town car by Fleetwood on a custom chassis built for the Atwater Kent (radio) family. Photo by Susan Scott.

A 1920 Twin Six town car by Fleetwood. Photo by Susan Scott.

A 1920 Twin Six Fleetwood town car. Photo by Susan Scott.

A 1920 Twin Six Fleetwood town car. Photo by Susan Scott.

Ask the Man Who Owns One

6

The Liberty

In 1917, for all its bustling automobile factories and proliferation of railroad lines, the United States was fourteenth among all the world's nations in aircraft production. Although American automobiles could now match any European or British effort, this was not the case in aviation. As France and Germany had earlier embraced and nurtured the automobile, so had they later supported aircraft refinement. While Britain and the Continent fielded 115 mile-an-hour SPADs, Nieuports, and Fokkers, America's most capable offering was the 75-mile-an-hour Curtiss Jenny.

In 1914, Packard President Henry Joy had seen enough in aviation to urge his company to develop an aero engine. When Alvan Macauley took over the company's leadership two years later, he continued to encourage the development of what would become the water-cooled Liberty.

Early prototypes were racing-car engines based on the Twin Six, which Jesse Vincent meant as stepping stones to Packard's new aero engine. Like the Twin Six, the first of these was a 60-degree, V-12 with cylinders cast in blocks of three (though with a 2 21/32 × 4 1/2 bore × stroke for 299 cubic inches). With an overhead camshaft for each cylinder bank and four valves per cylinder, the 500-pound engine developed 130 horsepower at 3300 rpm.

Installed in a single-seat racing car, this engine was the first in the 300-cubic-inch class to better 100 mph at the Indianapolis Speedway (116 mph on August 4, 1916). In November of 1917, Ralph De Palma drove it to beat the world's six-hour speed record set by a Sunbeam at Brooklands (616 miles in the allotted time). The car's last outing was the 1919 Indianapolis 500 in which De Palma managed sixth place. A Ferrari, in 1952, would be the only other 12-cylinder car to finish the Indy 500.

Three 40-degree, 905-cubic-inch (4 × 6 bore × stroke) V-12 prototypes were built in 1916-17. The second engine was put in a Packard racing car driven by Bill Rader. The car set new circular track records in July of 1917: the quarter mile in 13.95 seconds at 129 mph, the mile in 28.76 seconds at 125.1 mph, and 10 miles in 4:50.88 at 123.7 mph. At Daytona Beach in February of 1919, Ralph De Palma drove the 905 racer to a new world record for the mile, 149.73, beating the 141.73 mph set in 1911 by a Blitzen Benz.

Most of Packard's official racing program was centered around the development of what would become the Liberty engine. Except for noncompetitive speed trials, most earlier Packard efforts had been reliability runs and the like. Although Packard men like Jesse Vincent were racing fans, and many Packard owners sponsored their own cars in various events through the 1950s, Packard considered a factory racing team as unsuited to the image of a first-class producer of luxury automobiles. Rolls-Royce followed a similiar tack.

In any event, by 1928 Packard boasted that its engines had set more existing speed records than those of any other manufacturer in the world. While this was no doubt true, many of these were speedboat as well as automobile and aircraft runs. Jesse Vincent's house was built on the water's edge so he could walk downstairs to his own Packard-propelled powerboat.

Vincent's brother Charles had been chief final inspector at Hudson, and in 1915 helped develop the famed Super Six. In 1916, Charles Vincent became an experimental engineer at Packard, working on both the racing chassis and 299- and 905-cubic-inch prototypes. He remained at Packard until 1947, and was in charge of the reknowned Packard Proving Grounds. This home of the then fastest track in the world had a smoothly banked 2 1/2-mile oval.

The engine that became known as the Liberty was first called the U.S.A. Standardized Aircraft Engine. The former name was suggested by an admiral as commemorating Independence Day, the date the V-8 prototype was ready. Meanwhile, development of the 1100-cubic-inch, 45-degree V-12 (5 × 7 bore × stroke) prototype continued until it was ready on Thanksgiving Day, 1917. France and England were building dozens of different aero engines, resulting in limited production at high cost. Packard offered its engine as a standardized effort to be built by several manufacturers.

By turning over the fruit of its labors to the war effort, Packard gave away the opportunity to have its name synonymous with aviation (as were Rolls-Royce and Mercedes). Because the 20,478 Liberty V-12s built during World War I were built not just by Packard but also by other automobile makers (6500 Liberty V-12s were built by Packard, 6500 by Lincoln, 3950 by Ford, 2528 by Cadillac and Buick, and 1000 by Nordyke & Marmon), most historians forget that the Liberty design was a Packard effort.

French and English aviation officials visiting the Packard plant during Liberty development were impressed by Packard's quality, but thought the engine too heavy for its power. The idea was to build a series of Liberty engines in four-, six-, eight-, and twelve-cylinder forms with interchangeable parts for use in trainers, fighters, reconnaissance planes, and bombers.

While only 52 six-cylinder versions were built, one of these was installed in a Curtiss PN-1 night fighter. Because the result was not fast enough these engines were shelved. The 15 eight-cylinder versions built by Buick suffered vibration, and in any event could not counter the famed Hispano-Suiza V-8s. Hudson built a few four-cylinder versions but nothing came of them.

Even though Packard raised the Liberty's V-12 power to over 400 horsepower, the engine suffered a stigma brought on by early production difficulties. A quarter of its parts underwent engineering changes even as the engines were produced because of the Allies' desperate need for aero engines. Also, some of the early engines, problems and all, went into combat. Because the debugged Liberty went into the DH-4, already known as the "Flaming Coffin" for the tendency of its gastank to break loose and burst in a crash, the engine's reputation was further tarnished by being associated with that plane.

Although the wartime Liberty would have benefitted from a little more development time—which was not available—the engine nevertheless raised the DH-4's ceiling to 19,500 feet, and its top speed to 125 mph. The complicated Rolls-Royce Eagle VIII engine took the DH-4 another 2500 feet and 18 miles an hour faster. While Packard was a neophyte aero engine builder, Rolls-Royce was not. During World War II, Packard took another excellent, though terribly complex Rolls-Royce aero engine, and turned it into the finest example of liquid-cooled, piston-driven aircraft engine ever built.

The government impressed the urgency of the Liberty engine project on the leading civilians involved by having them commissioned as Army officers. By the war's end, Jesse Vincent had become a lieutenant colonel. Proud of his part in the Liberty program, he was ever after "Col. Vincent."

Although Charles Kettering of General Motors designed the Liberty's battery ignition system, and Ford Motor Company contributed bearing and cylinder design and production, Vincent oversaw the entire program from beginning to end. His efforts included heading a 25-member engineering team comprised of talent from Packard, Cadillac, Dodge, and Pierce-Arrow housed in offices in Washington's Bureau of Standards and assembled to check the V-12 plans.

If anyone other than Jesse Vincent was responsible for the final design that led to the production Liberty, it was Elbert Hall of Hall-Scott. Hall's company was already producing an 824-cubic-inch, 125-horsepower six-cylinder aero engine, the A-5, used in Russia, China, Japan, and England as well as the states. In five days and nights at the Willard Hotel in Washington, the two engineers designed the final version of the Liberty. Vincent's and Packard's roles in the now national effort were sublimated to the point that, before the engine was known as the Liberty, it was being called the "All-American" engine as an almost communal pride swept through the automobile industry.

Originally, William Crapo Durant, head of General Motors and a pacifist, refused to produce the Liberty. Henry M. Leland and his son, Wilfred, left Cadillac to found

A 1917 Model 3-25, seven-passenger touring car. Photo John A. Conde Collection.

A 1918 Twin Six landaulet. Photo John A. Conde Collection.

A 1924 Model 226 Second Series sedan. Photo John A. Conde Collection.

Lincoln—as a young man Leland cast his first vote for Abraham Lincoln and had revered the president ever since—expressly to manufacture the engine. It should be remembered that President Wilson was elected partly on his promise to keep America out of war, and that less than two years earlier, in December of 1915, Henry Ford funded the Peace Ship, an antiwar voyage to Europe of 150 prominent Americans. Similarly, Ford was opposed to the United States' entry into World War II. Once the nation entered the wars, however, he lost no time grinding out war materiel.

After the war, the Liberty distinguised itself by powering the US Navy flying boat,which made the first transatlantic flight, the first aerial circumnavigation of the globe, the first US airmail service, as well as a number of racing boats and cars. As late as World War II, the Liberty powered British tanks, and was built without license by the Russians, who called it the M-5 and used it in their tanks.

Packard was paid the same amount for Liberty engines as the other manufacturers ($5000 cost and $625 profit) despite all the development work the company had done.

Packard had been building trucks ever since mounting a panel body on a Model F in 1902. The company built 43,538 trucks over two decades until abandoning them in 1923 to concentrate on the more profitable automobiles. World War I was a boom to Packard's truck business. Only 10 percent of its total production was before the war. The trucks were thoroughly Packard quality, often comprised of motor car engines and components. Although the early models were chain-driven, the 1916 Packard offered the increasingly popular worm-drive to remain competitive. Other quality car builders, including Peerless, Pierce-Arrow, and Locomobile, offered trucks. Like Packard they left the field unable to compete with larger producers, like Mack and White, who could offer considerable fleet discounts.

Over half of Packard's truck orders were war business. Then the postwar recession hurt truckers who, in any event, could often buy military surplus trucks for much less. Packard's dealers were complaining about the factory's policy of forcing trucks on them based on the number of automobiles they sold. Also, the relatively sleek new Packards were better shown against a backdrop of potted palms than one of lumbering trucks.

With the advent of the Roaring '20s, Packard entered a remarkable period of peacetime profits never again realized. The new Packard single six and straight eight were built more profitably by precision machines. The trucks, like the large and expensive Twin Six, required a great deal of handwork.

Ask the Man Who Owns One

7
Quality and Competition

Although production of the venerable and well-liked Twin Six was continued through June of 1923, Packard could clearly see that competition would be coming increasingly from other than the ponderous offerings of Peerless, Pierce-Arrow, and Locomobile. General Motors was growing rapidly and setting the tone for the entire industry. Packard President Alvan Macauley could see that Cadillac would soon become a serious rival. In order to cope with congested traffic in suburban and urban areas, the new Packard model would be smaller and lighter than the Twin Six.

The production lessons of the Liberty engine would not be lost. President Macauley proposed that carefully designed and operated machines could produce an automobile of better quality than by hand. From its introduction in September, 1920 through August, 1928, Packard sold 150,000 Single Sixes. To its general acceptance as the master motor builder in the industry, Packard added nonpareil machine-tool design and practice.

A Cadillac V-8 was half the price of the Twin-Six and a Model T Ford cost a tenth the price. Choosing a car was a much tougher task than today's buyer faces. Alvan Macauley pointed out, "There are 10 million American-built automobiles, which means that nearly one out of every two families owns a motor car as an intimate part of its business and professional life. There are approximately 250 different kinds offered on the market. It's no wonder that the intending owner is oftentimes bewildered in making his selection."

Packard had some selecting to do as well. Although reduced in size and price from the 30, the 18 was otherwise a slightly smaller version of the same car and so cost nearly as much to build as the 30. Packard was able to sell the 18 for a thousand dollars less than the 30 because its mark-up was considerable. The economics and competition in the booming automobile business no longer allowed for such extravagance. The same had held true for the 38 and 48 models, and the 38 had been by no means a small car. Both the type of car and the way it would be built were crucial if the company was to make money. To offer a four-cylinder engine would not do in a marketplace becoming enamored with sixes and eights. Another V-12 would be both too costly and complex for a small, light automobile.

Cadillac was having success with its upper-medium-priced, 314-cubic-inch V-8 (3 1/8 × 5 1/8 bore × stoke, 70 hp at 2400 rpm; 122-inch wheelbase). They sold 19,000 of them in 1920, and it wouldn't do for Packard to parrot Cadillac. Because six cylinders were the least that could run in perfect balance, the choice was obvious. Packard didn't mention anything about an inline eight; that was yet to come.

The car that debuted was offered on a 116-inch wheelbase. The five-passenger touring car sold for $3640, the two-passenger roadster went for the same price, the five-passenger sedan cost $4950, and the four-passenger coupe sold for $4835. Before the Single Six was introduced, the board of directors authorized production of 20,000 cars a year. Of the 12,143 cars Packard sold in 1920, only 1042 were the new Single Six. The rest were Twin Sixes and trucks (now slacking off). In 1921, Packard sold only 6374 Single Sixes (or "116s," for the wheelbase). The solution was astonishingly simple. In 1922 the 116 became the 126. What had earlier appeared only a short and boxy cousin to the Twin Six now became a long, sleek car in its own right. And sales took off.

There was more to the Single Six's popularity than a 10-inch stretch of wheelbase. The simple, rugged L-head six was advertised as able to stretch as many as 20 miles to the gallon, 20,000 miles from a set of tires, and 500 miles to a gallon of oil. The Single Six engine grew a little from 241.5 cubic inches in the original 116 of

A 1925 Model 236 sedan. Photo John A. Conde Collection.

A 1925 Model 243 touring car. Photo John A. Conde Collection.

September, 1920 (3 3/8 × 4 1/2 bore × stroke; 4.8 compression ration, 52 hp at 24 rpm), to 268.4 cubic inches in the 1922-23 126 and 133 (half-inch longer stroke, 3 3/8 × 5; 54 hp at 2400 rpm), to its final 288.6 cubic inches in the 1925-26 326 and 333 (3 1/2 × 5; 60 hp at 3200 rpm). The final Single Six pumped out 81 horsepower at 3200 rpm. Late in 1923, Packard offered four-wheel brakes on the Single Six models 226 and 233 for 1924. This was fortunate because Buick and Cadillac, among others, already had them.

Buick had Packard's radiator shape, and Buick wasn't the only imitator. The 1922-24 Dagmar not only copied Packard's radiator shape, but the hubcaps' red hexagon, too. A letter to Dagmar from Packard's legal department warning that the latter was a registered trademark stopped that bit of copying, but the radiator imitation continued on the 1925 Star and the 1926 Flint Junior Six. William Durant formed a combine to challenge General Motors; his Star challenged Chevrolet while his Flint Junior Six was priced a little higher. One car that didn't copy the Packard's radiator was the new Chrysler 70 (so-called because it would do 70 miles an hour). It was an excellent product that was priced to give Buick tough competition ($1200 less than the Single Six). Because Packard was secure in its prestige, President Macauley no doubt viewed the abundant radiator copying as inexpensive advertising and never took any of the offenders to court.

In 1926, Packard offered its new hypoid rear axle. It was quieter and smoother still than the spiral bevel gears Packard introduced in 1913. In addition, the hypoid rear axle allowed a lower-profile car. This blended well with the new lacquer colors Packard used on its 1926 models. The new nitrocellulose lacquer was a Du Pont development called Duco. It was sprayed on General Motors' 1924 Oakland, and throughout the GM line in 1925. Before this development, automobile bodies had been varnished and had to dry for several days. Now automobile bodies could be painted in a matter of hours because Duco dried almost instantly.

General Motors and Du Pont were old friends. The 1920 depression sent GM stock tumbling, and William Durant stoked the firm with his own money and borrowed his way into tremendous debt. For the second and last time, Durant was out of GM (he had been dumped in 1910 for nearly bleeding GM dry when he had tried to buy nearly every automotive concern in sight). The du Ponts now bought 2 1/2 million shares of GM stock, Pierre du Pont became president and put Alfred P. Sloan, Jr. in charge of the corporation. Sloan built General Motors into the effective organization that dominated the industry. Each division was responsible for its own success yet was able to draw on corporate research, financial, and sales divisions.

In 1927, largely because of the new possibilities Duco offered, General Motors created its new Art and Color Department. Styling became as important as engineering. In 1925, when nearly four million cars were sold but only a million and a half were scrapped, Charles W. Nash, among others, worried that the automotive market had become saturated. But now with a dazzling array of new colors and more frequent models changes, there would be little to fear.

Although Packard was still referring to its cars by series rather than by years, the series were generally introduced year by year. Although Packard would entice owners of its cars to trade in, it would also update used cars with newer lights and accessories. Packard offered improvements as they came, and not always at the start of a new series. In addition, Packard advertised its Single Six as "the ten year car," and in 1925 promised that its cars would not look out of style in 1935.

In 1930 Packard's treatment of elderly and disabled workers attracted national attention. When an employee fell back on his job, he was counseled by the employment department. Sometimes only medical attention was needed to return him to his old job, and sometimes he was given a different job. In the case of older workers, a special department was set aside where each man worked according to his age, ability, and physical condition—and at his regular hourly rate. Any difference between this and regular production was made up from a special fund.

Packard found that by rewarding workers for a job well done by instituting a group bonus plan, the entire plant became an eagle-eyed inspection army. This and the thoughtful treatment of old and disabled workers accounted for a quality-nurturing atmosphere. When men are well treated and able to profit by the success their labor engenders, careful workmanship results. The stability of the Packard workforce was such that in 1930 37 percent of all employees in its Detroit factories had been with the company for five years or more and 15 percent had been Packard employees for 10 or more years. With that sort of background the claim of a "ten year car" takes on significance.

Packard quality was no accident.

Ask the Man Who Owns One

8
Lineage

In 1921, President Harding was the first president to ride to an inauguration in an automobile. He rode in a Twin-Six. While that model had further heightened Packard's stature and profits, it was not adaptable to the increasing "machine method" Macauley was introducing as the company's road to increased future production and profit. In June of 1923, Packard introduced the first inline eight-cylinder motor made by a volume producer. There was the limited-production Isotta Fraschini in Italy, and a handful of Duesenberg Model As, but the Packard effort would best either. For the next 31 years (other than during World War II), Packard marketed the most refined and dependable straight eights in the world.

Packard's new Single Eight was, like the six, both an L-head and cast en bloc. It developed 85 horsepower—a great deal in 1923—at 3000 rpm, and displaced 357.8 cubic inches (3 3/8 × 5 bore × stroke), had a nine-bearing crankshaft and had a 4.51 compression ratio.

Because in those days good things still came in big packages and length was everything, the new Packard Single Eight rode on 136- and 143-inch wheelbases; that was 10 inches longer than the two Single Six models. As when the company stretched the Single Six 116 to 126, the increased length meant sales. This time, however, the additional length was all in one place—the hood. Through the years, a long hood was to become one of the industry's great marketing ploys because it suggested a great and powerful engine and terrific speed. Unlike many cars produced even until recently, the Packard did have a relatively great and powerful engine, for its day, and the 80-miles-an-hour it delivered was twice the top speed of a Model T Ford and 20-30 miles an hour faster than most other makes. Performance without the sacrifice of docility had always been a Packard feature. The Single Six would do an honest 75 while, like its big brother, remain tractable around town.

And the two cars were brothers even if few customers realized it. Although the long, lithe Single Eight was a new car, the truth was that most of its tooling belonged to the Single Six, and Packard could switch production to either car as orders came in. Any production snags had been solved after 2 1/2 years of building Single Sixes. As in 1940, when all Packards ran down the same production line—120s and 180s sharing frames and all models (including the volume six-cylinder 110) sharing sheet metal—the company managed the illusion of producing vastly different automobiles.

In 1940, there were name changes. Since the Twin Six was dropped, as was the Twelve in 1939, the new and remaining cars alike were renamed to help the public forget the departed models. In 1924, the Single Six became the Packard Six, and the Single Eight became the Packard Eight. In the 1940, to erase the memory of the Twelve and aging Super-8, the 110, 120, 160, and 180 names denoted a clean break with the past.

Just as many auto buffs considered nothing after the ponderous and dated 1939 Twelve a true Packard, not so many years ago there were those who looked down at the Sixes and Eights of the 1920s. They considered them inconsequential offerings after the massive 48 and Twin Six. We are always hearing that such-and-such was the last "real Packard." Those who long only for the huge models of the Teens should remember than no one was building such cars in the Twenties. They were not competitive. Locomobile is an example of a make rooted in the past. Those who decry the One-Twenty forget that it was one of the most eminently roadable Packards and that it saved the entire company. Those who laud the Twelve of the 1930s don't realize that it was originally designed as a Buick-priced front-wheel-drive car for those upwardly mobile souls not greatly put out by the Depression.

A 1926 Model 326 touring car. Photo John A. Conde Collection.

Another comment on the Packard Eights of the 1920s and the company's products in general is that for all the "Sport Phaetons," roadsters, and the like, Packards were not sports cars or anything close. Advertising might have shown a young rake beside his new Eight touring car just as luxury car ads half a century later pictured a young man or woman in or next to the newest sheet-metal dream. Youth sells. The truth is that through the 1930s and even into the 1940s, the typical Packard customer was someone who came of age when horses were still the general mode of transportation, and they expected to be insulated from the world.

Because Packard engineering was awash with men who knew motors and were steeped in the company's performance legends, Packards would always be as fast or faster than any other production car. And this bespeaks reams for Packard engines because most of the firm's products were ratioed for flexibility in high gear. Such cars turned very high engine revolutions at top speeds. Lesser products could not do this or they could not do it for long.

In late 1926, the Packard Eight's bore was increased to 3 1/2 inches for a displacement of 385 cubic-inches. Through a number of name changes and models, this engine was offered through 1936; then it was called the Super Eight. It was a popular engine size, and not just for Packard. Chrysler and Pierce-Arrow fielded nine-main-bearing, 385-cubic-inch straight eights in 1931 and 1929, respectively. Though excellent engines, those who owned or worked on all three usually preferred the Packard.

Not only had the trucks and the Twin-Six died in 1923, so had William Doud Packard. James Ward Packard's older brother had provided much of the business guidance for both the electric works and the new automobile company. In 1928, James Ward Packard died at his estate in Lakewood, the Lake Chautauqua village his father had founded. Packard ran full-page elegy advertisements in several magazines. Beginning with the Sixth series in 1929, the company honored its founder by placing his family crest on the radiator shell.

Henry Bourne Joy became chairman of the board in 1916, placing former general manager Alvan Macauley in the presidency. In 1917, Joy left Packard, perhaps because he had talked merger with two former General Motors men, Charles W. Nash and James J. Storrow, who wanted to acquire Packard and create their own GM. General Motors tried to buy Packard as early as 1909, but the answer had always been no.

Henry Joy brought Packard to Detroit, rounded up capital (much of it his own), commissioned Albert Kahn, pushed for more cylinders, encouraged new engineering, and all the while kept alive James Ward Packard's dictum of quality first.

The patrician Macauley, conservative yet wide awake, would exemplify Packard through the next two and a half decades. A manager adroit with both men and machines, Macauley kept the spark of both evolutionary engineering and design even as production and marketing were guided under his almost paternal leadership. Most of all, he calmly planned and instituted while, during the Depression, automakers were panicking and dying.

The man who replaced Macauley in 1939, Max Gilman, had been with the company since 1919 (when he sold Packard trucks in Brooklyn).

It shows how serious Packard was becoming about its future survival in an increasingly tough industry that as the refined Macauley became chairman of the board his replacement should be a rough fellow whose favorite pastime in New York had been driving the streets in a beat-up touring car on the prowl for taxi drivers whose manners displeased him. The offending taxi was run into an El pillar, and Gilman drove away in search of another victim. But in April, 1942, an open manhole cover in Detroit sought revenge on Gilman for his earlier deeds. Also in the wrecked car was the wife of one of the members of Packard's advertising agency. Because Chairman Macauley would brook no scandal, his former hatchetman wound up at General Tire and Rubber Company, where he became president.

Gilman's replacement was George Christopher, a GM production man schooled in Buicks and Pontiacs. In 1949, Christopher was followed by Hugh Ferry, Packard's

The 1929 Eight 640 phaeton given by Earle C. Anthony to architect Bernard Maybeck for designing the San Francisco dealership. Photo courtesy William H. Friedrich.

treasurer. His first major act was to find another president. In 1952, James Nance, a Hotpoint executive, became the president of Packard Motor Car Company.

Somehow this lineage seems to sum up Packard. Founded by an inventor, nurtured by a "hands-on" venture capitalist (Henry Joy had locked himself in the shop for three days and nights with a pile of tomato cans and emerged with the Model L's carburetor), guided by a steady executive, and then, as General Motors became ever more the "power that be," run under first the helpless eyes of a street brawler, then those of a former GM production man, and finally those of a master appliance salesman—appropriately enough in the pushbutton Fifties.

Sic transit gloria automobile business.

9
Glimpsing the Past

We've looked at Packard's products and growth. Now it's time to see the company as buyers did. At the beginning of this chapter are reproductions of papers covering the purchase of a 1928 Fifth series Packard Six sedan from California distributor Earle C. Anthony's San Francisco dealership. The papers reveal an interesting glimpse into the past. The monthly payment of $130.20 is better put into perspective when it is remembered that the average monthly income of American factory workers in 1927 was $33 less.

As the new Packard Six and Eight built by machine methods further spread the Packard name throughout the world during the 1920s, it was appropriate that the company advertise in *National Geographic*. The gallery of ads found in this chapter shows Packard's high-toned yet simple approach.

Two eras of Packards. Photo by Susan Scott.

CALIFORNIA DISTRIBUTORS
Packard MOTOR CARS

SAN FRANCISCO
OAKLAND
LOS ANGELES

RADIO CENTRAL
SUPER STATION
K F I
LOS ANGELES

ANTHONY SERVICE
IN
DAYLIGHT SHOPS

San Francisco, Calif.
Nov. 19, 1927

Mr. R. J. Waters,
646 - 19th Ave.,
San Francisco,
California.

Dear Sir:-

We are enclosing you herewith triplicate copy of conditional sales contract, dated Nov. 17th, 1927, covering your Packard Sedan, Serial No. 136575, Motor No. 136846.

We are enclosing also copy of St. Paul Fire & Marine Insurance Company policy No. 04902, certificate No. 1132, which insures the above mentioned car for fire and theft in the amount of $2285.00, and for full coverage collision. In a few days we will forward to you the original policy for property damage, $1000.00 limit, and public liability $20,000.00 and $40,000.00 limit. This coverage attaches the date that car was delivered to you, and as we do not require to hold the original policy, it will be forwarded to you within a few days.

Thanking you for past favors, we are

Very truly yours,

EARLE C. ANTHONY, INC.
By- E.R.Tretheway

INVESTIGATE ANTHONY SERVICE

Dictated by-
E.R.Tretheway,
Credit Manager,
Typed by-T.D.

Courtesy Ross M. Lee Collection.

CALIFORNIA DISTRIBUTORS

Packard MOTOR CARS

SAN FRANCISCO
OAKLAND
LOS ANGELES

RADIO CENTRAL
SUPER STATION
K F I
LOS ANGELES

ANTHONY SERVICE
IN
DAYLIGHT SHOPS

Earle C. Anthony, Inc.

San Francisco
November 24, 1928.

Mr. R. J. Waters,
646 - 19th Avenue,
San Francisco, Calif.

Dear Sir:

    We are enclosing you herewith paid conditional sale contract, St. Paul Fire and Marine Insurance Company policy #1814688, certificate #1132, and certificate of ownership #04902, 1928 legal owners notice # 815900 attached, covering your Packard Sedan serial #136575, motor #136846.

    These papers were received by us today from the Finance Corporation of America.

    Thanking you for past favors, we are

Very truly yours,

EARLE C. ANTHONY, INC.

E. R. Tretheway
Credit Manager

ERT'M

INVESTIGATE ANTHONY SERVICE

Courtesy Ross M. Lee Collection.

SF-319

ORIGINAL

Must Accompany Applicant's Statement and Note

CONDITIONAL SALE CONTRACT

For use in all States except Colo., Mich., Mo., Ohio, N. J., La. and Va.

The undersigned SELLER hereby sells, and the undersigned PURCHASER hereby purchases, subject to the terms and conditions hereinafter set forth, the following property, complete with standard attachments and equipment, delivery and acceptance of which is hereby acknowledged by PURCHASER, viz:—

	New or Used	MAKE Trade Name	If Used, Year Model	Type of Body	Motor Number	Manufacturer's Serial No.
ONE	New	Packard		Sedan	136846	136575

For the Total Time Price of $ Twenty Eight Hundred Sixty One and 04/100 - Dollars, payable as follows:

Cash on or before delivery $ 698.64 Trade in for $ 600.00 Total $ 1298.64

Deferred balance $ 1562.40 payable as set forth in Schedule of payments on note of PURCHASER, hereinafter referred to, at the place designated on said note, with interest thereon after maturity at the highest lawful rate, and if this contract be placed with an attorney for collection, 15% of the amount due hereunder as attorney's fees, or if prohibited, the amount prescribed by law.

1. Title to said property shall not pass to PURCHASER until the total amount payable as aforesaid is actually paid in cash.

2. No transfer, renewal, extension or assignment of this contract or of any interest hereunder, or loss, injury or destruction of said property from any cause, shall release PURCHASER from his obligations hereunder.

3. PURCHASER shall keep the said property free of all taxes, liens and encumbrances; shall at his own expense make any and all repairs necessary to keep the said property in as good condition as it now is, reasonable wear and tear alone excepted; shall keep and use the vehicle in a careful and prudent manner and in strict conformity with the laws relating to or governing the same; shall not use or permit the same to be used for any illegal purpose or for hire; shall not remove the same from the State herein referred to as the residence of PURCHASER without permission of SELLER, and shall not transfer any interest in this contract or in said property. PURCHASER shall keep the said property insured against fire and theft, and, if required by SELLER, against collision (with a $100 deductible clause), said insurance to be in a company or companies designated by SELLER and in such amounts as will at all times protect SELLER'S interest herein. The proceeds of any insurance, whether paid by reason of loss, injury, return premium or otherwise, shall be payable to SELLER and at his option be applied toward the repair and replacement of the said property or toward the payment of the obligations of PURCHASER hereunder.

4. This writing constitutes the entire contract between the parties, there being no warranties or representations of any character except as set forth herein.

5. If PURCHASER shall default in the payment of any amount for which he shall be liable hereunder, and it is hereby agreed that time is of the essence of this contract, or shall violate or fail to perform any of the provisions hereof, or if any proceeding in bankruptcy, receivership or insolvency is instituted by or against PURCHASER, or if the said property is seized in any legal proceeding, or if at any time in the exclusive judgment of SELLER the rights of SELLER in the said property, or under this contract, shall be in any way prejudiced or rendered insecure, then in any such event SELLER may, without notice or demand, elect to consider the full amount remaining unpaid by PURCHASER as being immediately due and payable, and PURCHASER hereby authorizes any attorney at law to appear for PURCHASER in any court of record in the United States, waive the issue and service of any process, and confess judgment against PURCHASER for the amount due hereunder and attorneys fees for collection, as above specified, in favor of SELLER or his Assignee

6. If PURCHASER defaults in complying with any of the terms or provisions hereof SELLER may take immediate possession of said property, including any equipment and accessories thereto, and for this purpose SELLER may enter the premises where said property may be and remove the same, without notice or demand, and with or without legal process. SELLER may resell said property so retaken at public or private sale, without demand for performance, with or without notice to PURCHASER (if given notice by mail to address below being sufficient), with or without having such property at the place of sale, and upon such terms and in such manner as SELLER may determine. SELLER may become the purchaser at any such public sale. From the proceeds of any such public or private sale, SELLER shall deduct all expenses for retaking, including expenses incurred in locating said property, repairing and selling such property, including a reasonable attorney's fee, and any and all charges due thereon. The balance remaining shall be applied to the amount due. Any surplus shall be paid over to PURCHASER; in case of deficiency PURCHASER shall pay the same with interest, and PURCHASER does hereby authorize a confession of judgment in the amount of such deficiency.

7. PURCHASER agrees to execute a promissory note, which note, covering the said deferred payments, may be discounted or negotiated by SELLER, but such discount or negotiation of said note shall not be considered its acceptance as payment under any circumstances, and none of the unpaid installments provided for in this contract shall be deemed or considered as paid until actually paid in lawful money of the United States.

8. All remedies of SELLER whether provided for in this contract or conferred by law are cumulative rights and not alternative and may be enforced successively or concurrently; and repossession, retaking or sale of the said property pursuant to the terms hereof shall not bar an action for the recovery of any amount which PURCHASER may be required to pay hereunder, and the bringing of any such action, or the entry of judgment against PURCHASER, shall not bar SELLER'S rights to the repossession of the said property as herein provided. Any provision of this contract prohibited by law of any State shall as to said State be ineffective to the extent of such prohibition without invalidating the remaining provisions of this contract. The failure of SELLER, upon knowledge of any default or violation hereof by PURCHASER to enforce the rights or remedies herein given or conferred by law, shall not be construed as a waiver of any provision hereof, or any right or remedy of SELLER.

9. All the terms and provisions hereof shall be binding upon and enure to the benefit of the heirs, executors, administrators, successors and assigns of the parties hereto. Upon any assignment hereof by SELLER the assignee shall be entitled to all the rights of SELLER, it being expressly understood and agreed that the word SELLER whenever used in this contract shall be understood to include SUCCESSORS OR ASSIGNS.

10. PURCHASER hereby waives notice of any assignment of this contract and does also hereby waive any defense, set-off or counterclaim which may now exist or which may at any time hereafter arise to the covenants, obligations or undertakings of PURCHASER hereunder.

Executed in triplicate, one copy of which was delivered to and retained by PURCHASER this 17th day of November 1927

X R. J. Waters (L. S.)
(Purchaser's Signature)

By
(Official Title, if Company)

646-19th Ave., San Francisco.
(Purchaser's Residence Address—Street, Town, State)

C. Magner Jr
(Witness' Signature)

EARLE C. ANTHONY, INC. (L. S.)
(Seller's Signature)

By [signature]
(Official Title, if Company)

901 Van Ness Ave., San Francisco.
(Seller's Address—Street, Town, State)

[signature]
(Witness' Signature)

Schedule of Payments

$130.20 1 mo. after date
$130.20 2 mos. after date
$130.20 3 mos. after date
$130.20 4 mos. after date
$130.20 5 mos. after date
$130.20 6 mos. after date
$130.20 7 mos. after date
$130.20 8 mos. after date
$130.20 9 mos. after date
$130.20 10 mos. after date
$130.20 11 mos. after date
$130.20 12 mos. after date

$1562.40 San Francisco, California November 17, 1927
(City) (State) (Date)

On or before twelve (12) months after date I promise to pay to the order

—BEARER—

Fifteen Hundred Sixty Two and 40/100 Dollars

Payable in 12 equal monthly installments of $ Dollars

on the 17th day of each month beginning December 17 1927

at Wells Fargo Bank & Union Trust Co., Union Trust Office, San Francisco, California

Packard
(Make)

136575
(Mfrs.' Serial No.)

R. J. Waters
(Print or type Signer's name)

Signature X R. J. Waters

P. O. Address 646-19th Ave., S. F. Cal.
(Print or typewrite)

Wells Fargo Bank & Union Trust Co. Union Trust Office NOV 14 1928 Paid

Courtesy Ross M. Lee Collection.

PACKARD

A New and Improved Model of the Famous Single-Six

In the opinion of more than 30,000 enthusiastic Single-Six owners, this famous Packard cannot be greatly improved.

They see no opportunity for betterment in the car which has established for the entire motor car industry a new high standard of fine car performance, of economy, of beauty, of motoring comfort.

But it has been the unvarying policy of the Packard Company, for twenty-four years, steadily to improve its product.

In pursuance of this practice, it is now our privilege to announce a new model of the Packard Single-Six, including many important new features and refinements.

In the fundamentals of Single-Six engineering and manufacture, we agree that no desirable changes are possible.

We recognize, however, in four wheel brakes, an important advance in motor car design.

In fact, Packard Straight-Eight was the first prominent American car to carry four-wheel brakes as regular equipment.

From this time, all Packard cars will be equipped with four-wheel brakes.

To insure greater durability, long life and economy of upkeep, the new Single-Six is provided with a newly designed and heavier transmission.

It is exceptionally quiet and smooth in operation.

Artillery type wheels of heavier construction contribute enhanced appearance.

To make the battery most accessible, it has been located on the running board, as in the Straight-Eight, and enclosed in a theft-proof box.

There are also several important refinements in regular equipment, including—

Gasoline gauge on the instrument board;

The use of adjustable window regulators on the rear windows of Sedans and Sedan-Limousines;

The adoption of an efficient stop-light for all types;

Larger steering wheel;

A more beautiful instrument board, with walnut finish;

An interior tonneau light for all open models.

The brilliant beauty of design and color, which have made the Single-Six the most notable—and the most imitated—car on the market, remain unchanged.

With these important improvements, the Packard Single-Six is, in our opinion, an even more outstanding value than in the past.

PACKARD MOTOR CAR COMPANY

Ready January 1, 1924
To be exhibited at all National Automobile Shows

Advertisements courtesy Ross M. Lee Collection.

ROUND THE WORLD FLIERS CHOOSE PACKARD EIGHT

On November 9, 1924, Mayor Dever, on behalf of the citizens of Chicago, presented Capt. Lowell H. Smith and Lt. Leslie P. Arnold each with a Packard Eight sport model—the car of their choice.

The Packard Motor Car Company acknowledges one of the finest compliments ever paid to any motor car manufacturer.

Five of the six round the world fliers, when asked which among all of the motor cars in the world they would like as gifts in recognition of their history-making flight, voted for the Packard Eight.

To have these men, who entrusted their lives to the Liberty aeroplane motor—first developed by Packard —choose the Packard Eight, is an endorsement which cannot be taken lightly.

Copyright by Underwood & Underwood

Above: Captain Lowell H. Smith

Below: Lieutenant Leslie P. Arnold

Packard Six and Eight both furnished in ten body types, open and enclosed. Packard's extremely liberal monthly payment plan makes possible the immediate enjoyment of a Packard, purchasing out of income instead of capital.

ASK THE MAN WHO OWNS ONE

GLIMPSING THE PAST 47

PACKARD

SUPREME—AIR, LAND AND WATER

Packard motors drove the giant Navy dirigible Shenandoah on its record-breaking flight of 8100 miles.

Packard motors enabled the seaplane PN-9 to nearly double the previous world's record for non-stop sea-plane flight by traveling 2230 miles in 28 hours, 35 minutes, 27 seconds—with a starting load of nearly ten tons.

A standard Packard marine motor drove Rainbow III 1064 miles in 24 hours, a distance greater by 276 miles than any boat of any kind or size ever covered in one day.

Packard's quarter century of experience in the design and manufacture of motors is available to all in the Packard Six and the Packard Eight.

Ask The Man Who Owns One

Advertisements courtesy Ross M. Lee Collection.

Mastery of Power

Ask the man who owns one

THE new series Packard Eight brings a new zest for motoring to those who long ago ceased to drive for pleasure.

Smooth, quiet, truly beautiful in performance, it is pleasing to sense your mastery of its eighty horse-power.

The new Packard steering and front spring suspension at all times assure your safety and ease on low-pressure tires.

And like a great, healthy animal the new Packard Eight requires little attention to be always in the pink of condition. The chassis lubricating system and the oil rectifier make that attention almost automatic. Together, they double the life of the car.

Behind the wheel of a Packard Eight you may learn the true meaning of luxury, comfort and distinction in travel.

The Packard Eight is provided in nine body types—four open and five enclosed. Packard dealers welcome the buyer who prefers to purchase out of income instead of capital.

The Packard Eight five-passenger Sedan is illustrated, $4750 at Detroit

PACKARD

What Price-Class?

PACKARD

ASK THE MAN WHO OWNS ONE

The important thing to consider in purchasing a car is the cost of *owning*—not the cost of *buying*

Unfortunately people have grouped cars into "price-classes." There is the "$1000 price-class," the "$1500 price-class," the "$2000 price-class," and so on.

This informal classification is misleading. It lays entirely too much emphasis on the *relatively* unimportant first cost of any car and none on the very important cost of ownership and use. Hence people delude themselves as to how good a car they can afford to own.

Paying for a Packard Without Owning One!

Here is a carefully considered statement which may astonish you: If you have been in the habit of paying ten or twelve hundred dollars or more for your motor cars, then you can easily afford a Packard Eight! In fact, *you are very likely paying for a Packard without owning one!*

It can be demonstrated to you that you may own and drive a Packard Standard Eight *at no greater cost,* over a period of four or five years, than the expense of owning your present "price-class" car.

Most of the items of cost in *operating* a car are the same as between a Packard Eight and any car down to *half the cost of a Packard.* And if you will use even *half* the mileage we build into your Packard your depreciation charge will be so low that *the saving will completely offset the original cost difference.*

The Packard Eight Has No Price-Class

The Packard Eight is not in a "price-class." We build it as well as a motor car can be built. We build it to last—and we price it fairly. Then we protect the investment of our owners. No radical changes have depreciated Packard cars from year to year. Our owners keep their Packards—and *enjoy* keeping them—nearly twice as long as they have been in the habit of keeping their "price-class" cars. And in doing so they drive Packard Eights at no extra charge!

If you want a Packard Eight—buy one! You may buy it out of income—and there is no better investment. Remember you are very probably paying for a Packard no matter what car costing over $1000 you may be driving. Packard dealers everywhere have the facts and will gladly give them to you.

You *can* afford a Packard.

· · I suppose I have owned every really fine car built in this country. And I even imported a couple. You know I drive myself and always get a lot of real pleasure out of my cars — not just transportation. A fine car appeals to me as much as a good horse. I quit experimenting three years ago and went back to my first love. That car has everything I want or expect in the way of looks and performance. You'll always be glad you got a Packard. I wouldn't drive anything else.

Illustrated above is the Packard Eight 645 Five-Passenger Phaeton

ASK THE MAN WHO OWNS ONE

PACKARD MOTOR CAR COMPANY
DETROIT - - - MICHIGAN

Advertisements courtesy Ross M. Lee Collection.

Serving America's Aristocracy

America has its aristocracy of intelligence and culture, of achievement and wealth, of taste and talent. Every community has its leaders of thought and action. And historic Washington—drawing its leaders from every section of the Union—is representative of the aristocracy of them all.

There in the world's greatest capital it is natural to find Packard cars honored by marked preferment—now as for a generation past. That five of the distinguished jurists of the United States Supreme Court own Packard cars is but an indication of this preference among those whose taste and judgment is unquestioned.

The list of cabinet members, senators, ambassadors and congressional leaders who consistently favor Packard with their patronage reads like the roster of an American peerage. Packard could cite no stronger credentials.

PACKARD
ASK THE MAN WHO OWNS ONE

Advertisements courtesy Ross M. Lee Collection.

"The supreme combination of all that is fine in motor cars."

Beauty

It has been said that "beauty is in the eye of the beholder". And yet, while tastes differ, there are some things the beauty of which is agreed upon the world around.

The graceful proportions and distinguished simplicity of Packard design seem to command universal admiration. At home they long ago established a style which other manufacturers sincerely flattered by imitation. Abroad, both the Packard Six and the Packard Eight have time after time won first award in International Car Beauty Contests—being acclaimed by foreign judges as superior in grace and beauty to the finest custom designs of their own countrymen!

The improved Packard retains the famous lines which have been characteristically Packard for a decade—with refinements of detail which provide still more alluring appearance and luxurious comfort. Its aristocratic beauty is in keeping with the improved Packard's unrivaled mechanical performance.

PACKARD
ASK THE MAN WHO OWNS ONE

Charm · That women of wealth and social position the world over have shown so pronounced a preference for Packard cars is a tribute to Packard's grace and beauty.

There is an irresistible charm in the simple dignity of Packard lines — a slender, thoroughbred appearance as appealing to the man of affairs as to the woman of fashion. But the real secret of Packard's universal attraction goes beyond the design and proportions which have been so widely imitated.

The prestige reflected by a generation of distinguished owners; the reputation achieved through more than a quarter century of engineering leadership, the luxurious fineness in every detail of body and chassis; the super-power of the smooth and silent motor, its alert response on hill or crowded boulevard—

These qualities all contribute to that charm which leads the discriminating man or woman to Packard ownership.

ASK THE MAN WHO OWNS ONE

PACKARD

DEPENDABILITY— Thousands of families have not been without the faithful service of a Packard for a generation.

To these and many other families of more recent ownership Packard cars have come to mean far more than fine, efficient machines of transportation. They have gained some part of that affection men feel for faithful dogs and high-bred horses.

For the Packard is, above all, *dependable*. Owners learn to trust the unfailing performance of this fine car—day after day—year after year—with its surprisingly small cost of maintenance and simplest sort of routine care.

The famed beauty and distinction of the Packard, its roomy comfort, great power and long life—all have had a part in establishing its priceless reputation. But underlying all these is the Packard dependability which for twenty-seven years has made the name Packard synonymous with quality motor cars.

ASK THE MAN WHO OWNS ONE

PACKARD

Advertisements courtesy Ross M. Lee Collection.

GLIMPSING THE PAST 51

"The supreme combination of all that is fine in motor cars."

ASK THE MAN WHO OWNS ONE

THE RESTFUL CAR

Distinction · · A man or a motor may gain notoriety, even popularity, almost over night—and lose them just as quickly. But distinction comes only with time and a long series of notable achievements.

The distinction which Packard cars enjoy is the result of more than a generation of leadership in engineering and in body design—a quarter century of patronage by an illustrious clientele.

Pride in Packard ownership is natural, and few would care to change the famous lines which proclaim their cars as Packards. But there are those who wish an individual distinction. To them Packard offers the masterpieces of the foremost body designers and unlimited choice in color combinations, upholstery and the refinements of equipment.

Thus those who would add the final touch of luxury and personality to supreme comfort, beauty and distinction can gratify their ultimate desire in a custom-built Packard.

PACKARD

Advertisements courtesy Ross M. Lee Collection.

Luxury · The improved Packard Eight is the supremely luxurious car. It is designed and built for those favored few who may and do demand the comfort and ease of their own drawing rooms in motor travel.

Fast or slow, flashing through the maze of metropolitan congestion, or smoothly annihilating distance at almost aircraft speed in the open, Packard passengers know the luxury of truly restful transportation.

The graceful beauty of Packard lines, the roominess of the car's interior, the quiet good taste of its upholstery and appointments, the silent ease of motion, and the sense of security which comes with tremendous power under sure control—all contribute to the mental satisfaction and physical repose of the Packard Eight owner.

Here, the discriminating man or woman finds ideal performance, beauty, distinction and comfort perfectly combined.

PACKARD
ASK THE MAN WHO OWNS ONE

52 PACKARD

"The supreme combination of all that is fine in motor cars."

Prestige · The Packard owner, however high his station, mentions his car with a certain satisfaction —knowing that his choice proclaims discriminating taste as well as a sound judgment of fine things.

For the Packard is one of the world's few fine cars universally approved by the enthusiastic owners of other famous makes.

Recognized everywhere as supremely typifying America's genius for perfection in things mechanical, Packard cars go further in possessing to a marked degree that subtle attribute— prestige.

Packard prestige, sensed if not defined by every Packard owner, is reflected in the car's aristocratic beauty, its distinction, its luxury and comfort, its superb performance—unexcelled in traffic or on the open road.

PACKARD

ASK THE MAN WHO OWNS ONE

Advertisements courtesy Ross M. Lee Collection.

"The supreme combination of all that is fine in motor cars."

ASK THE MAN WHO OWNS ONE

Pride of Possession · There are those who understand the subtle pleasure, the inner satisfaction, gained from the ownership of things which the whole world approves and acknowledges to be fine and genuine.

A gown by Poiret; an etching by Whistler; an authentic Chippendale; a blooded hunter; a service of Sèvres porcelain—such possessions mean far more to those of taste and discrimination than the sums they cost.

Is it strange that such people turn instinctively to Packard for their motor cars—that they count their Packards among their most prized possessions?

Packard, for a generation, has built its cars for such a clientele.

PACKARD
THE RESTFUL CAR

"The supreme combination of all that is fine in motor cars"

The Greek mathematician and inventor, Archimedes, discovered and used many of the principles of mechanical engineering two hundred fifty years B.C.

Simplicity — More than ten years ago Packard started not only the modern trend in body lines but the intensive simplification of design so universally sought after today. The mechanical simplicity of Packard cars has since been as much copied as has their famous beauty.

True engineering genius, years of research and experiment, are required to reduce any machine to its simplest and most efficient form. But once achieved, as in Packard cars, such simplicity is of the greatest value. It means lower first cost, exceptionally low maintenance expense and long life.

Packard simplicity and high precision workmanship, together with such features as "Instant" chassis lubrication, are responsible for the years of luxurious mileage every Packard owner enjoys.

PACKARD
ASK THE MAN WHO OWNS ONE

IN ONE generation automotive engineering has revolutionized civilized life. Yet many of the fundamentals of the science are older than the Christian era.

The spiral bevel gears, which Packard developed and was the first to use commercially, are based on the principle of Archimedes' screw—in use 2,000 years ago. Today these gears are found in nearly every motor car except the very lowest priced.

They are but one example of the hundreds of advanced steps Packard has pioneered in the 28 years it has held engineering leadership. For Packard engineering no less than Packard beauty of line has been widely imitated.

The greatest achievements of Packard engineers and designers are the new Packard Six and Packard Eight—the finest, the most beautiful and the greatest performing cars Packard has ever built.

PACKARD
ASK THE MAN WHO OWNS ONE

Advertisements courtesy Ross M. Lee Collection.

PACKARD

Ability and achievement have ever won permanent place in those organizations consecrated to one high ideal

Packard men bear the imprint of the Packard organization. They are selected and schooled for but one quality of work and service. It shows, and it pays—both them and Packard.

From skilled machinist to designing engineer, Packard cars are produced by men who know and love fine things—men brought up in the interpretation and application of quality ideals.

From suburban dealer to manager of sales, Packard's clientele is served by men who uphold the Packard principles—men who know that the patronage of the discriminating brooks no compromise with quality either in product or in service.

For a single standard of high quality is ever uppermost in the minds of the Packard management—and the Packard organization is the guardian of a priceless reputation.

ASK THE MAN WHO OWNS ONE

Advertisements courtesy Ross M. Lee Collection.

The ancient craft of fine leather-working found expression in the seventeenth century in the cavalier's equipment.

IN leather selection and upholstery work Packard standards are as high and exacting as in the precision manufacture of motor parts.

These requirements prevail in the studios and shops of America's foremost body builders who make a complete selection of custom bodies for both the Packard Six and Packard Eight.

Each body is truly custom-made in the strictest sense of the word. Each bears the name plate of its distinguished maker, signifying that in beauty, comfort and distinction it is one of his masterpieces.

The All-Weather Town Car is one of the most interesting offerings. This may be readily converted from closed to open use by removing the driver's compartment roof and folding back the leather top and quarters.

Custom body builders have long preferred to design creations for Packard chassis. No others afford the slender lines so necessary for yacht-like beauty.

PACKARD
ASK THE MAN WHO OWNS ONE

GLIMPSING THE PAST 55

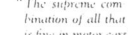

"The supreme combination of all that is fine in motor cars"

Long life is probably the most outstanding characteristic of the Packard car. It is a quality which new owners mention very frequently as the reason for their choice.

For the enduring excellence of Packard transportation is the foundation of Packard's greatly broadened market. Thousands buy these fine cars with the calculated intention of keeping them at least five years—and with the

ENDURING!

knowledge that on such a basis Packard ownership costs no more per year than they have paid for half price cars of far less comfort and distinction.

Packard makes it easy and desirable for its owners to keep their cars. No radical design changes intrigue them annually. And Packard beauty, of line, finish and upholstery, endures as surely as the sturdy precision of its famous chassis.

Ask The Man Who Owns One

PACKARD

Advertisements courtesy Ross M. Lee Collection.

You are paying for a Packard Why not own one?

Before buying an automobile consider these two facts: After costs are not less because first cost is less. A car priced at twice as much does not cost any more if driven twice as long.

Many motorists have been kept from Packard ownership because they thought it too expensive. Yet records prove that it costs no more to enjoy the luxury of Packard transportation.

CONFIRMED BY OWNERS IN ATLANTA

There are eight items of cost to consider in owning any car. Compare these costs as between a Packard Standard Eight and any car of its size down to half its price and you will find:

That the license cost for the Packard is little, if any more.

That garage cost is the same.

That insurance may be slightly higher. But this applies principally to collision coverage—a very small sum annually.

That the three operating items—gas, oil and tires—show no advantage for either car. The Packard Standard Eight gives 10 to 12 miles or more to the gallon of gasoline; 1,000 miles or more to the gallon of oil; 15,000 to 20,000 miles or more to the set of tires.

That Packard repairs actually cost less. This is due, first, to the simplicity of Packard design which makes repair work quick and easy; second, to Packard quality which makes less repair work necessary;

and third, to Packard's advanced motor and centralized chassis lubrication systems which protect factory-built-in precision.

And finally you will find that depreciation on a Packard costs no more because country-wide records prove that Packard cars are driven far longer—in Atlanta, Ga., for example, much more than twice as long as the lower priced cars traded in on them.

Atlanta motorists have learned that Packard transportation costs no more. There, three out of four buyers of Packard Standard Eights turn in other makes of cars. And, if past records are an indication, they will remain in the Packard family indefinitely, as only 3 percent of Packard owners in Atlanta have changed to other automobiles.

Figure out your own costs of motoring and compare them with the costs of owning a Packard. The Packard dealer in your city has the facts. You may find that you, too, can enjoy the luxury and distinction of Packard transportation at no increase in your motoring expense.

PACKARD MOTOR CAR COMPANY
DETROIT - - - MICHIGAN

ASK THE MAN WHO OWNS ONE

—and now at Monte Carlo

THOSE who have been in Europe during the past few seasons will remember the car beauty contests which have been a fad at all the famous watering places on the Continent. *Concours d'Elégance-Automobiles* they are called in France.

In these contests, held where the wealth and fashion of all nations gather at play, the most luxurious special bodies, the world's finest motor cars, are judged for beauty and distinction.

Americans will be proud to learn that a standard American motor car has won first prize in such a competition—not once but eleven times!

Packard cars, entered by their private owners, have won first place for grace and beauty at Vichy, at Le Touquet and at Aix-les-Bains in France. At Wiesbaden, Neuenahr, Trier, and Baden-Baden in Germany. At Oporto in Portugal. And now at Monte Carlo—that cosmopolitan center of luxury and beauty on the Riviera!

Such international acclaim confirms America's verdict—that the unchanging beauty and distinction of Packard lines have yet to be equaled or surpassed.

PACKARD
Ask the man who owns one

Advertisements courtesy Ross M. Lee Collection.

PACKARD

Each Packard is built to the exacting requirements of the world's most discriminating clientele

Packard, like its patrons, demands and selects only the best the world provides.

Discriminating taste, experience, exact knowledge and scientific equipment, combine to aid in the selection of the diverse materials which Packard craftsmanship finally molds into the modern miracle of luxurious transportation.

There are artists in other fields than color, form and fabric. Packard has also its connoisseurs in steel, in bronze, in aluminum, in wood, in a score of other highly specialized departments. These men pick Packard materials with a fine appreciation of their responsibilities in upholding a priceless reputation.

Fine workmanship demands and deserves the best of materials. In things unseen as in things seen, a Packard must measure up to the one standard of quality which Packard knows the highest.

ASK THE MAN WHO OWNS ONE

PACKARD

Only where talent and industry are rewarded, can the highest standard of quality craftsmanship be maintained

Packard men are carefully chosen. Their native skill is enhanced by Packard training. Inspection is rigid, but supervision is friendly and helpful. Initiative is fostered—aptitude rewarded. Merit may always be sure of recognition.

The human element is all-important. No other factor—design, engineering, methods or materials—overshadows craftsmanship in its contribution to the high quality of Packard cars.

And so at Packard there has been developed an organization of automobile artisans, schooled to one standard of quality workmanship—the highest.

Thousands of Packard craftsmen have been at their duties for five and more years—hundreds upwards of a decade. Their loyal and intelligent co-operation has helped measurably to build Packard's priceless reputation for outstanding leadership in the fine car field.

ASK THE MAN WHO OWNS ONE

Advertisements courtesy Ross M. Lee Collection.

How Many Buyers Can Judge *Value*?

NEARLY every man has his visions of finding the ideal motor car. He anticipates the true mastery of the roads at last, and the prestige of being *right* at every point of his motoring.

For the man who wants the Packard qualities in his motoring, only the Packard Car will do. While if his taste and sense of values are not up to the Packard, some other car will do.

The Packard Twin-Six really is as true and fine as anyone ever assumed any car to be.

It occupies, alone and sufficient, the place it has made for itself. It stands aloof equally from the car that obviously can be no better than it looks, and from the car that strives to look better than it is.

The dominant place of the Packard is not a thing of chance. For twenty-one years the Packard has been delivering *intrinsic value*—the soundest value a motor car has ever given.

During the War, inspecting officers spoke of the Packard plant as a manufacturing marvel. The only automobile plant in the world to produce high-grade cars on a quantity basis.

Why this tremendous plant investment? Simply to produce a car of Packard grade at a price within reason. If built by piecemeal methods the Packard would be the highest priced car in the world.

PACKARD MOTOR CAR COMPANY ⋅ DETROIT

Performance: THE TWIN-SIX ENGINE—More reserve power at all car speeds than any other stock car engine built

"Mention The Geographic—It identifies you"

World Supremacy

A new regime in Madrid has not lessened Spanish appreciation of the luxury and distinction of Packard transportation. Packard cars in Spain outnumber those of every other fine American make. Among families of rank and prominence there, as throughout the entire world, Packard is the supreme fine car

The new Packard Light Eight is a strikingly handsome car. In appearance it belongs unmistakably to the distinguished Packard family. Yet it is smartly new and original in its youthful grace of line and proportion—as is well illustrated by the popular Convertible Coupe below. ¶ When you first inspect the Packard Light Eight, you will be surprised at its size and roominess. It is a big and substantial car, with wheelbase of 128 inches. It is "light" only in comparison with other cars of the Packard line—the Standard Eight, the Eight DeLuxe and the new Twin Six. ¶ Richly appointed and upholstered, truly advanced in all mechanical features, the Packard Light Eight now offers the luxury of *fine car* transportation to those motorists who have been accustomed to paying from $1500 to $2000 for their cars. For here is an eight—"Packard" in personality, prestige and performance—factory-priced at the astonishing range of $1750 to $1795. ¶ Before buying *any* car be sure to *see* and *drive* the Packard Light Eight. You will thrill to its velvety, 110 horsepower motor, its Silent Synchro-mesh Transmission, *quiet in all three speeds*, its simple, *safe* Finger-Control Free-Wheeling. Why not take your old car to your Packard dealer today? He will allow you all that it is worth—and, if you wish to buy out of income, you will find the payments surprisingly small.

PACKARD — Ask the man who owns one

Advertisements courtesy Ross M. Lee Collection.

Mr. W. K. Jewett of Pasadena
*is one of more than 1000 distinguished owners through whose gateways
Packards have passed for 21 years or more*

Packard Twelve Cabriolet with Body by LeBaron

HERE is perhaps the greatest tribute that could be paid to the quality that Packard has maintained through the years . . .

. . . more than 1000 distinguished families have owned Packards continuously for 21 years or more.

Such a record is the greatest possible proof of the luxury Packard affords, the service Packard gives, the prestige Packard carries.

It is proof, too, that Packard has succeeded in its greatest aim—to make each new Packard finer and more beautiful than the one before.

And America is agreeing with that opinion. Since the introduction of these brilliant new cars, Packard has received a greater share of the fine car business—both here and abroad—than ever before in its history. And while it may be a coincidence, more people have been buying fine cars during these months than at any time in years.

If you, like so many of these people, have driven your present car far longer than usual, why not join them now in the joy of owning a new 1935 Packard? . . . Just telephone your Packard dealer—he will gladly bring one of these new cars to your door for a trial.

PACKARD EIGHT · SUPER EIGHT · TWELVE

· Ask the man who owns one ·

—get the *plus* of a Packard

THE ADVANCED PACKARD TWELVE
...the *finest* car that money can buy

THE new Packard 12 for 1937 is not just an improved version of last year's model. It is a new car—*greatly reduced in price*—and so revolutionary in its performance that it makes all previous standards of fine-car motoring obsolete.

This achievement is the result of *Packard's Completely Re-balanced Design*—a sweeping advance which affects all phases of performance.

This *Re-balanced Design* takes the finest individual wheel suspension ever created—*Packard's own Safe-T-Flex*—and makes it function as no other suspension has ever done before. Riding comfort and handling ease reach heights never before attained in any automobile.

This *Re-balanced Design* assists the Packard-improved hydraulic brakes to perform in a way that is new and wonderful. A mere toe-touch brings this great Twelve to a velvety stop.

This *Re-balanced Design* makes the new Packard Double-Trussed Frame—*a frame some 400% more rigid*—contribute a stability and roadability never before enjoyed in a motor car.

Anticipating the tremendous interest this new car will arouse, Packard has given it a most attractive price—a price hundreds of dollars less than last year's Twelve. Your Packard dealer is eager to show you the new Twelve. See it—drive it—and you will know why we say: For 1937—"*Get the plus of a Packard!*"

PACKARD TWELVE $3420
and up, at the factory
ASK THE MAN WHO OWNS ONE

AND—A BRAND NEW PACKARD SIX
...upsetting all former standards in this price class

SHOWN ABOVE is the new Packard Six—a car destined to completely re-shape America's lower-price car picture.

It is, Packard believes, the most astonishing value ever offered the public.

It is a high-powered car, yet a marvel of operating economy. It is the safest car of its weight ever built. Heir to Packard's 37 years of experience, brother of the great Packard 120, the Packard Six brings to its price class for the first time the important combination of qualities—*long mechanical life coupled with long style life.*

Built deliberately into your Packard Six is all the long mechanical life for which Packards are famous. And guarding this long mechanical life are the lines that assure long style life—the lines that keep Packards looking like Packards, year after year.

Here are quick facts about this astonishing car . . .

Overall length: 192 inches. *Weight:* 3450 lbs. *Motor:* Packard designed and built, to Packard precision standards, with a compression ratio of 6.4 to 1. *Horsepower:* 100. *Brakes:* hydraulic. *Front Suspension:* Packard Safe-T-Flex individual wheel suspension. *Body:* Packard designed and built.

We urge you to go to your Packard showroom and drive this car yourself. Find out how easily it can be bought out of income. We believe you'll soon be saying, "I'm driving a Packard."

NOW AT ALL DEALERS
PACKARD SIX $795
and up, at factory. Standard accessory group extra.

Every Tuesday Night—THE PACKARD HOUR starring Fred Astaire—NBC Red Network, Coast to Coast, 9:30 Eastern Daylight Saving Time

Advertisements courtesy Ross M. Lee Collection.

Advertisements courtesy Ross M. Lee Collection.

GLIMPSING THE PAST

Illustrated: Packard One-Twenty Touring Sedan, $1161* (white sidewall tires extra)

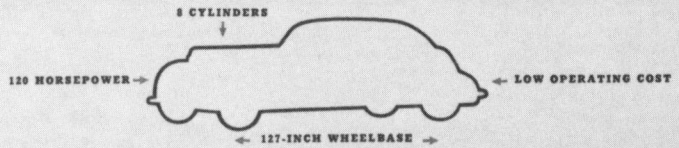

It crowds other eights out of the picture, the stunning PACKARD 120

IN THE EYES of almost anyone who knows the smart, new Packard 120, there *is* no other eight in the 1940 picture.

For to its loyal owners, this superlative car is in a class by itself. On a dollar-for-dollar value basis, no eight can match it. You can't own it without feeling for it an almost personalized affection. It's precisely *that* sort of an eight.

See it, and you'll know why. Its newly-styled lines will stir you to admiration—if you've an eye for a blue blood. But to *really* experience something new, something exciting (and that's a promise') step in and press the starter.

Trees, houses, humdrum cars slip past with the unreality of a dream. Pitted roads iron out into boulevards. You'll get that luxurious feeling of riding smoothness, of greater roominess, which its *extra length* imparts.

Above all else, do *this*: ask any owner of a new 1940 Packard 120 what he thinks of its operating costs! He'll tell you that he's amazed and delighted at the mileage his 120 clocks on a tankful of gasoline—that oil consumption is negligible.

And if he has had the car long enough to require any routine service operations, he can tell you that Packard 120 charges are comparable—not merely with other cars at its price—but with *those of much smaller, cheaper cars.*

Because One-Twenty owner enthusiasm and One-Twenty value are both at an all-time high, signs point to the greatest year in Packard history! Better join the Spring swing to Packard.

ASK THE MAN WHO OWNS ONE

PACKARD 120
$1038

AND UP. *Packard 110, $867 and up. Packard 120, $1038 and up. Packard Super-8 160, $1524 and up. Packard Custom Super-8 180, $2228 to $6330. *All prices delivered in Detroit, State taxes extra.*

Collier's, The National Weekly 1940

It's happening on a thousand Main Streets!

1. THIS YEAR, something has been happening on Main Streets all over America. For increasing thousands of average-income motorists have discovered that they don't have to keep on buying ordinary cars... they can own a truly *fine* car. Take the case of the Harry Browns... typical Americans. Our close-up shows their first eye-opener—the discovery that their neighbors in the modest house next door have bought a Packard!

2. A FEW DAYS LATER, the Stedmans took them riding. "Such a big, roomy car!" admired Mrs. Brown. "Watch her go," said Bill Stedman. Miles slipped by. Hills bowed down... rough spots vanished magically.

3. GHOSTING HOMEWARD, Harry fired questions at his neighbor... found that Bill hadn't had to pay a penny down! His old car *more* than covered the down payment, so that his monthly payments were unbelievably low. (This happens 4 times out of 5.)

4. NOW—weekends find this note in the Brown's milk bottle. They have a beautiful, smart new Packard of their own. Its flashing performance and its astonishingly low operating costs delight them. And this same experience can be yours.

THE SWING'S TO PACKARD!

This year, thousands of new owners have joined the Packard family.

Ask *any* of them what he thinks of his 1940 Packard. Then *try* to break away from his enthusiasm for the newly-styled Packard lines, for the car's verve and spirit, its all-around fineness. And operating costs? He'll declare his Packard a veritable miser on gasoline—and that he can hardly remember when he last had to "add a quart" of oil!

Add these owner facts to what your Packard dealer will *show* you: that service charges on a big, roomy Packard actually compare favorably with even those of the so-called "economy cars". But drive a new 1940 Packard *yourself*—and you'll know—*immediately*, why this promises to be Packard's biggest year!

ASK THE MAN WHO OWNS ONE

PACKARD
$867

AND UP. *Packard 110, $867 and up. Packard 120, $1038 and up. Packard Super-8 160, $1524 and up. Packard Custom Super-8 180, $2243 to $6000. All prices delivered in Detroit, State taxes and white sidewall tires (as shown) extra.*

Advertisements courtesy Ross M. Lee Collection.

Illustrations: Custom *Super Clipper*

- **For a world-famed architect who knows the measure of perfection**

It is only natural that a man who has devoted his life to *creating* beauty should be attracted by the restrained elegance of the Packard *Super Clipper*.

And even though his unerring judgment led him to choose this motor car because of its beauty, he knows full well that its famed Packard crest is the hallmark of still *other* attributes which a man of means expects and demands in the car of his choice...

...a silken-smooth 165-horsepower Packard engine which responds with a brilliance of performance literally tops on the road today... and an uncompromising mechanical excellence which adds new lustre even to Packard's tradition of craftsmanship.

In short, we are certain that a visit to your Packard dealer's will quickly confirm what you probably suspect right now: Once you have seen and driven this distinguished motor car, nothing short of such perfection can ever again fully satisfy you!

★ ASK THE MAN WHO OWNS ONE ★

PACKARD *Super Clipper*

Now, for the first time in nearly 4 years

AMERICA'S No. 1 GLAMOUR CAR

is rolling off the Packard assembly lines!

Until today, that title—"Glamour Car of America"—was proudly held by the last, prewar, Packard Clipper.

But now that title passes on to a still more glamorous car—*the brand-new 1946 Packard Clipper!*

These new cars, now rolling off our assembly lines, are *the finest Packards ever built!*

And they *should* be! For they have everything that made the *last* Clipper tops in design and performance. "Fadeaway" fenders! Functional streamlining with wider, roomy interiors! Plus new postwar beauty! Plus...

new mechanical perfection!

Our wartime experience—building combat engines to measurements as fine as millionths of an inch—adds new luster to Packard precision craftsmanship. And new materials will mean better quality, longer life.

When you buy a 1946 Packard Clipper, it's more than ever...

a "long haul" investment

In style, and engineering, the new Clipper is truly ahead of its time. We predict that when you see this dazzling new 1946 Packard, you won't be happy until you own one... and you'll always be glad you bought one!

★ ASK THE MAN WHO OWNS ONE ★

See **PACKARD** FOR 1946

Advertisements courtesy Ross M. Lee Collection.

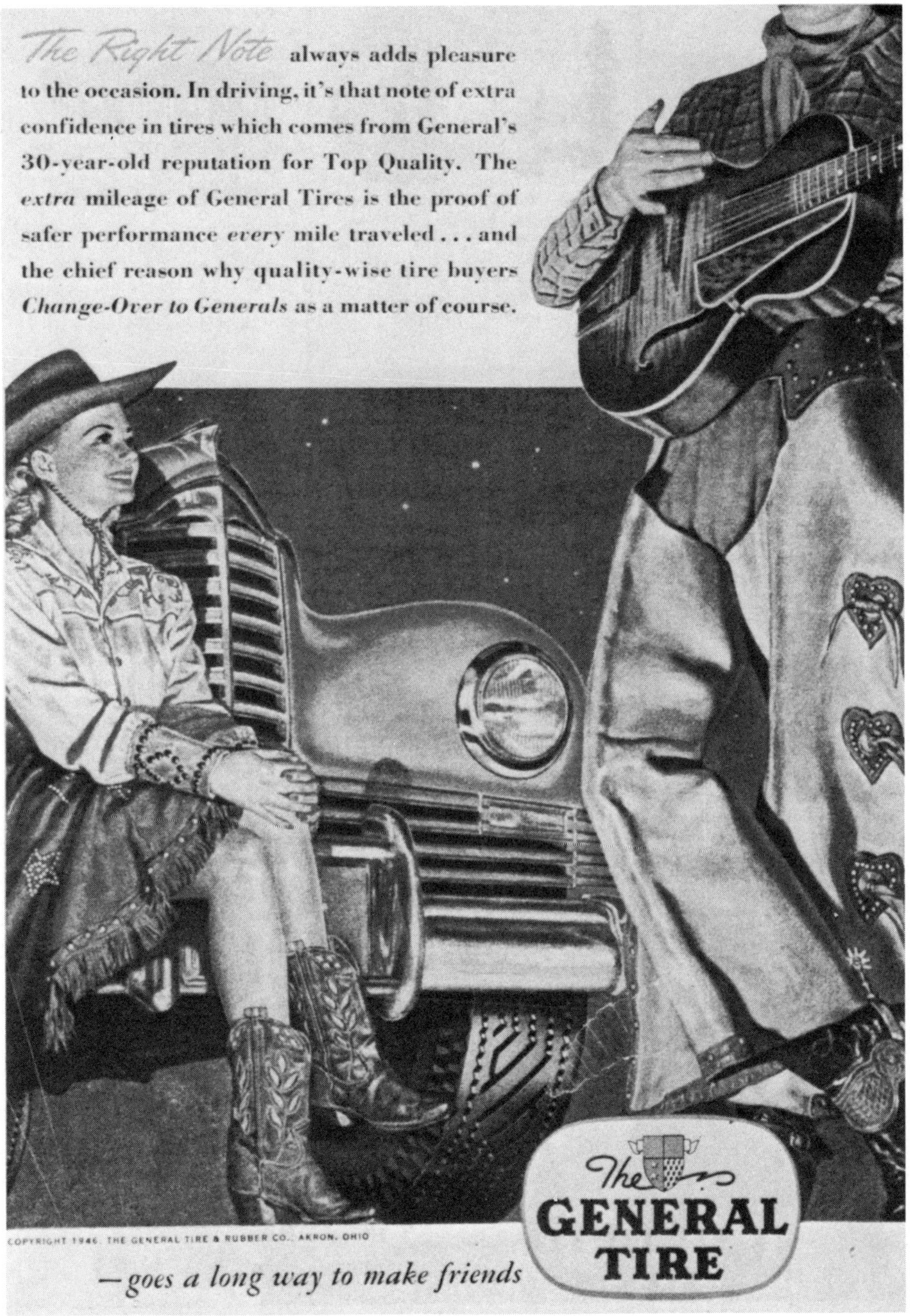

Advertisements courtesy Ross M. Lee Collection.

Advertisements courtesy Ross M. Lee Collection.

It crawled from the sea.

GLIMPSING THE PAST

Advertisements courtesy Ross M. Lee Collection.

Advertisements courtesy Ross M. Lee Collection.

GLIMPSING THE PAST

the New PACKARD
with Sensational Torsion Level Ride

THE *Patrician*
260 HORSEPOWER
AMERICA'S MOST DISTINCTIVE SEDAN

THE *Four Hundred*
260 HORSEPOWER
SPIRITED AND ELEGANT HARDTOP

Greatest Engineering Advancement in Automotive History!

Outstanding leadership in creative engineering has been a Packard tradition ever since the automobile came upon the American scene at the turn of the century. No achievement in all this time has been greater than the *new* Packard Torsion-Level Ride. And *only* Packard gives you Torsion-Level Suspension that eliminates conventional springing and *automatically levels the load... smooths the road*.

This sensational ride is on all Packard models... the Caribbean, designed for excitement and pure pleasure... the Patrician, regal and classic... the Four Hundred, sophisticated and distinctive.

These newest of all the fine cars are distinctive not only in appearance but in *every* respect. For example, Packard's new V-8 is the most powerful American passenger car engine, for it delivers the greatest driving force at all road speeds. This powerful engine is linked to the *new* Packard Twin Ultramatic, smoothest and most responsive automatic transmission ever built. It gives you a choice of starts at your finger tips... smooth, cruising glide or lightning getaway.

Before you buy any fine car, drive the *new* Packard... the *one* new car that has created a higher concept of motoring pleasure and comfort.

"ASK THE MAN WHO OWNS ONE"

Take the key and see
Let the Ride Decide

Why not call your Packard dealer now? He will be happy to give you the key to a better ride by placing a new Packard at your disposal.

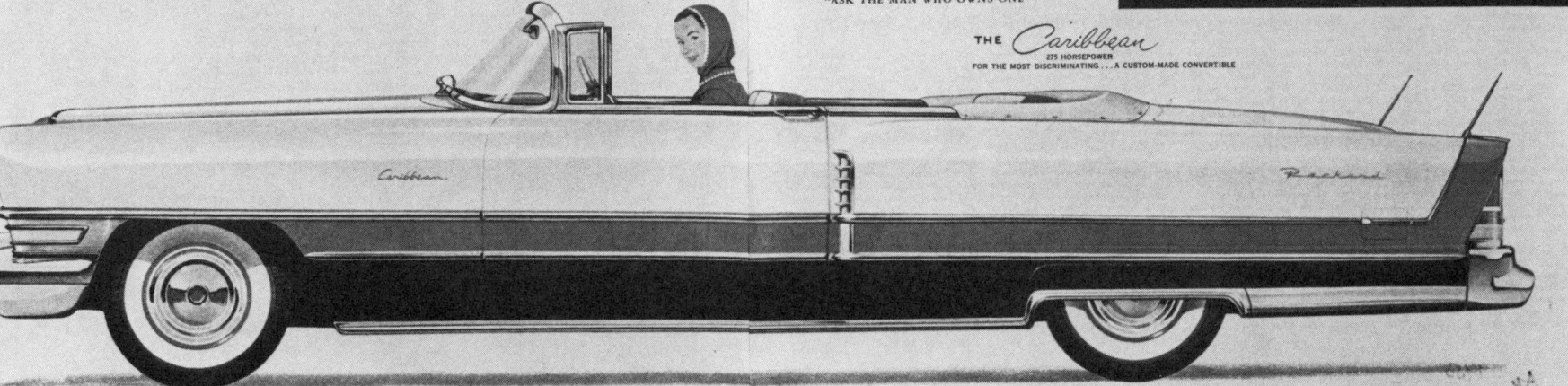

THE *Caribbean*
275 HORSEPOWER
FOR THE MOST DISCRIMINATING... A CUSTOM-MADE CONVERTIBLE

Advertisements courtesy Ross M. Lee Collection.

Another Revolutionary Advance from PACKARD the TWIN-TRACTION SAFETY DIFFERENTIAL!

Vastly increases your anti-skid safety on wet, slippery roads. Pulls you out of mud, sand, snow and ice—because if one wheel starts to slip, your power is instantly transmitted to the other wheel, the one with *traction*. No more being stuck, as in other cars, with one wheel spinning helplessly, the other standing still.

Enjoy these other features that are increasing the high resale value of Packards and Clippers faster than any other car—as much as 9.6% in the past year alone:

NO OTHER CAR COULD MAKE THIS HILL. Without Twin-Traction, no car could make this test hill at Packard Proving Grounds (its left side was dangerously iced). With this now available feature, Packards and Clippers move easily up and over—a feat so incredible that you must try a Packard or Clipper to really believe it.

TORSION-LEVEL SUSPENSION. Bounce and sway are minimized by long, resilient Torsion bars which replace now-outmoded coil and leaf springs. So smooth-riding it will change tomorrow's cars.

UP TO 310 HP—most powerful on the road in actual wheel-driving force. Delivers up to 15% greater economy and mileage through a superbly efficient power-train—a product of Packard precision.

ELECTRONIC TOUCH-BUTTON DRIVE. The only Selector that requires just a feathertouch—and it's placed *at* the steering wheel. Gives you instant control of Twin-Ultramatic—finest of automatic transmissions.

PACKARD DIVISION • Studebaker-Packard Corporation Where Pride of Workmanship *Still* Comes First

Advertisement courtesy Ross M. Lee Collection.

Ask the Man Who Owns One

10

Boom and Bad Years

The Packard Eight was as powerful as the Twin Six, and its long hood and generally long, flowing lines helped buyers forget the earlier model. The production simplicity possible with the Six and Eight paid off; sales went from 3589 cars in 1919 to 49,698 in 1928. In 1920, there were 200 Packard dealers and distributors, and by 1932 there were nearly 1000.

Packard's careful marketing and sales policies were matched by a strident service organization. In 1920, Packard had $5 million in service buildings alone (not including tools and other equipment). By 1931 that figure had quintupled. Packard service departments often would not charge a Packard owner from another area. They strove to create a good will that would keep owners in the family for years to come. The company left no aspect of ownership overlooked, and such tactics continued to pay off in repeat and new sales. For decades, Packard had the highest level of repeat owners in the industry.

Packard's sales growth was reflected by the number of stockholders. In 1919, 3000 people held Packard stock, by 1931 the number had grown to 99,000, and in 1933 there were 107,000 stockholders. Packard became the most widely held stock after General Motors (which had 360,000 stockholders).

After the inexpensive and voluminous Ford, Packard was the most recognized automotive name in the world. Lindbergh and other heroes rode Packards through Wall Street tickertape parades; senators, presidents, and Supreme Court justices rode in them, as did captains of industry, hoodlums, Hollywood, kings, dictators, and maharajas. On their famous camping trips, Thomas Edison, naturalist John Burroughs, Harvey Firestone, and Henry Ford traveled in a Packard Twin-Six touring car. But it was the simple, reliable, and rugged Six and Eight that were to spread Packard across the globe as never before. All the day's custom-body automakers mounted their work on Packard chassis. In 1928, its final year, you could buy the Fifth series Six 526 for $2275 to $2425, and choose from a phaeton, runabout, sedan, coupe, or convertible coupe. The 533 sold for from $2385 to $2785 with a choice of seven-passenger touring car, sedan, or limousine. Also available were the five-passenger club sedan, the four-passenger coupe, the two-four-passenger runabout, or the five-passenger phaeton.

If that wasn't enough, and you wanted to spend from $3550 to $5150, you got two more cylinders in addition to the above bodies. Although Packard listed 20 designs by Rollson, Holbrook, Dietrich, LeBaron, Judkins, Derham, Murphy, and Fleetwood in the custom coachwork catalog, prices could run thousands more if the customer visited one of the custom-body automakers and specified a one-off production.

Although almost 154,000 Packard Sixes were sold during its eight-year run, the company saw that it was expedient to again offer more cylinders. Its replacement was called the Standard Eight even though it was basically the same car as the Six. Actually the car's firewall was indented so the new engine would fit. The new motor was a shorter version of the 385-cubic-inch Eight, made possible by decreasing the bore to 3 3/16 inches. The Standard Eight engine displaced 320 cubic inches, and it kept the 5-inch stroke of the larger engine.

Two more cylinders and 10 more horsepower for the price of the old Six was a bargain many couldn't pass. By again simplifying production while offering more car, Packard was rewarded with more sales. The 1928-29 Sixth series run of 54,992 cars—43,130 of them the new Standard Eight—was the company's biggest so far. Although Packard would sell more cars in years to come, 1929 was to be its most profitable ($25,000,000) year.

A 1928 fifth series Six sedan. Photo John A. Conde Collection.

A 1928 Model 443 roadster. Photo John A. Conde Collection.

A 1929 Standard Eight Model 633 runabout. Photo John A. Conde Collection.

A 1930 745 roadster. Photo John A. Conde Collection.

Paring production costs enabled Packard to offer its famous name at increasingly attractive prices. A straight-eight Packard for no more than the old Six filled showrooms and company coffers. A similar coup in 1937 led to the biggest year in units sold in Packard's history. A six-cylinder car based on the popular One-Twenty was offered for the price of a Hudson or bottom-line Buick. That year Packard sold 109,518 cars, well over half of them the new 115-C. At 76,927, model year 1940 was the second biggest prewar year in terms of unit sales. Each time the company had such a banner year, however, it seemed to lose a little of its original exclusive allure. As Packards became closer to the realm of affordable cars, they also became a little more common—in both senses of the word.

Cadillac was now Packard's chief competitor and not likely to go away. Cadillac's lower-price offshoot was the eight-cylindered LaSalle; it was the first result of General Motor's new Art and Color Department under Harley Earl. With its crib of the Hispano-Suiza's lines and even that car's stock hood ornament, the new LaSalle was a success.

Selling cars by playing off a traditional name was to prove a marketing boomerang (as Packard would find out in years to come). Cadillac made a wise, long-term move by giving its lower-price version a free-standing name. If it sank it was a LaSalle; if it swam it was a Cadillac-LaSalle. The Standard Eight, and the Six before it, had been Packards in every sense of the word. But Packard men with an eye on future market penetration were watching the LaSalle with great interest.

Some 1930 model details. Photo by Susan Scott.

This was before October 29, 1929. After that, reaching into lower-price levels of the market would not just be another way to make money, but the only way to survive.

Into the Thirties, Packard offered cars from just under $2500 to over $10,000 if the customer wanted to commission a custom body. The 320-cubic-inch eight occupied the lower tiers, and the 385-cubic-inch eight with a factory body on the shorter wheelbase started at around $3500 in 1931. While wheelbases ranged up to 142 1/8 and 147 1/8 inches on the 1932 Ninth series 903 and 904, with prices as high as $7250 for custom bodies sold through the Packard factory, the smaller engine on the 134 1/2-inch wheelbase also offered on the 1931 model as an "Individual Custom Eight" for those poor souls who either had no more than $5175 to spend or had to keep a low profile.

Even as broken businessmen were sleeping under bridges at night and peddling apples by day, Packard skillfully covered every innuendo of the remaining luxury market. From Packard's 47,855 cars in 1929, to 28,386 in 1930, and 12,922 in 1931, about 22 percent were the larger-engine, more-expensive models. From 1925-28, the portion of more expensive Eights had been only about 16 percent. What business there was Packard cornered, and didn't forget the playboy cadre and the image of vitality that would bring. A speedster was offered in 1929 and 1930. The 626 and 734 speedsters were rakish open affairs combining a high-output version of the big eight with the short chassis driving through axle ratios as tall as 3.31 (usual Packard ratios in the other lines ranged from 4.07 to 5.08, open and lighter cars generally having the higher speed axles).

But the profit and romance the speedsters brought Packard wasn't justified by the expense of turning out fewer than 150 cars. The high-speed axles proved sluggish around town at a time when even the most inexpensive new cars were geared to move smartly away. There were few open roads for the speedster owner to try for 100. If he should try for long, the long stroke hammering the primitive bearings (by today's standards) would doubtless take its toll. A number of 734 speedsters were unsold at the end of the year. Also, the new convertible coupe and convertible sedan were to replace roadsters and phaetons in the Thirties.

Just after the 1929 stock-market crash, Cadillac brought out its V-16. It was not built to sell itself so much as to spread prestige over the other Cadillac products. Packard's more expensive cars had always added ambiance to its lesser lines; this was nothing new. The Depression reinforced a trend that had been growing all through the Twenties: the increasing market share of lower-priced cars.

By the opening of the Thirties, most medium and upper-medium-priced products were becoming smooth, fashionable cars thanks to engineering improvements disseminated by streamlined production methods, and wrapped in colorful styling. The difference between traditional-quality cars and the rabble was not as drastic as it had been, and an increasing number of wealthy buyers were driving the improved lower-priced cars. Packard had studied the feasibility of entering price ranges still lower than its Six during the Twenties, but continued success in the fine-car field made such tack unnecessary.

A 1931 phaeton. Photo by Susan Scott.

The impressive snout of the 1931 phaeton. Photo by Susan Scott.

The radiator grille stoneguard on a 1931 phaeton. Photo by Susan Scott.

A 1931 Phaeton. Photo by Susan Scott.

Mechanical refinements and economics of manufacture had continued to meld the industry to the point that Cadillac, once a medium-price offering, was now Packard's serious rival. In 1931, even Buick was marketing nothing but eight-cylindered automobiles. The top-of-the-line Buick displaced 345 cubic inches (3 5/16 × 5 bore × stroke) and would outperform a Packard costing twice as much.

The early Twelve prototype had front-wheel drive both because of its performance image and because it was envisioned as being more economical to manufacture than a conventional transmission with separate differential and driveshaft.

A V-12 allowed for the Buick's power but in a smoother and more compact package that would make for a nimbler, easier-handling car. But there were development snags in the new transmission, and Packard was eager to remind a public—impressed with new multicylindered cars—who the leader still was. So the excellent new V-12 was dropped in the Deluxe Eight's chassis. But the original 376-cubic-inch Buick beater, however fine, was not deemed suitable as Packard's new world-class luxury motor until it was enlarged to an introductory 445 cubic inches (3 7/16 × 4 bore × stroke; 160 hp at 3200 rpm, 322 ft. lbs. of torque at 1400 rpm).

Because the new Twin Six, as it was called for 1932 only, cost more than Packard's Deluxe Eight, the company still needed a lower-priced car. The solution was the attractive new Light Eight; it was the Standard Eight engine placed in a short (127 1/2-inch) new wheelbase. Priced under $2000, the new Light Eight was

Another view of a 1931 phaeton. Photo by Susan Scott.

BOOM AND BAD YEARS 79

Some 1932 Gothic chrome.
Photo by Susan Scott.

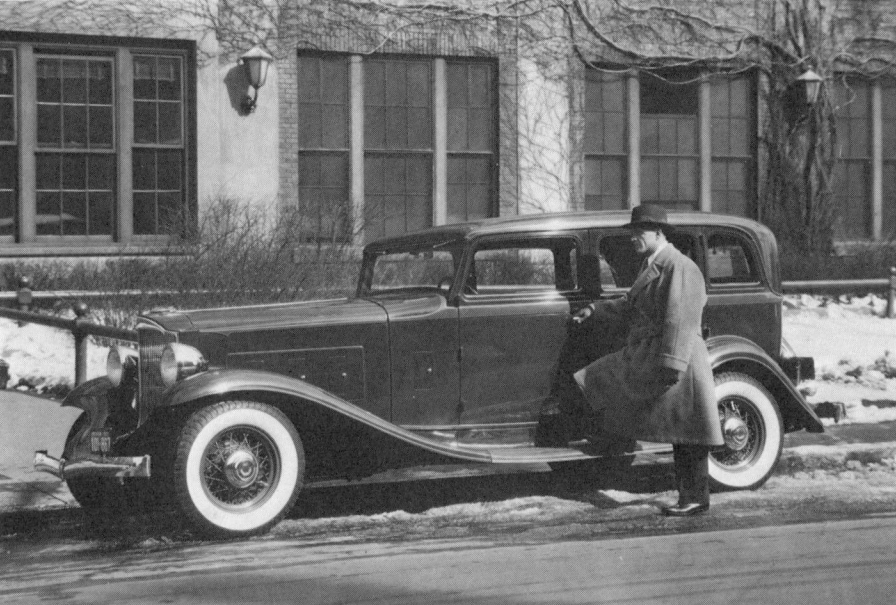

A 1932 Light Eight. Photo John A. Conde Collection.

A 1932 Eight sedan. Photo John A. Conde Collection.

A 1932 Light Eight roadster golf club compartment. Photo by Susan Scott.

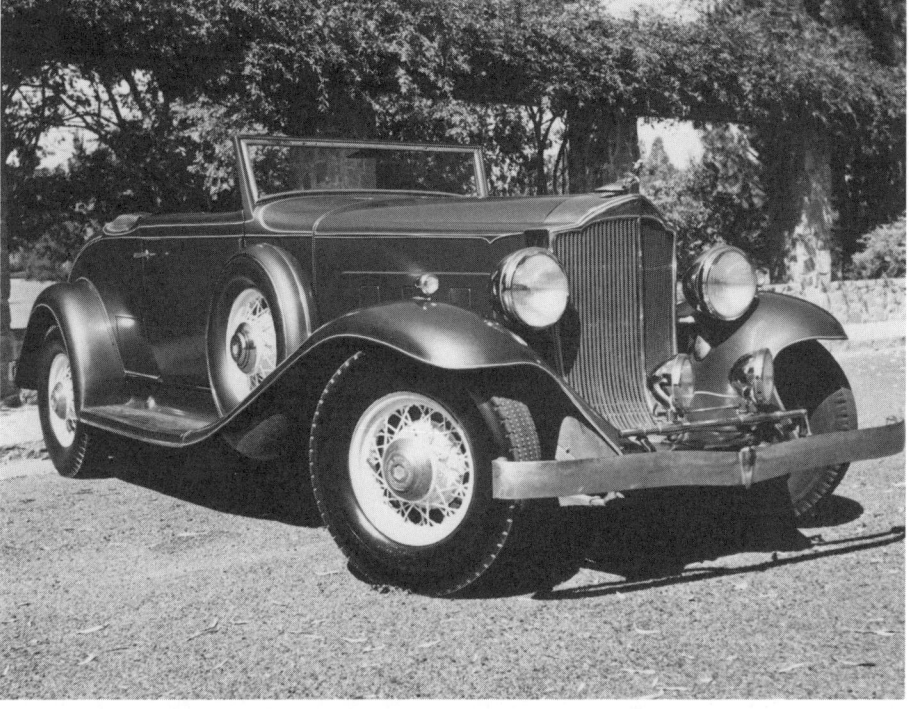

A 1932 Light Eight. Photos courtesy William H. Friedrich.

an immediate success. With the same horsepower as the Standard Eight but 600 less pounds, it was an excellent performer. Many people, including Al Jolson, were buying it just for that reason, and not because of its lower price.

The Light Eight wasn't really priced low enough to lure Buick and other medium-priced buyers. Rather, it was siphoning sales off its bigger brothers. And since the Light Eight cost Packard nearly as much to build as a Standard Eight, though lacking the profit margin, it was hardly a commercial success. Nevertheless, it was a valuable lesson to the company. The Light Eight was dropped for the 1933 Tenth series. Its new chassis became the lowest line of the Standard Eight.

Packard could see that, if it was to enter the medium-price field in earnest, it would need an entirely new automobile—and it would have to be re-engineered from the wheels up.

11

Weathering the Depression

The 1933 Tenth series lasted only from January 6, 1933 through August 20, 1933. The bottom-line Eight offered the remnants of the Ninth series Light Eight (now priced more profitably, opening at $2150). Introductory Light Eights a year earlier had been as low as $1750, but that base had to be increased to $1895 in June of 1932 to make up for a lack of volume. The rest of the Tenth series Eights were on the 136-inch wheelbase at prices up to $3085. For the less-deprecating Eight, Packard dropped the Standard Eight name.

The Deluxe and Custom Eight appelations were also dropped; they were replaced simply by Super Eight. The 385-cubic-inch engine was offered on a 135-inch wheelbase (sedan only, $2750). All other body styles were offered on the 142-inch chassis for prices as high as $3600 (formal sedan).

The Twelve offered the new monobloc 67-degree V-12 (introduced as the Twin Six in the preceding year) with its novel canted valve arrangement. The engine was similar to that of the Auburn V-12 and later the Lycoming Cord 810-812 V-8. Prices ran $3650 to $7950 for touring, phaeton, sport phaeton, convertible sedan, club sedan, coupe, convertible victoria, sedan, and coupe roadster bodies on the 142-inch wheelbase, and on the 147-inch wheelbase, sedan, limousine, all-weather cabriolet, all-weather landaulet, all-weather town car, all-weather town car landaulet, or Dietrich factor custom bodies including stationary coupe, sport phaeton, convertible sedan, convertible roadster or convertible victoria.

If you insisted on spending more than $7950, you could have most any of these bodies styled to your tastes on the longer wheelbase under the "Individual Custom" series.

As the Depression deepened, Packard introduced the Eleventh series on August 21, 1933. The company hoped that the fanfare would excite people who still had money. There weren't many changes except for minor appearance details. In a sensible production move, the Super Eight and the Twelve shared the same chassis for the same bodies. Calendar 1932 brought only 9,010 sales of all Packard lines, 1933 was good for a mere 9893, and 1934 was lower still.

Packard introduced Ride Control on the 1932 Ninth series. A knob to the left of the steering wheel adjusted the shock absorbers for a taut ride over rough or winding road or a soft ride over boulevards. Even the wealthy seemed to have lost their humor during the Depression as Packard received complaints over Ride Control's dash-mounted instruction plaque: In—Hard Out—Soft. As of 1983, General Motors planned to offer an adjustable ride on future models; it remains to be seen how GM will handle its "Ride Control"

From 1926 through the 1936 Fourteenth series, Packard offered Bijur chassis lubrication. Basically, this was an oil pump connected to copper lines running to lubrication points. Both Ride Control and Bijur chassis lubrication were dropped on the 1937 Fifteenth series models.

In August, 1934 Packard brought out its Twelfth series. The Eight was now offered on four chassis: 127 inches ($2385); 134 inches ($2470 to $5240); 139 inches ($2630 to $5385); and two 160-inch commercial chassis. The Super Eight ran on 132 inches ($2990), 139 inches ($2880 to $5670), 144 inches ($3265-$5815), and a 165-inch commercial chassis. The Eight was up to 130 horsepower, and the Super Eight had risen to 150 (both at 3200 rpm). The Twelve was enlarged to its final size of 473 cubic inches (3 7/16 × 4 1/4 bore × stroke) with horsepower up to 175 at 3200 rpm, 6.0:1 compression ratio, and 180 horsepower with optional high compression heads of 7.0:1 (actual output was closer to 200). Torque was now 366 ft. lbs. at 1400 rpm.

A 1933 Eight victoria. Photo courtesy William H. Friedrich.

Because of improved roads and increased horsepower, owners were driving their cars on longer and faster trips. An important engine change was the new copper-lead, steel-backed connecting rod bearings not just in the Packard Twelve but in the long-stroke Eights as well. A stock Packard Eight sedan equipped with the modern bearings was run wide open at the Packard Proving Grounds track for 25,000 miles at a time when Rolls-Royce and Mercedes were warning owners to avoid continued high speeds on the new Autobahn.

If the Packard Eight and Super Eight were among the most durable and refined motors in the world, the Twelve was nonpareil. The 1935 Twelfth series offered it in a 132 1/4-inch wheelbase, five-passenger sedan and in a full selection of other body styles on 139 1/4-inch and 144 1/4-inch wheelbases—factory Dietrich and LeBaron customs among them—as in the 1934 Eleventh series. The 12 prices ranged from $3820 for the short-wheelbased sedan to $6435 for the seven-passenger LeBaron, all-weather town car.

As building owners skip the 13th floor, so would Packard omit the "Thirteenth series." On August 10, 1935, the company offered the virtually unchanged Fourteenth series. While 1934 had been the lowest production year for Packard with only 6265 cars sold, calendar 1935 netted 52,045 sales. Of that total, 45,294 of them

11-2. A 1933 Eight, seven-passenger phaeton (with nine passengers). Photo courtesy William H. Friedrich.

A 1933 Twelve coupe-roadster. Photo courtesy William H. Friedrich.

A 1934 Twelve Dietrich convertible sedan. Photo courtesy William H. Friedrich.

A 1934 Super Eight coupe-roadster. Photo courtesy William H. Friedrich.

were the new One-Twenty, which debuted in January, 1935 as a Twelfth series product.

As Packard weathered the Depression, other automakers were going out of business. In 1934, Packard sent its stockholders a booklet entitled, appropriately enough, *Packard And Its Future*.

The last year Packard offered exclusively high-priced automobiles was 1934. Although the company led all other quality car builders, there was not enough luxury business to sustain even the leader. Because increasing mechanical sophistication was quickly closing the performance gap between high-priced and low-priced cars, even as the Depression lifted there would never again be as great a luxury market.

Even as Packard continued to dominate the dwindling carriage trade, the company was clearly staking its future on its new 120. The annual report for the year ending December 31, 1934 shows this.

A 1934 Twelve Bohman & Schwartz town car. Photo courtesy William H. Friedrich.

The remains of one of three 1934 Twelve 1106 sport coupes built. This one caught fire en route from Washington D.C. to Tennessee. Please carry a fire extinguisher. Photo courtesy William H. Friedrich.

WEATHERING THE DEPRESSION

Why pay the price of a Packard?

PERHAPS *you* are debating this very question with yourself:

"Why pay the price of a Packard when I can get a good car for several hundred dollars less?"

Then read this story of Fred C. Dierking, a Chicago Packard Salesman, and the 65 Packards he sold in 1928.

The story of 65 Packards

Every one of those cars was sold on the basis of "pay a little more—keep the car much longer."

"Operating costs on a Packard," Mr. Dierking pointed out to those Chicagoans, "are no greater, and frequently smaller, than on a 'compromise car.' The heaviest expense of automobile ownership is the depreciation cost you pay when you trade in your car every two or three years. Pay Packard's slightly higher price and keep the car longer—*keep it at least five years*—and you will be money ahead in the end."

Thus spoke Mr. Dierking in 1928. How true were his words in the light of the intervening five years?

What a census disclosed

Here is a census of those same 65 cars made a few weeks ago: Two owners have moved away from Chicago. Three have died. Three have disposed of their cars and now own no automobiles at all. Six have traded in their Packards on other makes—a surprisingly small number in an era of shifting fortunes and positions. Eight have replaced their 1928 Packards with new Packards.

But here is the most amazing thing. *42 of the 65 owners, or two out of every three, are still driving their original 1928 Packards!*

If you were to carry such a census throughout the country, you would probably find a similar situation everywhere. You would find owner after owner who *knows*, through years of experience, that Packard is the wisest motor car investment he has ever made!

The finest Packards ever built

You would expect the Packard of today to be finer than the Packard of 1928. And it is — infinitely finer. In fact, the new 1934 Packards are the finest cars ever to bear the Packard name — cars deliberately designed to give America a yardstick with which to measure *all* fine car values, American or European.

Today, see these great cars at your Packard dealer's. Ride in one — the new Packard Eight, the new Packard Super-Eight, or the new Packard Twelve. Compare it with any other fine car.

And remember that this Packard which so thrills you today will keep on thrilling you for years to come. Mechanically it is built to last, not five years, but far longer than that. And it has the famous Packard lines whose beauty never fades.

Yes, ride in a 1934 Packard— and compare it. We believe your question, "Can I afford to own a Packard?" will become, "Can I afford *not* to own one?"

PACKARD 1934

THE YARDSTICK WITH WHICH TO MEASURE ALL FINE CAR VALUES

The Packard 8 · Super-8 · 12

Ask the Man Who Owns One

Packard urges you to borrow this yardstick

IF YOU plan to buy a fine car this year, Packard has a yardstick it wants to lend you.

That yardstick is the new 1934 Packard—a car deliberately designed to be the standard of value with which to judge all fine cars, American or European.

And this year, more than ever, the fine-car buyer needs such a yardstick.

For, within the past three years, there has been a revolution in automotive values. Engineers, taking the depression as a challenge, have accomplished miracles of improvement. The progress of a decade has been compressed into three "hard times" years.

Old prejudices should no longer influence you in your choice of a fine car. Habit and hearsay are not safe guides, if you want to get the most for your money. Packard believes that this year, of all years, you should *know*!

And the best way to know is to ride in every other fine car America can offer you. But ride in a Packard *first*.

Use the knowledge you get behind the wheel of a new 1934 Packard to judge every other fine car. Measure your dollars in terms of what Packard gives you for them. Then see if you can match Packard value in any other car— on either side of the Atlantic.

And while you marvel at the performance of this new Packard, remember this — if you buy a Packard, you can plan to keep it at least five years. Five years from now your 1934 Packard will still give you peak performance. And five years from now your Packard will still be smart — for the lines of a Packard never wear out.

Why not telephone your Packard dealer today and ask him to bring a new Packard to your home? Take your choice of the new Eight, the new Super-Eight, or the new Twelve.

Drive it. Dare other fine cars to match it. Do this, and we'll leave it to you which car you'll want to own. We believe it will be a Packard.

PACKARD 1934

THE YARDSTICK WITH WHICH TO MEASURE ALL FINE CAR VALUES

The Packard Eight · The Packard Super-Eight · The Packard Twelve

Advertisements courtesy Ross M. Lee Collection.

A 1934 Twelve Dietrich convertible sedan. Photo by Susan Scott.

A 1934 Twelve Dietrich convertible sedan. Photo by Susan Scott.

A 1935 Eight phaeton. Photo courtesy John A. Conde Collection.

A 1935 Eight. Photo by Susan Scott.

AN analysis of sales tendencies over the last several years shows a steady increase in the proportion of automobile sales that have been secured by the low priced cars. It has been our experience over a period of more than 30 years, that, with a return to more prosperous conditions, this tendency will be checked, since there is no indication that people financially able to buy the best in motor cars, or, for that matter, any other product, have permanently lost their desire to do so.

Nevertheless there is not now, and for a time past there has not been, available a sufficient volume of high priced car business to enable any of the higher priced manufacturers to show a profit on higher priced cars alone. Packard has, in the course of its successful history, met somewhat similar conditions before, how successfully can best be judged by analyzing its history, the strength of its present cash position and the reputation it has maintained throughout the world.

For the purpose of using its manufacturing facilities to better advantage and enhancing its solidly established reputation, Packard has intensified its development program and will produce a line of cars in a more popular and lower priced class. These cars will be built to Packard standards and will be of thoroughly Packard quality.

While it is expected that, as conditions improve, the demand for cars in the price class Packard has always operated in, will recover and increase in proportion to the greater prosperity, Packard's new additional line in a price class of large volume should produce for Packard a far greater number of sales and improve its already strong financial position. That such cars will be welcomed by the public is strongly indicated by the interest attracted by our preliminary announcements.

Packard's operations in the first six months of the year show a loss, but a considerable portion of this is in reality investment in

1—The intensive preparations made for the perfection and manufacture of the new line of lower priced cars.

2—The preparation of an elaborate new line of new model cars of the price class in which Packard has maintained a leading position. This will be announced to the public in the coming fall, as usual.

(To date no penny of the cost of our new models, which will be known as Twelfth Series cars, and none of the costs involved in the preparations for the design, manufacture, etc., of the new lower priced cars has been capitalized. It has all been charged off.)

Our loss is partially attributed to

3—The decline in high class business available at this time.

4—The operations of the Motor Vehicle Retailing Code, which, as enacted, may work to the advantage of lower priced cars but certainly operates to the great disadvantage of all high priced cars.

During the last part of the year we shall be marketing our new Twelfth Series models which will be helpful to our financial position. The preparation expenses will stop and we shall have the advantage of the stimulated demand that has always followed the introduction of new model cars. Those who have had the privilege of seeing our new model Twelfth Series cars are very much impressed with their attractiveness. They are beautiful, luxurious, and can be counted upon, we believe, to enhance Packard's outstanding reputation in the fine car field. In styling, they embody the best of modern tendencies without, however, entirely departing from the well known Packard characteristics.

Our new line of cars in the lower price field, non-competitive with the above, will be completed as to engineering and testing, and preparations will be effected for their manufacture as rapidly as that can be done. We shall take time to do both thoroughly and well. When the cars are ready for the market they will be recognizable as the products of Packard and they can be counted upon to be outstanding in their several price classes.

Of course this means that expenditures for tools and other preparations for this lower price line of cars will continue through the fall and until the cars are in production and on the market, when we anticipate these new products will become very real assets to the company and to its distributers.

It is remarkable that in view of the magnitude of the engineering and other preparation efforts of the company and despite substantial losses for the first six months, the loss in actual cash position is but $524,397.64. As of July first, cash and marketable securities were valued at less than market, at $14,636,963.83, compared with $15,161,361.47 at January 1, 1934. Some of this accumulation can be expected to flow out into new tools, factory preparations and inventories for all of the various new models during the next six months, but the end of the year will find us still in a strong cash position with ample facilities to carry on any programs of new models or new cars that we may find necessary or advantageous in maintaining a satisfactory position in the industry.

We count this year as one of constructive effort looking to a prosperous future. This belief is based upon our successes of the past and our intensified development program, as outlined here, to broaden our field. Thus we will use our manufacturing facilities to greater advantage and enhance a reputation which has been one of our greatest assets and which will be as jealously guarded in the future as it has been in the past.

Alvan Macauley
President

To the Stockholders of the
Packard Motor Car Company:

This report covers the operations of the Company for the fiscal and calendar year of 1934. Our report for the preceding year (1933) showed net profit and other additions to Surplus of $506,433.91.

Our operations for 1934 show up less favorably from an earnings point of view largely because of the huge program undertaken in order to better adapt the Company's affairs to the changing times. It is well known that the demand for automobiles has been increasingly for those in the lower price brackets. This is a movement that has continued unchecked through the depression years. It has been a serious handicap to manufacturers of high priced fine quality cars. This classification is usually considered to include all cars having a list price of $2,000 and over. It is the price class in which we have been operating with our three lines of cars: the Eight, the Super Eight and the Twelve. In this fine car class during the year 1934 Packard continued not only to hold its high prestige but sold a greater percentage of all the high priced business available than in any previous year. In 1933 we secured 38.4% of all high price business available. In 1934 this rose to 42.7%.

But the sales available to all manufacturers in this field continued to decline through the year with the result that the volume available to us was less than in the preceding year. The popularity of the fine cars is probably as great as ever. Certainly they are very wonderful vehicles, but fewer people feel that they can afford to buy them in these times. It still seems as true as ever it did, that with the return of real prosperity the sales of high priced cars will benefit correspondingly.

In view of existing conditions your directors decided more than a year ago to add a completely new line of Packard cars to sell in the $1,000 price class. You may recall that in our Annual Report to you of last year the Company announced its determination to enlarge its market with a new line of quality cars of much lower price. The development work on these had then begun and has been diligently followed through during the past year. It was decided to call this new line of cars the Packard One Twenty, because that is the length of its wheelbase, and they are as you doubtless know now on the market. At this writing they are being shipped at the rate of 150 cars daily and are making a very fine impression on those whom we have so far been able to supply.

During the year we developed and perfected two new One Twenty chassis, one for cars and with seven new body types, and the other of longer wheelbase for commercial use and allied lines. This, too, is now on the market.

In addition, we developed a right drive chassis for sale in England and other countries preferring the driver's seat on the right side of the car. Some of these, too, have been shipped and have been exceptionally well received by our British distributer.

The export market for the new car is opening up splendidly, for the One Twenty seems to be specially adapted to export markets. Exports of Packard cars increased 22.8% in 1934 over the previous year, and **again were more than the total for all other American cars combined in the high priced class.** Reinforced now with the One Twenties our export market can be expected to expand many times over.

The Packard One Twenty is not a small car despite the fact that prices range from $980 to $1095.

PACKARD TWELFTH SERIES CARS

Packard Eight—Packard Super Eight—Packard Twelve

Our new Twelfth Series cars priced from $2385 to $4950 were announced during September 1934 and have met with cordial approval. With these cars the Company inaugurated a new style cycle, the fifth in the thirty years in which it has kept its identifying lines. Ordinarily new styles are announced from year to year, only relatively minor changes in body designs being necessary. But about once in five years, or thereabouts, it is necessary to inaugurate a new style cycle, in order to maintain style leadership. It was decided under this principle that Twelfth Series cars should inaugurate a new style cycle in body designs while still retaining the essential features of traditional Packard appearance. Accordingly all of the forty bodies for Twelfth Series cars were redesigned and modernized and gotten into production and necessarily at large expense for designing, tooling and preparation. Our owners who have purchased these new Twelfth Series cars praise them highly. We believe there is nothing so fine in appearance or in operation manufactured anywhere else in the world. An examination, or better yet, a trial trip in one of these new cars by our stockholders will, we believe, confirm our high opinion of them. The increased attractiveness of our new Twelfth Series cars will, we think, be undoubtedly reflected in their increased popularity.

A YEAR OF CONSTRUCTIVE PROGRESS

The magnitude of the program undertaken by the Company in 1934 can hardly be appreciated by one not familiar with the industry. To design the different bodies for the Twelfth Series cars, to build or otherwise secure the highly special tools required for their manufacture, to revamp and rearrange the factory facilities so as to enable them to be produced efficiently—this of itself was a large undertaking. But on top of this we designed, perfected and produced tools for seven new bodies and two chassis of the One Twenty and, in addition, purchased or built the thousand or more tools and facilities required for its manufacture; these, together, constituted a program such as Packard has never before undertaken. No new buildings were erected in connection with either program. Use was made of existing buildings and of existing facilities so far as they were appropriate.

1934 OPERATIONS

The size of the Company's operations for 1934 involved the expenditure of large sums of money and because the cost and expenses of designing, preparation, factory rearrangement and, above all, tools, were not capitalized, they adversely affected our Profit and Loss Statement. Without these operations our showing would have been vastly better but the Company would not now be in the greatly improved position that it is, competitively and otherwise. We are now certain of a much greater volume of business and volume is the keystone to prosperity in these highly competitive times.

This somewhat lengthy statement of the Company's 1934 programs is necessary in order to make it clear that much of the loss from the Company's 1934 operations was a constructive loss and that it was deliberately and carefully undertaken for the purpose of improving the Company's position. Our operations for last year showed a loss of $7,290,549.26. Simply and briefly this is accounted for approximately as follows:

Expense Incidental to Model 120	$3,541,500.00
Twelfth Series Tools	1,559,975.00
Branch Losses Due to Low Volume	438,827.00
Factory Loss Due to Low Volume	1,750,247.00
Total	$7,290,549.00

ASSETS

Cash on Hand, United States Government Securities, Municipal, State and Canadian Bonds stand at $12,395,680.36 compared with $15,161,361.47 a year ago.

Accounts Receivable have declined from $605,761.50 to $506,643.57.

Deferred Installment Notes are practically the same as last year.

Inventories of Raw Materials, Work in Process, Etc., have increased $310,873.04 on account of preparation for the manufacture of the One Twenty.

The item of Finished Motor Carriages decreased from $2,789,405.90 to $1,805,121.17, or $984,284.73. We produced fewer cars and naturally carried a smaller inventory of finished cars.

Mortgages and Miscellaneous Items were reduced $119,186.00. This includes land and buildings formerly used for service purposes in Long Island City and sold by us. Partial payments have reduced the amount of this mortgage.

Deposits in Banks and Trust Companies Closed or Under Restriction are fully covered by the Reserve set up for that purpose. Additional payments are expected from time to time.

To clarify our Property Account we are showing it this year in greater detail. Of the $27,842,292.14, $1,947,132.10 is the cost of Detroit land acquired by the Company many years ago; and the buildings, plant equipment, productive machinery, tools, power plant and power producing equipment, office furniture and fixtures, etc., are now carried on our books at $14,200,760.15.

The Company owns twenty-eight well chosen properties located in strategic cities throughout the United States and one in London, England, which are used for purposes of distribution of our products. Eleven of these properties are rented under leases to independent distributers. The remainder are for the most part used by our Branches for sales and service purposes. The land is carried at the price paid for it. Some of it was purchased more than twenty-five years ago.

The item of Deferred Charges to Future Operations has increased $64,394.62. This approximately represents pre-payment for tools to one of our vendors and the amount is to be amortized pro rata as the finished material is delivered to us.

LIABILITIES

Current Liabilities are substantially the same as last year except for two items.

Current Accounts Payable and Pay Rolls have increased $1,253,239.02 chiefly on account of larger pay rolls and purchases of raw materials, machine tools and equipment in preparation for the manufacture of the One Twenty.

The other item is that of Tool Commitments of Model One Twenty amounting to $1,198,734.00, which is substantially the remaining amount to be paid for completion of the One Twenty tools, etc.

The Item Miscellaneous Liabilities, Not Yet Due, is just about the same as last year.

Reserve for Miscellaneous Items is $96,481.65 less than last year.

The Reserve for General Purposes is unchanged and in our opinion is more than adequate to take care of all unrecorded liabilities.

The Reserve for Deposits in Banks and Trust Companies Closed or Under Restriction is slightly less than last year. Further payments as the closed banks and trust companies liquidate are certain to be made.

Capital Stock account is unchanged.

The Surplus which at the beginning of the year stood at $8,904,685.23 has been reduced by the losses recorded and chiefly on account of the Company's expansion program, to $1,614,135.97. But it is the expectation as forecast in notices calling this meeting that the stockholders will return to Surplus the remaining $10,000,000 that was transferred some years ago out of Surplus to Capital. With this accomplished the Surplus at December 31, 1934 would be $11,614,135.97 and Capital Stock $50,000,000.

GENERAL

In planning for the production of our new lower priced line we reinforced our organization by selecting additional men experienced and skilled in the engineering, in the manufacturing, and in the distribution of low priced cars. So that our organization now consists of highly trained specialists in all the lines we are offering to the public. We have as a whole what we have good reason to believe is a very efficient organization.

Factory production of One Twenties commenced in February and from a small beginning has increased to the rate of 150 daily mentioned elsewhere. Production will constantly and rapidly further increase until we satisfy the market demand. We are about 6000 retail orders ahead of our production and orders are still coming in faster than we can produce the cars.

Since January first we have added 402 new dealers to our distribution forces and more are being signed up daily.

The first quarter of 1935 can be expected to show a loss, because there has been a heavy concentration of expense and expenditure in that period, due to One Twenty operations and with only the beginnings of production. But from April first on, we shall be in substantial and still increasing production and the heavy items of expense and expenditure will be behind us. So far as we can now see, all extraordinary disbursements will have been made and costs will more nearly resume the normal expectation.

The last three quarters of the year look promising. A full year at substantially maximum production would produce a pleasing result. Like other manufacturers we shall, of course, be dependent upon the degree of prosperity throughout the country.

March 27, 1935.

President

PACKARD MOTOR CAR COMPANY
AND SUBSIDIARY COMPANIES

Consolidated Balance Sheet as of December 31, 1934

ASSETS

CURRENT ASSETS:

Cash in Banks and on Hand			$ 2,747,101.61	
Investments, Less Reserve to Adjust to Market Value—				
United States Government Securities		9,139,118.75		
Municipal, State, and Canadian Bonds		509,460.00	$12,395,680.36	
Accounts and Notes Receivable, Less Reserve—				
Accounts Receivable	$ 506,643.57			
Deferred Installment Notes	976,719.40		1,483,362.97	
Inventories, at or Below Cost—				
Raw Material, Work in Process, Etc.	$ 2,972,267.57			
Finished Motor Carriages	1,805,121.17		4,777,388.74	
Total Current Assets			$18,656,432.07	

MORTGAGES AND MISCELLANEOUS INVESTMENTS: 656,732.00

DEPOSITS IN BANKS AND TRUST COMPANIES CLOSED OR UNDER RESTRICTION: 641,544.63

PROPERTY ACCOUNT:

Land, at Cost—				
For Manufacturing Purposes	$ 1,947,132.10			
For Distribution Purposes	4,418,375.69	$ 6,365,507.79		
Buildings, Plant Equipment, Etc., at Cost—				
Manufacturing Properties	29,088,108.24			
Less—Reserve for Depreciation	14,887,348.09	14,200,760.15		
Distribution Properties	9,608,829.91			
Less—Reserve for Depreciation	2,332,806.71	7,276,023.20		
Rights, Privileges, Franchises and Inventions		1.00	$27,842,292.14	

DEFERRED CHARGES TO FUTURE OPERATIONS:

Prepaid Insurance and Other Expense   403,949.05

    Total Assets $48,200,949.89

LIABILITIES

CURRENT LIABILITIES:

Current Accounts Payable and Pay Rolls		$ 2,787,122.86
Miscellaneous Liabilities, Not Yet Due		533,349.23
Reserves—		
Tool Commitments of Model 120		1,198,734.00
Miscellaneous Items		162,218.35
U. S. Federal and Canadian Income Taxes of Subsidiary Companies		13,844.85
Total Current Liabilities		$ 4,695,269.29

RESERVE FOR GENERAL PURPOSES: 1,250,000.00

RESERVE FOR DEPOSITS IN BANKS AND TRUST COMPANIES CLOSED OR UNDER RESTRICTION: 641,544.63

CAPITAL STOCK:

Common (Authorized 25,000,000 Shares)
No Par Value—Issued 15,000,000 Shares   40,000,000.00
(Includes 8,660 Shares Issued to Trustee for Account of Company, and not Carried as an Asset)

SURPLUS:

Balance at December 31, 1933	$ 8,904,685.23	
Deduct—Net Loss for the Year Ended December 31, 1934	7,290,549.26	1,614,135.97
Total Liabilities and Capital		$48,200,949.89

PACKARD MOTOR CAR COMPANY
AND SUBSIDIARY COMPANIES

STATEMENT OF INCOME
For the Year Ended December 31, 1934

PARTICULARS			Amount
FACTORY SALES:			
Carriages and Service Parts			$14,618,742.77
Cost of Sales			17,315,064.67
Gross Loss			$ 2,696,321.90
Deduct—Other Income:			
Discount on Purchases	$	64,036.51	
Rentals		5,856.51	
Interest Earned		302,311.48	
Profit on Sale or Disposal of Capital Assets		35,190.10	
Miscellaneous		7,249.10	$ 414,643.70
GROSS LOSS LESS OTHER INCOME			$ 2,281,678.20
Add—Selling, General, and Administrative Expenses			2,094,874.51
LOSS BEFORE APPLYING FACTORY DEPRECIATION AND SPECIAL ITEMS			$ 4,376,552.71
Deduct			
Reduction in Reserve for Depreciation in Value of Investments	$	546,002.76	
Profit on Sale of Investments, Etc.		18,234.45	564,237.21
			$ 3,812,315.50
Add			
Depreciation of Factory Properties	$	1,840,671.81	
To Reserve for Tool Commitments of Model 120		1,198,734.00	3,039,405.81
LOSS FROM FACTORY OPERATIONS			$ 6,851,721.31
LOSS FROM OPERATIONS OF BRANCHES AND SUBSIDIARY COMPANIES			438,827.95
LOSS FOR THE YEAR ENDED DECEMBER 31, 1934			$ 7,290,549.26

Price, Waterhouse & Co.

RESIDENT PARTNER
T. JACKSON
CERTIFIED PUBLIC ACCOUNTANT

PENOBSCOT BUILDING

DETROIT

March 4, 1935

To the Board of Directors,
 Packard Motor Car Company,
  Detroit, Michigan.

We have made an examination of the consolidated balance sheet of Packard Motor Car Company and subsidiary companies as at December 31, 1934, and of the statement of income for the year 1934. In connection therewith, we examined or tested accounting records of the companies and other supporting evidence and obtained information and explanations from officers and employees of the companies; we also made a general review of the accounting methods and of the operating and income accounts for the year, but we did not make a detailed audit of the transactions.

In our opinion, based upon such examination, the accompanying balance sheet and related statement of income fairly present, in accordance with accepted principles of accounting consistently maintained by the companies during the year under review, their combined position at December 31, 1934, and the results of operations for the year.

Price, Waterhouse & Co.

PACKARD MOTOR CAR COMPANY
DETROIT, MICHIGAN

Incorporated under the Laws of Michigan

Directors

Truman H. Newberry
Henry E. Bodman
Alvan Macauley
James T. McMillan
Robert B. Parker

President
Alvan Macauley

Vice-President and General Manager
M. M. Gilman

Vice-President of Engineering
J. G. Vincent

Vice-President of Manufacturing
E. F. Roberts

Assistant Vice-President of Manufacturing
G. T. Christopher

Vice-President
Lee J. Eastman

Comptroller
Eugene C. Hoelzle

Vice-President and General Counsel
Henry E. Bodman

Vice-President and Secretary
Merlin A. Cudlip

Treasurer
Hugh J. Ferry

Vice-President and Patent Counsel
Milton Tibbetts

Assistant Secretary and Assistant Treasurer
A. C. Bennett

Subsidiary Companies

Packard Motor Car Company of New York
Packard Buffalo, Inc.
Atlanta Packard Motors, Inc.
Packard Motor Car Company of Canada, Limited
Packard Motors Export Corporation
Packard Motor Sales Company
Packard Limited, London, England
Packard Motor Car Company of Chicago
Packard Rochester, Inc.

Auditors—Price, Waterhouse & Co.

Ask the Man Who Owns One

12

Enduring Identity

When Packard stock fell from 129 points in early 1929 to below two points in 1933, serious planning for a popularly priced car began. The resulting One-Twenty outsold nearly every Eight in its price class during its first eight months. Exceptions were the least expensive Buick and the Pontiac (which was actually a lower-priced car). In 1936, the One-Twenty outsold even the Pontiac Eight and carried Packard from twelfth to tenth place—past both Nash and Chrysler.

The One-Twenty engine was not similar to Pontiac's, other than being an L-head inline eight (the Pontiac was a 77-horsepower, cast-iron piston affair). The General Motors employees Packard recruited in 1934 were cost specialists brought in to ensure that the One-Twenty would be built and priced competitively. Jesse Vincent engineered a car, every bit a Packard, that was in many ways superior to the senior models. The One-Twenty's new Saf-T-Flex independent front suspension was adopted by the senior Packards in 1937, and by Rolls-Royce, Bentley, Daimler, and Lagonda after the war. The introductory 257-cubic-inch (3 1/4 × 3 7/8 bore × stroke) straight eight was the most refined volume motor yet seen on the market. Its 110 horsepower was increased to 120 for 1936 when the engine was enlarged to 282 cubic inches (3 1/4 × 4 1/4 bore × stroke), in which form it would be used through the final 1947 Clippers.

The new model's name came from its 120-inch wheelbase. Although targeted as an $850 3000-pound automobile, Vincent and other Packard men insisted on so many usual Packard features that the $980 (for base business coupe) 3500-pound car that was unveiled was more a production man's Packard than the typical medium-priced, eight-cylinder Detroit automobile of the day. Thousands of orders poured in from people who hadn't even seen the car. Models included the business, convertible, sport, and touring coupes, and sedan, club sedan, and touring sedan. Prices ran to $1095.

The 1936 One-Twenty (120-B) was introduced in August, 1935 with the rest of the Fourteenth series, observing Packard's longtime tradition of offering its models before the rest of the industry. Because Packard's series generally coincided with year models and the company often added features or made changes without regard to either series or year model, calendar-year production figures have been given unless otherwise noted. These were the figures followed by both industry and government. Also, the profit from calendar totals was included in the annual report. In 1936 there were 80,978 Packards sold. The total included 965 Twelves, 3420 Super Eights, 2147 Eights (dropped in August), 50,928 One-Twenties, and (already) 23,518 of a new Six not even put on the market until September.

The One-Twenty had never been a low-priced car; it was to become an upper-medium-priced product. The convertible sedan introduced for 1936 was priced at $1395. Although the Depression was dissipating, registrations in the strictly luxury market Packard had for so long dominated had fallen from 10 percent in the early 1920s, to 2 percent in 1933, and now to only half a percent. Sobered, and also heartened by the One-Twenty's runaway success, Packard introduced a still lower-priced model—the six-cylinder 115-C.

At a time when many of Packard's competitors had long since gone out of business, the company sent a message entitled *The Car of Enduring Identity* to its stockholders.

The 1936 Twelve sport phaeton. Photo by Susan Scott.

A 1936 One-Twenty club sedan. Photo courtesy William H. Friedrich.

A 1936 Eight sedan. Photo courtesy William H. Friedrich.

A 1936 Eight sedan. Photo courtesy William H. Friedrich.

A 1936 Super Eight Dietrich convertible sedan. Photo courtesy William H. Friedrich.

A 1936 Twelve sport phaeton. Photo by Susan Scott.

A 1936 Twelve sport phaeton. Photo by Susan Scott.

The Car of Enduring Identity

A MESSAGE TO
PACKARD STOCKHOLDERS

WE ARE pleased to enclose your dividend check due July 1. On February 11, 1936, Packard paid a dividend of $1,500,000. On July 1, 1936, Packard is paying a dividend of $2,250,000.

In the first six months of 1936 Packard's net earnings will be approximately the same as for the entire year of 1935 which were $3,315,622.

This excellent showing is due mainly to the great popularity and increased sales of Packard cars.

During the first six months of 1936 Packard's sales will have totaled about 34,000 cars, an increase of some 16,700 cars, or 97 per cent over the corresponding period of 1935.

In May, 1936, the last month for which complete figures are available, deliveries of Packard cars passed the previous all-time monthly record made in August, 1929.

Packard's sales for cash are in almost inverse ratio to the industry as a whole. Whereas two in every three cars are generally bought on time, but one in every three Packards is bought on deferred payments. Your company has a time-payment plan which matches any other in fairness and has unusual flexibility, and will undoubtedly contribute to greater sales.

You, as a stockholder, may wish to bring this plan to the attention of your friends and associates.

We are also pleased to inform you that, the efficiency of our factory having reached a high rating, we were able on June 1, 1936, to put into effect additional labor policies beneficial to all hourly rate factory employees. These included: 1, vacations with pay; 2, separation pay (allowances to workers laid off), and 3, retirement pay.

Much favorable comment has been received by the management for initiating these policies. In working directly to the benefit of factory employees we believe the policies also serve well the efficiency and stability of your company.

Factory workers continuously employed for one year will receive a week's vacation with pay. Over 7,000 of our men are now looking forward to such vacations with their families this year. Our men who have worked steadily without opportunity for vacation unless taken at their own expense are enthusiastic over the prospect. Those anticipating and receiving vacations with pay are bound to be more interested in their company and in their work.

If, due to no fault of his own, but due to reduction of the factory schedule, a factory worker must be laid off, he will receive a certain amount, in addition to the pay due him, as separation pay.

The giving of retirement pay is in keeping with Packard's long-standing policy to reward faithful service. Factory employees 65 years of age or over with 15 or more years of service will receive $25 for each year of past service when they leave the company.

Packard stockholders and Packard owners have written in commending your company for establishing these policies. One writes: "When I read of your action, I was proud I had bought a Packard."

That industry generally is thinking and acting in terms of generosity and justice to its employees is revealed by the wide interest that has been shown in Packard's labor policies on the part of many companies in different fields of endeavor, as well as by research organizations, colleges and others.

Packard is looking forward to a successful year.

Alvan Macauley
President

PACKARD MOTOR CAR COMPANY • DETROIT, MICHIGAN • JUNE 27, 1936

PACKARD TWELVE . . 13 Luxurious Body Types
Priced from $3820 to $5050 at the factory

PACKARD SUPER EIGHT . 13 Handsome Body Types
Priced from $2880 to $4010 at the factory

PACKARD EIGHT . . 13 Beautiful Body Types
Priced from $2385 to $3400 at the factory

PACKARD ONE TWENTY . 7 Popular Body Types

2-Passenger Business Coupe	*Priced at* $ 990
2 or 4-Passenger Conv. Coupe	*Priced at* $1110
2 or 4-Passenger Sport Coupe	*Priced at* $1030
5-Passenger Touring Coupe	*Priced at* $1040
5-Passenger Sedan	*Priced at* $1075
5-Passenger Club Sedan	*Priced at* $1090
5-Passenger Touring Sedan	*Priced at* $1115

at the factory, standard accessory group extra

PACKARD ONE TWENTY CONVERTIBLE SEDAN
With Special Custom Body *Priced at $1395*
at the factory, standard accessory group extra

ASK THE MAN WHO OWNS ONE

The purchase of Packards by you, our stockholders, has long been of mutual advantage. The suggestion made with our last dividend check that you give us names of associates and friends who are contemplating the purchase of a car bore fruit. Again we ask you to send us names of prospective buyers. With better times here and ahead, your neighbors and friends are thinking of a new car. Urge them to "match Packard against the field."

Packard

Ask the Man Who Owns One

13

Changes

Introduced with the rest of the Fifteenth series in September, 1936, the new Packard Six sold even better than the One-Twenty. At $795 for the business coupe, the 115-C (named for its wheelbase and use of the 120's body, now in its third year) came in below the One-Twenty's original target price. Other body styles included sport, touring, and convertible coupes, sedan, touring sedan, and station wagon. A $1295 price tag was the most expensive. The Six engine displaced 237 cubic inches, (3 7/16 × 4 1/4 bore × stroke) and pumped out 100 horsepower. It was an excellent and rugged engine that was used even through 1949 in 141-inch-wheelbase taxis and as a marine engine.

Even the Packard Six was not, strictly speaking, a low-priced car. And, or course, there never was a "cheap" Packard. Underneath their attractive shells, the junior cars boasted thorough Packard engineering. Hudson, Buick, Oldsmobile, and Pontiac offered eight-cylinder cars for less than the One-Twenty, and Dodge, Studebaker, and Pontiac sixes undersold the Packard Six. Until the thrill was gone, Packard could bank on the pull of its name.

The company dropped Ride Control, Bijur chassis lubrication, and the 385-cubic-inch engine as it focused most of its attention on the Six and One-Twenty and moved to consolidate all models on one assembly line by 1940. All 1937 Fifteenth series models used the Saf-T-Flex front suspension introduced on the One-Twenty. Packard had already decided to phase out its old senior lines. They began by putting the 320-cubic-inch Eight in 127-inch, 134-inch, and 139-inch chassis and calling this the Super Eight. The 320-cubic-inch Eight was now putting out 135 horsepower (15 horsepower shy of the discontinued 385-cubic-inch motor) and the new car was lighter than previous Super Eights. Cadillac outsold Packard for the second time in 12 years in 1936, but the company continued to wring all the prestige it could from the remaining senior Eight and the Twelve. Super Eight prices now ran from $2335 for a five-passenger touring sedan, the only model available on the 127-inch wheelbase, to $3350 for a five-passenger convertible sedan on the 139-inch wheelbase. The most expensive was a five-seven-passenger (jump seats) LeBaron town car for $4990.

The Twelve came in three wheelbase increments: the 132-inch and 139-inch lengths shared with the Super Eight, and a longer 144-inch frame. Prices ran $3420 to $5900. As usual, these figures could be much higher if the buyer wanted a one-off custom body. Many of the custom bodies seen on Packards and other luxury cars were actually limited-production catalog customs akin to designer jeans.

By the late Thirties, coachbuilders weren't selling many singular creations to particular customers or limited runs of revamped factory bodies to Detroit. They were often reduced to ordinary body-shop work. What custom bodies were being ordered were most often seen on Packard chassis. Some of these bodies claimed excellent craftmanship, but many—some of the biggest names included—were strictly for appearance, with many tacks and much lead used.

Although the 109,518 cars sold during 1937 more than doubled 1929's tally, the $3 million profit was less than one-eight of 1929's. Nevertheless, 1086 Twelves, 4883 Super Eights, 47,230 One Twenties, and 56,319 Sixes found homes.

The 1938 Sixteenth series was offered in September, 1937, and continued the strategies and changes that kept Packard from going the way of Pierce-Arrow (whose equipment was auctioned the following year for a mere half a million dollars). Except for the Packard Twelve, the Pierce-Arrow Twelve had been the best luxury automobile in the world. Pierce-Arrow made last-minute plans to market a medium-price car and had even undertaken the manufacture of camping and house trailers,

A 1936 Super Eight convertible sedan. Photo John A. Conde Collection.

A 1937 One-Twenty sedan driving through water at the proving grounds. Photo John A. Conde Collection.

A 1937 Six convertible coupe. Photo by Susan Scott.

but the firm's devotion to the carriage trade had been its undoing.

In the fall of 1937, few at Packard needed vindication that their company had made the right move. In 1930, Packard had its usual 900 plus dealers and distributors (with the lowest turnover in the industry). Depression ravages dropped the number of sales outlets to 500 in 1933, but the core of 75 distributing corporations (four of which Packard owned) and the success of the One-Twenty led to 1700 outlets. There were another 280 in 95 other countries. Foreign business accounted for 8 percent of Packard's dollar sales. Also, Packard's 11,500 employees more than doubled the number working in its factories before the One-Twenty was produced.

The Sixteenth series Twelve was offered on two chassis shared with the Super Eight (134 and 139 inches, prices from $4135 to $8510). The Super Eight on those two chassis ranged from $2925 to $3970. The higher figure was for the five-passenger convertible sedan on the 139-inch wheelbase. Because the Super Eight and Twelve now shared both bodies and chassis, the price differential of identical factory semicustoms shows the value Packard put on its Twelve. The Rollston All-Weather Cabriolet on the 134-inch-wheelbased Super Eight cost $5790, and on the 134-inch Twelve it cost $6730. Likewise the Brunn All-Weather Cabriolet, Brunn Touring Cabriolet, and Rollston town car on the 139-inch-wheelbased Super Eight ran $7475, $7475, and $5890. On the 139-inch Twelve they ran, respectively, $8510, $8510, and $6880. The Super Eight also offered a 127-inch wheelbase in only one model—a five-passenger touring sedan for $2790.

Although the senior cars were on shorter chassis than was the practice only a few years earlier, independent front suspensions and the resulting forward mounting of the engines left as much and often more body room. The earlier senior Packards might have seemed more elegant, but the long ladder-type frames necessarily needed a bit of flex to absorb road shock. Packard announced that its new frames introduced in 1937 with independent front suspension were "400 percent more rigid."

As the modern suspension absorbed more road shock, the frames could actually be stronger, giving the later cars a more solid feel and a more insulated riding quality. But independent front suspension, as well as rubber mounting of the engine, allowed smaller, lighter, inexpensive cars the ride and smoothness found earlier only in luxury cars. The extra cost of the senior Packards, and other big cars, increasingly outweighed any benefits.

As the senior cars faded, the Six and One Twenty wheelbases grew to 122 and 127 inches, respectively, while the One Twenty was renamed the Eight. The junior cars were given new all-steel bodies, and the entire Packard line had a unified look that included new pontoon fenders and divided windshields.

The 1938 (One-Twenty) was now a thoroughly upper-medium-priced car with prices beginning at $1160 for the business coupe to $1575 for the convertible sedan. The 1937 Fifteenth series One-Twenty offered a pair of seven-passenger cars on a 138-inch chassis. The touring sedan sold for $1835 and the touring limousine sold for $1985. In 1938, these were again offered at the same prices, although as Sixteenth series Eights and on longer 148-inch chassis.

A 1937 Twelve convertible coupe owned by Beverly Ferreira. Photo by Susan Scott.

The Six engine displacement was up to its final 245 cubic inches as the bore had been increased to 3 1/2 inches. Horsepower was still listed as 100; low end torque was said to have improved. Prices ranged from $1075 to $1235.

The 1938 recession hurt the entire industry; average production down nearly 48 percent from 1937. In 1938, 323 Twelves, 2545 Super Eights, 18,287 Eights, and 29,105 Sixes left the Packard plant (for a calendar total of 50,260). The company reported a $1,638,000 loss for the year, and could no longer afford to keep the senior lines—at least in present form.

The 1939 Seventeenth series models totaled 46,405 (9313 fewer than the Sixteenth series). Increased sales of the facelifted 1940 Eighteenth series cars introduced in August gave 1939 a half-million-dollar profit. The last Packard Twelves were the 446 of the 1939 Seventeenth series. They were merely a continuation of the Sixteenth series with column shift and alternately painted grille bars. Models and prices remained those of 1938.

The old Super Eight, which had in 1938 shared chassis with the Twelve, was gone. The new, replacement Super-8 (this abbreviated, modern numeric practice foreshadowed 1940 practice) was the old 320-cubic-inch engine placed in the One-Twenty's body and chassis. The result was prices starting at $1995 for the two-four-passenger club coupe to $2600 for the touring limousine on the 148-inch-wheelbase (which was still less expensive than 1938's least expensive Super Eight).

The new Super-8 attracted 3962 status-starved folk who evidently didn't mind paying up to $790 more than a One-Twenty for otherwise basically the same car.

A 1937 Twelve formal limousine. Photo courtesy William H. Friedrich.

A 1937 Twelve formal limousine. Note the rear window and trunk rack. Photo courtesy William H. Friedrich.

A 1938 Twelve Brunn touring cabriolet. Photo courtesy William H. Friedrich.

The Super-8 had 10 more horsepower and a few minor trim variations (including alternately painted grille bars). In May of 1939, Packard lowered Super-8 prices by $300. But the company had established the dollar-drawing value of the Super-8 name, which would be invaluable in pricing and marketing the 1940 models, and it had gotten rid of a number of increasingly obsolete engines.

The 1938 Eight served its prestige-building purpose. Although the 1939 One Twenty lacked 10 horsepower from its Super-8 counterpart, it also weighed over

A 1938 Eight (120) Rollston All-Weather panel brougham. Photo courtesy William H. Friedrich.

Brunn touring cabriolets. Photo courtesy William H. Friedrich.

King George VI and Queen Elizabeth in a 1939 Packard Twelve phaeton. Photo John A. Conde Collection.

A 1939 Six with an aftermarket air cooler. Photo by Susan Scott.

Band leader Ray Noble's 1939 Twelve Brunn touring cabriolet. Photo courtesy William H. Friedrich.

A 1939 Twelve Brunn touring cabriolet. Photo courtesy William H. Friedrich.

300 pounds less and was the better performer of the two. Prices ran from $1200 for the base two-passenger business coupe to $1955 for the touring limousine on the 148-inch wheelbase.

The 1939 Seventeenth series Packard Six ran from an even $1000 for the business coupe to $1195 for the convertible coupe. The 1939 model was Packard's first year of overdrive (offered on all lines but the Twelve) and column shift, but a floor-mounted "cane" shift was still available.

A 1939 Packard ad asked and answered: "'Which car do you consider best-looking?'—An independent fact-finding organization, showing pictures of all U.S. cars with identifying marks concealed, put this question to motorists in a nation-wide study survey—a survey using the methods of Dr. George Gallup and checked by this famous election forecaster. Packard got more votes than any other 1939 car."

That Packard felt a need to run and then advertise such a survey is telling. The company had to at once offer its traditional acclaimed lines but without appearing stagnant. The 1940 and 1941 models were facelifted. A wholly new design was fronted by a stylized version of the Packard hallmark radiator grille.

Beginning in 1931, the following was stamped on the cowl identification plates of many Packards:

PACKARD MOTOR CAR COMPANY OF CANADA, LIMITED
Windsor, Ontario

Throughout the 1920s, the economic climate of many countries, Canada included, allowed a confidence leading to relaxed tariffs, increased quotas, and in general, freer trade by the removal of protective measures. Canadian tariffs on imported American automobiles fell to an all-time low of 12 percent. The Canadian distributor, Packard Ontario, located on Toronto's Bay Street, was doing a thriving business with the products of Packard's Detroit plant.*

After the stock market collapsed, the American government introduced the

---

* Thanks to Paul L. Waaland and Technical Vice President Robert L. Trueax of the Contemporary Historical Vehicle Association for ensuring that credit for this look at Canadian Packards go to *Packard Came to Canada in 1931*, by Arthur James, writing in the March/April 1981 *Action Era Vehicle*, published by the CHVA, Inc., Box 40, Antioch, TN 37013.

A 1939 Super Eight sedan. Photo courtesy Ross M. Lee.

A 1939 Super Eight Darrin victoria. Photo John A. Conde Collection.

protective Hawley-Smoot Tariff in June of 1930. To counter, Canada's new Conservative government increased tariffs to 30 percent on imported cars costing up to $2100, and 40 percent on luxury cars with higher prices. Packard was, of course, hurt because its base price was $2375, well into the 40 percent range.

The Canadian government offered some relief from the tax to American automakers willing to open Canadian branch assembly plants. Because Packard and Pierce-Arrow had traditionally good markets in Canada, both firms crossed the Detroit River to open plants in Windsor, Ontario.

Before the end of 1931, Packard assembled 500 cars in a pair of remodelled buildings on Windsor's Church and Chatham Streets. L.L. Roberts, from Packard's Detroit operation, became general manager. In 1932, the expanding production necessitated a move to larger quarters: the Fisher Body Building on St. Luke Road. Production reached a high of 2556 cars in 1937. After 1935, the Canadian plant built only Sixes and One-Twenties. War clouds slowed production until a final 1425 Packards were assembled in 1939. In 1936, Canadian tariffs had returned to a healthier 17 1/2 percent. With volume nearly at the break-even point, Packard decided it was better business to export than build. They closed the plant.

Although Packard was listed with the Canadian Manufacturers Association as a manufacturer from 1931 to 1939, many claimed the Company's focus was still Packard Ontario's Bay Street distributorship because Packard "only put the wheels on in Windsor."

Interestingly, the 1931 model wasn't the first Packard auto assembly in Canada. In 1900, 10 years after the Packard brothers began Packard Electric Company in Warren, Ohio, they opened Packard Electric Co. Ltd., in St. Catharines, Ontario. The automobiles produced in Packard Electric Co. Ltd.'s "Motor Car Department" weren't Packards; they were Oldsmobiles. The Olds Motor Works of Lansing, Michigan contracted Packard to build its 1905 through 1907 models under license. Though the name plates read Oldsmobile, the vehicle plates read "Made by Packard."

Nor was 1939 the last year that automobiles with Packard ties were assembled in Canada. In 1957, about 200 "Packardbakers" were put together at the Studebaker Hamilton, Ontario plant.

Ask the Man Who Owns One

14

Dutch Darrin's Designs

The first Packard Darrin was a 1937 120 two-seater sold to actor Dick Powell. Darrin had returned to the states from Paris to remodel production automobiles for the rich and famous, realizing that custom-bodied cars were dying. Many of the great coachbuilders of the Twenties and early Thirties were reduced to body and fender work just to keep their doors open.

Darrin's idea of producing semicustoms from production cars is easily understandable. As for using the Packard One-Twenty, Darrin remarked, "Its chassis was unimpeachable, and its classic grille a great starting point."

While the chassis might have been unimpeachable, Darrin's first effort was plagued with water leaks and too much body flex. He hired two fine auto body craftsmen, Paul Erdos and Rudi Stoessel, and went in a large building on the Sunset Strip. Darrin's showroom had been a bottle factory. Rather than redecorate, Darrin knocked out the remnants of broken plate glass and put up flat, painted plywood, displaying his revamped One-Twenties simply and regally.

Darrin preferred One-Twenties because they were less expensive and easier to alter. In a 1978 interview, Darrin said, "I liked the Packard One-Twenty best of all Packards," as he wondered " . . . why it isn't a classic. But I'm glad it isn't, I can pick them up cheaper!"

Perhaps the One-Twenty's nimbleness, operating economy, and rugged performance against the aging Super Eight, with its two-piece block, would further endear his cars (although a few 1938-39 Super Eights were modified, too). Taking a business coupe, Darrin cut off the roof, sectioned the body 3 inches, angled the rear fenders, and cut the rakish side notch in the beltline. Rudi Stoessel, who is today involved with the restoration of fine cars—many of them Darrin's old efforts—designed an aluminum cowl that took care of the body flex. Darrin demonstrated the cowl's strength to Alvan Macauley by jumping up and down on it.

No more than 16 to 18 1938-39 Packard Darrins were built. They ranged from $4200 to $5300 when finished. The only problem Darrin now had was producing enough of them. That led him to drive one to the Packard Proving Grounds dealer show, parking the damaged car's good side out, and blending into the dealer crowd where he could gauge his car's acceptance. The dealers loved it, quite ignoring the production models parked about the grounds. And so the 1940 catalog carried the Packard Darrin, which was now built in the old Auburn plant in Connersville, Indiana.

After Dick Powell's Darrin, the next car was built for Clark Gable. It was the first five-passenger Darrin. All Darrin victorias through the end of 1942 were this model. Among the purchasers of the other 1938-39 Darrins were Al Jolson, Chester Morris, and Rosalind Russell.

The 1940 factory semicustom was the Darrin that attracted, and still attracts, the most attention. It was the purest and smoothest of the lot, and it had the additional advantage of being hyped by Packard in *Collier's, Fortune,* and *Country Life* as "Glamour Car of the Year." That was certainly true enough. Although a 1940 Lincoln Continental was one of 10 cars displayed by the Museum of Modern Art as the highest forms of automotive art, the 1940 Packard Darrin's automotive mystique reduces the prow-nose Continental to a pretty motor launch—albeit a delicate and well-balanced one. Something about the Packard Darrin's hallmark grille, creased hood, and general rolling elan is at once stolid and graceful. Clearly it is the highest form of automobilia. There are few automobiles that have reached this exalted realm of purity. One is the 1938 Talbot-Lago coupe (which inspired the XK-120 Jaguar). Another is the Jaguar E-type.

A mark of a good painting is one that leaves you wanting to add something

A 1938 Eight (One-Twenty) Darrin. The fifth victoria built and Darrin's personal car, it was driven by his friend, Gene Tierney, Photo courtesy William H. Friedrich.

The Dutch Darrin/Gene Tierney Packard. Photo courtesy William H. Friedrich.

(though perhaps you know not what). And so you stand there, drawn in, searching, involved. Usually when Detroit—Packard included—reached such a plateau, they blew it by not trusting instinct. Usually they festooned chrome baubles and last-minute, sheet-metal nervous tics onto the potential hallmark.

The 1941-42 Darrins were produced by hearse, ambulance, and special bodycrafter Sayers & Scoville, of Cincinnati, Ohio. They were all built on the One-Eighty chassis, as half the 1940 victorias had been, because President Macauley wanted as much prestige as possible. Perhaps this was meant to partly plug any hole left since the Twelve's departure.

To account for the Packard Darrins, the first, and only, two-seater was made for Dick Powell in 1937. The second Darrin, and first five-passenger model, was Gable's. These two were One-Twenties, as were all but a few of the 16 to 18 1938-39 Darrins.

The 1940 Connersville factory semicustoms numbered 40 victorias, divided between One-Twenty and One-Eighty chassis. On the longer 138-inch wheelbase One-Eighty chassis only, there were two sport sedans and five convertible sedans. These seven 138-inch wheelbase models, and the original two-seater, were the only non-five-passenger Victorias built.

The first 35 One-Eighty-only Victorias built by the Sayers & Scoville works appeared in 1941, and 15 more were made in 1942. Like all Darrin Victorias since the beginning, these were on 127-inch wheelbases (the One-Twenty and standard wheelbase Super-8s using the same frame).

Darrin teamed with custom auto body builder Thomas Hibbard as Hibbard & Darrin in the 1920s. They crafted and sold custom Mercedes-Benz, Rolls-Royce, Hispano-Suiza, Delage, Minerva and other expensive cars out of a Parisian Minerva dealership. Before Hibbard left in 1931 to work in General Motors' styling department, he and Darrin consulted for Citroen and Renault in France, Minerva in Belgium, Rolls-Royce, Armstrong-Siddeley, and Barker in England, Mercedes-Benz in Germany, and Stutz and GM in America.

Darrin admitted that when he and Hibbard designed and built custom bodies, they were only "two young kids in Paris," and had never expected their products to last more than 10 years.

After Hibbard left to join GM, Darrin formed Fernandez et Darrin, and continued customizing expensive European automobiles. In 1937, he returned to America, landing on Los Angeles' Sunset Strip, where he became "Darrin of Paris."

Despite his association with Packard, Darrin never worked for Packard. Nor was he ever paid for his consulting work on the Clipper, which appears now to be mainly Darrin's design.

Darrin was asked to design in 10 days the new car that would become the Clipper. He thought he could handle it and agreed, though demanding $1000 a day. After Darrin submitted, on time, a quarter-scale model of his Clipper, Packard's purchasing agent offered to increase his Packard Darrin order rather than pay him. Packard later canceled the order. That left Darrin with understandably unfond remembrances

A 1940 Darrin victoria. Photo John A. Conde Collection.

of Packard management until his death in 1982 at 84.

Under what the Supreme Court terms "broad construction," the Packard Darrins are no more or less than radical California customs (being an alteration of company designer Werner Gubitz' traditional theme). Dutch Darrin's fresh styling for the 1941-47 Clipper is more nearly a "Packard Darrin," with some production changes by designer Phil Wright of 1933 Pierce-Arrow, Silver Arrow fame.

Rather than retire early, which by age 50 he could easily afford to do, Darrin went on to design additional automobiles. He even came up with a sliding-door, four-seater proposal for Packard in 1955 that included a traditional grille. His most-remembered postwar efforts were for Kaiser. The 1951 Kaiser was a mechanically uninspiring creation. It was propelled by a forklift motor with daylight-seeking pistons and was saved, if possible, only by Darrin's flowing design that featured the largest amount of glass of any passenger car at the time. Marginal mechanics notwithstanding, the fiberglass Kaiser Darrin, with its sliding doors, is still as popular today.

But if Dutch Darrin had done nothing else, he would be remembered for the Packard Darrin.

15

The Super-8 Arrives

Ask the Man Who Owns One

The 1940 Packards (introduced in September, 1939) accounted for the firm's second biggest prewar model run (after the 1937 Fifteenth series) with a total of 98,000 even. The 1951 Twenty-Fourth series was the biggest single-year postwar run (discounting the extended 1948-49 Twenty-Second and 1949-50 Twenty-Third series) with 100,713, making 1940 the third biggest sales model in Packard's history.

Mechanically the Six and One-Twenty were much the same; axle ratios were a bit longer-legged and the overdrive was simplified. All 1940 Packards were built on a common assembly line, and prices were substantially lowered on all models because of this. The Six was called the 110, the One-Twenty kept its designation, the Super-8 was called the 160, and the 180 (or Custom Super-8) was a plusher version meant for all-out luxury and to replace the Twelve as top of the line.

The 110 prices plummeted to a mere $867 for a business coupe, to only $1087 for a convertible coupe, $975 for a four-door sedan, and $1195 for the station wagon (first offered in 1937).

The 120 prices dropped to only $1038 for a business coupe, to $1238 for a convertible coupe (but $3800 for the now factory-offered Darrin victoria), $1146 for a four-door touring sedan, and $1397 for the station wagon. A four-door convertible sedan cost $1550.

The new Super-8 160 boasted the most powerful eight-cylinder engine in the industry: 160 horsepower at 3600 rpm, and 292 ft. lbs. of torque at 1800 rpm. This new eight was designed along similar lines as the proven 120 motor. It displaced 356 cubic inches (3 1/2 × 4 5/8 bore × stroke), had a nine-main-bearing crankshaft, and (with Cadillac shared Wilcox-Rich) hydraulic valve lifters. The 160/180 shared main body stampings with the 110, and shared everything with the 120 but engine, trim, and some driveline and suspension components.

The 127-inch-wheelbase 160 ranged from $1524 for a business coupe to $1632 for a four-door touring sedan and $2050 for a convertible sedan. Long wheelbases were no longer offered through the 120 line because of the low prices possible on the new Super-8 160: $1895 for the 138-inch, five-passenger touring sedan; $2026 for five-eight-passenger touring sedan; and $2154 for five-eight-passenger touring limousine on the 148 inch chassis.

In 180 guise, 127-inch-wheelbase cars were $2228 for a club sedan and $4570 for the Darrin victoria (the only models offered on the short wheelbase). The 138-inch 180s ran $2395 for a five-passenger touring sedan, $2825 for a five-six-passenger formal sedan, $4450 for a five-seven-passenger All-Weather Cabriolet factory custom by Rollson, $6300 for a Darrin convertible sedan, and $6100 for a Darrin sport sedan. The 148-inch 180s were a five-eight-passenger touring limousine for $2654, $2526 for a five-eight-passenger touring sedan, and $4575 for an All-Weather Town Car factory custom by Rollson.

Packard was the world's first production car to offer air-conditioning; it was available on closed body styles of the eight-cylindered cars for $275. The 2000 1940-42 cars so equipped were subcontracted to Bishop & Babcock, a Cleveland firm. The bulky evaporator was mounted in the trunk beneath the rear-seat package shelf. The compressor was mounted on the engine, and it ran continuously unless the drive belt was removed; there was no automatic disconnect clutch. The faster the car went the cooler it became. Packard didn't offer air-conditioning again until a more modern unit was available in the 1953-56 models.

With their all-steel bodies and independent front suspensions, prewar cars were becoming more like the modern cars we know. Buick's cloverleaf grille seemed a harbinger of little more than trust in marketing backed with only enough engineer-

A 1940 Super Eight 160. Photo John A. Conde Collection.

A 1940 One-Twenty touring sedan. Photo John A. Conde Collection.

ing for lively straight-line performance—and that only in the Century 60, Roadmaster 70, and Limited 80 series. Cadillacs of the era seem sound—more than adequate—but lack refinements found on Packards. Packard refinements such as Saf-T-Flex front suspension and a fifth rear shock absorber to help control body sway were subtle, and lost on many buyers as they headed for Buick and Cadillac showrooms.

Other automobiles, though promising much, fell short of Packard's reality. The Cord's coffin nose was an apt warning of the underfunded development engineering within. None of the handcrafted, high-quality British and European cars matched Packard's, and, in fairness, many other American makes' reliability and proven

The Edward Benson Family's 1940 One-Twenty. Photo by Susan Scott.

Another view of the Benson Thoroughbred.

The interior of the 1940 One-Twenty.

Packard's famed mascot "Winged Goddess of Speed" or "Flying Lady" on the Edward Benson Family's 1940 One-Twenty. Photo by Susan Scott.

The 1940 160 limousine ordered by the Navy for Admiral Nimitz. Photo courtesy Ross M. Lee.

engineering. Hence the popularity of Packards overseas.

Chrysler, though long synonymous with thorough engineering, nevertheless used siamesed cylinders while Packard had full-length water jacketing. Chrysler sixes and eights had longer strokes than their Packard counterparts, and generated greater heat (reflected by the Chryslers' necessarily larger cooling systems). To Chrysler's credit, it introduced overdrive in 1934 (on the ill-received Airflows). The overdrive would have made more efficient high-speed cars of the pre-1939 Packards. Had Chrysler products been better styled, they might have been more of a threat to Packard. Nevertheless, throughout the '30s and '40s Chrysler was the number two automaker.

During August, 1939, Packard became the first major automaker to settle with the United Auto Workers; 74 percent of the company's rank and file voted for representation by an outside union. There had been a skeletal "Employee Representation Plan" long before the tide of unionism that swept the industry in the late 1930s. Even before the unions over 90 percent of Packard workers got at least 40 weeks of work a year, and by 1937 95 percent of them got 48 weeks a year. With clean, modern plants and wages above the industry average, Packard workers had fewer reasons for grievances than most. Packard reduced seasonality when it brought out its new models in autumn years before the rest of Detroit. Seeing the inevitable, Packard concentrated on building automobiles while, with baseball bats and thugs, Ford's antiunion campaign became a national disgrace.

Packard's treatment of its workers helped ensure a quality product. Too often, unions have been scapegoats for inept management. Packard's management was wise enough to see that a work force at odds with the company would hardly be as motivated to maintain high work standards. Much is made of design and engineering, but it is the workers who assemble the product.

In September, 1939, 87 percent of Briggs Body Company voted for union representation. Later that month, after putting up a mild fight in comparison with Ford and GM standards, Chrysler settled with an 81-percent vote. General Motors didn't settle with the UAW until a year after Packard. Ford held out until May of 1941.

Somehow it is not surprising that when the entire nation united to fight fascism, it was Packard's lot to build the highest mechanical echelon of war materiel; Rolls-Royce Merlin liquid-cooled aero engines. As the annual report for 1940 shows, Packard was already building both aviation and marine engines for our allies. Automobile production for the 1940 line broke down to 62, 300 110s, 28, 138 120s, 5662 160s, and 1900 180s.

If there was any doubt about the new Super-8s, Packard held a race at the prov-

130 PACKARD

A 1940 180 formal limousine. Photo courtesy William H. Friedrich.

To the Stockholders of the
Packard Motor Car Company:

Consolidated net earnings for the year 1940 were $774,147.36, after all charges including depreciation and federal income taxes. Factory sales of motor vehicles, service parts, marine engines, etc., amounted to $69,235,169.01.

These operating results compare with net earnings of $545,867.42 and factory sales of $63,425,062.82 for the previous year, 1939.

CAR DIVISION OPERATIONS

We produced 76,927 Packard cars during the year 1940 as compared with 76,573 for the previous year. Total deliveries of new Packard cars to customers were 77,552, as against 69,719 for 1939, representing a gain of 11.2% for the year. New cars delivered in the United States showed an increase of 14.7%; however, foreign and Canadian deliveries declined due to market restrictions resulting from the European War.

In comparison, the total production of passenger cars for the entire industry amounted to 3,802,454, an increase of 27.8% for the year 1940. Retail deliveries in the United States, represented by new car registrations of all makes of cars, showed an increase of 28.7%.

The gain in our volume of business, measured in terms of retail sales, while larger than for some of the other companies in the industry, cannot be considered satisfactory because it was less than the industry average, and because our volume is not large enough to enable us to take full advantage of the profit possibilities of our factory investment.

Our new model cars, introduced in the early fall of 1940, are attractive, well engineered, and have been well received by the public. However we determined that the addition of a newly styled Packard car to our line, which should represent a distinct departure from traditional Packard styling, was a desirable forward step toward further increasing the demand for our cars.

Accordingly we have been working for some time in collaboration with independent designers and stylists to this end. We are just beginning production of this new Packard car. We believe we have been successful in creating a very desirable new style cycle for Packard. Although our early production of these cars will of necessity be limited, we plan to have a sufficient number of them available for distribution this spring, and our spring merchandising program has been built around them.

Production schedules are being held as closely as possible in line with anticipated sales requirements. Packard dealers and distributers with but few changes continue a loyal, efficient organization. We have been working for some time to increase Packard representation in the smaller communities.

Relations with Packard employees have continued to be satisfactory due principally to a mutual desire to cooperate and a willingness to bargain collectively.

MARINE ENGINE DIVISION OPERATIONS

In our report a year ago, we advised our stockholders that the Company had re-entered the special engine field and had undertaken the development and production of a small number of high powered marine engines for the United States Navy.

To date we have signed contracts totalling approximately $17,500,000 for these marine engines and engine parts. Contracts are covered by suitable deposits. The engines are built and tested in a separate factory unit with 85,422 square feet of floor space devoted exclusively to this purpose. Originally set up for production of 5 engines a week, this was increased to 10 engines weekly, and is scheduled to be

(2)

The Packard Motor Car Company annual report for the year ending December 31, 1940.

increased to 15 engines a week in May 1941. Currently there are about 750 employees working full time on the project. We believe that we may reasonably expect to receive additional substantial orders for these engines requiring further expansion of facilities and production schedules in the near future.

The initial loss sustained in getting under way on this undertaking has been recovered and a satisfactory profit has accrued. The outlook for this division is promising.

AIRCRAFT ENGINE DIVISION OPERATIONS

During the latter part of 1940, the Company accepted the assignment of producing 9,000 Rolls-Royce aircraft engines. Under present contracts, 6,000 engines are to be built for Great Britain and 3,000 for the United States. Stockholders' interests were carefully considered in all of our negotiations to formulate the contracts for this undertaking. The necessity for this is evident when it is considered that the estimated cost of plant expansion, machines, equipment, tooling, etc., is more than $35,000,000 and that the value of the engines to be produced will probably exceed $165,000,000.

The undertaking is being financed by the contractees in accordance with present contractual agreements, and the Company has no added plant investment in the enterprise. It does, however, have certain portions of its property including land, buildings, and facilities, reserved exclusively for aircraft engine production under the terms of the related contracts. The contracts provide for payment on a cost-plus-a-fixed-fee basis.

Three new buildings for aircraft engine production are approaching completion. Altogether about 1,000,000 square feet of floor space will be devoted to building these engines, of which approximately 400,000 square feet represent available floor space in our existing plant.

Currently we are still in what is called the "make ready" stage of this project. Our tooling program is being carried forward on schedule. Parts are being run in preliminary set-ups for the first few test motors. We have some 1600 employees working full time on aircraft engine processing, plant layout, tool making, material purchasing and control, and other activities including actual production of engine parts. In addition several thousand employees in vendors' plants are working on the orders we have placed with them for machines, tools, engine parts, etc. We estimate that we will require 14,000 production employees for the aircraft engine division when we reach full production schedules.

Our preparatory work will be completed by the time the new buildings are finished. We are already proceeding with the installation of machinery and other production equipment. Present plans schedule the first production engine to be built on July 20.

The engine we are building is the latest model of the Rolls-Royce Merlin aircraft engines which the Rolls-Royce Company started to produce last April. The Merlin engine has been thoroughly tested and has given a good account of itself. It is used exclusively in the British Spitfire and Hurricane fighting planes and also in some bombers.

COORDINATION OF CAR MANUFACTURING AND DEFENSE PRODUCTION ACTIVITIES

Carefully coordinated planning permits all of our car manufacturing and defense production activities to be carried on simultaneously and independently. Our marine engine, aircraft engine, and car manufacturing divisions are separate factory units. Each has its own functional organization. This is desirable because the methods and machinery used in the manufacture of cars are not suitable for the production of these high powered, special purpose engines. Altogether different facilities, standards, and processes are required.

There has been no lessening of our motor car engineering and development activities. On the contrary, never before have we undertaken a larger development program than we now have well underway. Car production and related engineering programs are proceeding uninterruptedly and in accordance with projected schedules. Production for defense is our first objective during this emergency period; however, we believe that our car manufacturing programs can also be carried through to completion.

(3)

INCOME STATEMENT

Factory Sales — Sales for 1940 were $69,235,169.01 as compared with $63,425,062.82 for 1939

Factory Operating Expense — Administrative, selling and general expense amounted to $4,563,233.71 compared with $2,933,262.99 for 1939. The increase is in general accounted for by a change in accounting practice reflecting advertising expense at the total amount, whereas in previous years, expense was credited with a fixed amount for each car shipped.

Recoveries from Closed Banks — Claims for deposits in closed banks were reduced by payments amounting to $183,273.40. Recoveries for the previous year were $16,420.10.

Depreciation — Provision for depreciation of factory properties amounted to $1,309,656.24 as against $1,449,351.56 for 1939.

Provision for Federal Income Tax — Provision for federal income taxes includes $225,000 additional assessment for prior years from 1935 through 1939 due principally to capitalizing of amounts which we had considered as expense, and lower depreciation rates used by the tax examiner in computing the tax returns. In our opinion most of these adjustments will be claimed as deductions in future years when tax rates will probably be higher.

BALANCE SHEET

Cash Position — Cash and marketable securities totaled $37,866,326.27 at December 31, 1940. Of this amount, $35,015,111.01 was cash which included deposits of $24,115,806.25 by customers under aircraft engine contracts. At the previous year end, cash and marketable securities totaled $13,055,586.13.

Receivables — Accounts and notes receivable were $5,455,804.50 compared with $3,699,083.13 for 1939. The difference is occasioned by an increase in the time sales paper carried by our subsidiaries, and accounts with customers arising from marine and aircraft engine and other government business.

Inventories — Total inventories were valued at $10,118,436.42 as compared with $9,242,444.89 at the previous year end.

Current Assets — Total current assets were $53,440,567.19 as compared with $25,997,114.15 at December 31, 1939, an increase of $27,443,453.04 due principally to the funds advanced by customers as noted above.

Current Liabilities — Total current liabilities amounted to $34,836,961.75 as against $8,389,425.17 at the previous year end. The increase is due chiefly to the $26,151,306.25 net advances of customers under contracts.

Net Property Investment — The net property investment in land, buildings, plant equipment, etc., was $25,790,069.41, or $488,342.83 less than at the end of 1939, due to provision for depreciation at established rates in excess of plant additions for the year; also to the fact that the land and building of our distributer in London, England, which are owned by the Company, were shown as a separate investment at December 31, 1940, due to the war conditions prevailing.

This does not include any added investment in special aircraft engine plant facilities.

Deferred Charges — Deferred charges to future operations, consisting principally of prepaid insurance and engineering developments, totaled $487,324.03 as compared with $354,943.44 at the close of the previous year.

Surplus — Capital and surplus at December 31, 1940 amounted to $44,222,949.56 and was equivalent to a book value of $2.95 a share on the common stock outstanding.

(4)

SEGREGATION OF SURPLUS ACCOUNT

The Board of Directors have found it necessary and in the best interests of the Company to segregate the consolidated surplus of the Company and its subsidiaries as at January 1, 1941 and have authorized its segregation into capital surplus and earned surplus.

The last Annual Report and previous financial statements have shown that $20,000,000 of accumulated earnings was transferred in 1929 from the parent company's surplus account to capital account. In 1932 by direction of the stockholders $10,000,000 was re-transferred from capital to surplus and in 1935 a like amount was similarly re-transferred by direction of the stockholders from capital to surplus (total $20,000,000). Such Annual Report further explained that the consolidated surplus account has reflected the annual profits, losses and dividends paid; that $5,713,122.77 included in the parent company's surplus account represented the balance remaining of the amount ($20,000,000) so transferred from capital to surplus. The difference between these amounts, or $14,286,877.23, was used to absorb operating losses accumulated during the period from October, 1931 to May 1, 1935, which losses were included in the amounts shown in the published annual reports covering that period.

After the segregation of the consolidated surplus into two accounts, the capital surplus account at January 1, 1941 will include $5,713,122.77, being the remainder of $20,000,000 transferred to surplus mentioned above, and in addition the balance of the capital and earned surplus of the subsidiaries as of May 1, 1935. The consolidated earned surplus account will include net earnings of the parent company and subsidiaries since May 1, 1935 (less dividends paid since that date amounting to $10,493,938) which date is the first day of the month following the last transfer from capital to surplus referred to above (April 15, 1935). In order to segregate the surplus accounts and to charge accumulated losses against capital surplus, in the manner indicated above, present day accounting procedure and the Securities and Exchange Commission require that the surpluses of the subsidiaries as of May 1, 1935 shall be included in consolidated capital surplus regardless of whether such surplus prior thereto was earned surplus or capital surplus.

As the result the balances in these accounts as at January 1, 1941 will appear as follows:

Capital surplus	$10,766,721.20
Earned surplus since May 1, 1935	3,456,228.36
	$14,222,949.56

The action of the Board of Directors is in the best interests of the Company and the approval of the stockholders is requested.

THE OUTLOOK

We believe that the number of cars we will produce in 1941 will be as large as our output for 1940. The volume of our marine engine business will be considerably larger for 1941. We expect to ship a reasonable number of aircraft engines during the last six months of the year. The increase in dollar volume of our business should favorably affect earnings. We are hopeful that we will be in a position to resume dividend payments during the year.

We recognize the exacting nature of the dual responsibility of carrying on defense work and car production, and have accepted the task with confidence that we can successfully accomplish both objectives.

W. W. Gilman,
President.

March 18, 1941

BALANCE SHEET

Packard Motor Car Company
(A MICHIGAN CORPORATION)
and Subsidiary Companies

Consolidated Balance Sheet as of December 31, 1940

ASSETS

CURRENT ASSETS:

Cash in banks and on hand (including $24,115,806.25 of funds advanced by customers under aircraft engine contracts, of which $5,569,596.77 is subject to lien to secure performance)			$35,015,111.01
Investments, at lower of cost or quoted market value—			
United States Government Securities		$ 1,878,981.24	
Municipal and Canadian Government Bonds		972,234.02	2,851,215.26
Accounts and Notes Receivable, less reserves—			
Accounts Receivable		$ 2,472,248.34	
Deferred Installment Notes		2,983,556.16	5,455,804.50
Inventories, at or below cost—			
Raw Material, Work in Process, etc.		$ 5,530,801.53	
Finished Motor Vehicles		4,587,634.89	10,118,436.42
Total Current Assets			$53,440,567.19

OTHER ASSETS:

Mortgage and Miscellaneous Investments			$ 312,199.40
Claims for Deposits in banks and trust companies closed or under restriction	$ 103,460.49		
Less—Reserve	103,460.49		
Dividends Received From Closed Bank, on Deposit With Trustees		94,616.02	406,815.42

INVESTMENT IN AND ADVANCES TO WHOLLY-OWNED ENGLISH SUBSIDIARY, AT COST (Represented Principally By Distribution Properties in London, England) 185,135.26

PROPERTY ACCOUNT:

Land, at Cost—			
For Manufacturing Purposes		$ 1,954,666.30	
For Distribution Purposes		4,402,192.96	$ 6,356,859.26
Buildings, Plant Equipment, etc., at Cost—			
Manufacturing Properties	$22,381,818.96		
Less—Reserve for Depreciation	8,726,173.18	13,655,645.78	
Distribution Properties	$ 9,251,573.09		
Less—Reserve for Depreciation	3,474,009.72	5,777,563.37	
Rights, Privileges, Franchises and Inventions		1.00	25,790,069.41

SPECIAL AIRCRAFT ENGINE PLANT FACILITIES:

Buildings, Equipment and Rearrangement Expenses paid for directly by customers or from funds received from customers			$ 2,343,824.69
Unexpended Balance of Funds received from customer for purchase of special facilities			18,347,494.74
Total			$20,691,319.43
Less—Amounts Received From or Paid By Customers			20,691,319.43
Remainder			Nil

DEFERRED CHARGES TO FUTURE OPERATIONS:

Prepaid Insurance and Other Expense			487,324.03
Total Assets			$80,309,911.31

LIABILITIES

CURRENT LIABILITIES:

Current Accounts Payable and Pay Rolls			$ 5,568,636.80
Miscellaneous Liabilities Not Yet Due			610,537.28
Reserves for Miscellaneous Items			1,929,529.08
Advances by Customers Under Sales Contracts for Marine Engines			2,035,500.00
Advances by Customers Under Aircraft Engine Contracts	$24,800,219.71		
Less—Accumulated Costs in Respect of Such Contracts	684,413.46		24,115,806.25
Provision for Income Taxes			576,952.34
Total Current Liabilities			$34,836,961.75

RESERVE FOR GENERAL PURPOSES (Note 1) 1,250,000.00

CAPITAL STOCK:

Common (Authorized 25,000,000 Shares of No Par Value)

Issued 15,000,000 Shares 30,000,000.00

(Includes 8,660 Shares issued to Trustee for Account of Company, Not Carried as an Asset)

SURPLUS (Note 1):

Balance at December 31, 1939	$13,448,802.20		
Add—Net Profit for the Year Ended December 31, 1940, per Statement Attached	774,147.36		14,222,949.56

Total Liabilities and Capital $80,309,911.31

(See accompanying notes to financial statements)

Packard Motor Car Company
(A MICHIGAN CORPORATION)
and Subsidiary Companies

STATEMENT OF INCOME

For the Year Ended December 31, 1940

FACTORY OPERATIONS:			
Sales of Motor Vehicles, Marine Engines and Service Parts, etc.			$69,235,169.01
Deduct—Cost of Sales			62,535,300.93
			$ 6,699,868.08
Add—Other Income—			
Discount on Purchases	$ 202,499.79		
Interest and Rentals	47,459.84		
Miscellaneous	6,753.54		256,713.17
			$ 6,956,581.25
Deduct—Selling, General and Administrative Expense			4,563,233.71
Profit Before Applying Factory Depreciation and Special Items			$ 2,393,347.54
Add—			
Recoveries on Claims for Deposits in Closed Banks		$ 183,273.40	
Reduction in Reserve for Depreciation in Value of Investments		89,630.22	272,903.62
			$ 2,666,251.16
Deduct—			
Depreciation of Factory Properties		$1,309,656.24	
Provision for Unrealized Foreign Exchange Loss		35,316.96	
Provision for Federal Income Taxes—			
Additional Provision for Prior Years' Taxes Including Interest	225,000.00		
Estimated Provision for Normal Income Tax (1940)	250,000.00	1,819,973.20	
Net Profit From Factory Operations			$ 846,277.96
Deduct—Loss From Operations of Branches and Subsidiary Companies			72,130.60
Net Profit for the Year Ended December 31, 1940			$ 774,147.36

(See accompanying notes to financial statements)

Packard Motor Car Company

(A MICHIGAN CORPORATION)

and Subsidiary Companies

Notes to Financial Statements—December 31, 1940

NOTES:

1. Consolidated surplus of $14,222,949.56 includes $8,408,813.19 Parent Company surplus and $5,814,136.37 surplus of subsidiaries. The last annual report and previous financial statements have shown that $20,000,000 was transferred in 1929 from surplus to capital account on the Parent Company's books. Subsequently, a like amount was by authority of the Stockholders re-transferred from capital to surplus account. There is included in the Parent Company surplus $5,713,122.77 being the remaining balance of the amount so transferred to surplus which may not be distributable by way of dividend; also, surplus of subsidiary companies includes capital surplus of $881,763.23 which may not be so distributed by the subsidiaries.

    However, since December 31, 1940 the directors of the company have authorized, and the stockholders have been requested to approve, a segregation of the consolidated surplus balance as at January 1, 1941. After the segregation of the consolidated surplus into two accounts the balances in these accounts as at January 1, 1941, will be as follows:

Capital Surplus	$10,766,721.20*
Earned Surplus Since May 1, 1935	3,456,228.36
	$14,222,949.56

    *All undistributed earned surplus of subsidiary companies from dates of acquisition to May 1, 1935 is included in consolidated capital surplus.

    The reserve for general purposes, $1,250,000, was created prior to May 1, 1935.

2. Current assets and current liabilities in Canada have been included in the consolidated balance sheet at the prevailing rate of exchange at December 31, 1940. Fixed assets have been included at approximate U. S. dollar cost at date of acquisition. The monthly operating accounts of the Canadian subsidiary have been converted into dollars at the month-end rates of exchange throughout the year. On the foregoing basis the net assets in Canada as at December 31, 1940, amounted to $578,130.41, consisting of net current assets of $559,727.89 and fixed and other assets of $18,402.52.

    The accounts of the English subsidiary have not been included in the consolidated balance sheet at December 31, 1940, but the investment in and advances to that company, represented principally by distribution properties in London, England, have been included at cost. The operating accounts of the English subsidiary have not been included in the accompanying statement of income.

    Of the total consolidated sales for 1940 approximately 7% represented sales for foreign destination.

3. Other than commitments in the ordinary course of business, the company had as at December 31, 1940 unfilled orders for the manufacture of aircraft engines in the approximate aggregate amount of $165,000,000 and had made arrangements for the purchase of substantial amounts of raw materials, parts and supplies in connection with these unfilled orders, for which the company is entitled to reimbursement by customers. In the opinion of the company's officials the unexpended advances received from customers under these contracts were sufficient to cover any contingent liability of the company as at December 31, 1940 under these commitments.

    The company had also made arrangements for the purchase of plant facilities, machinery and equipment for use in aircraft engine production, to be owned by customers and to be paid for from funds advanced by them. The unexpended balances of funds received from customers were sufficient to cover the cost of these items.

(9)

PRICE, WATERHOUSE & CO.

RESIDENT PARTNER
A. J. BLOODSWORTH
CERTIFIED PUBLIC ACCOUNTANT

PENOBSCOT BUILDING

DETROIT

March 5, 1941

To the Board of Directors,
Packard Motor Car Company,
Detroit, Michigan.

We have examined the consolidated balance sheet of Packard Motor Car Company and its subsidiary companies as at December 31, 1940 and the statement of income for the year then ended. In connection with our examination, we reviewed the system of accounting control and procedures of the companies and examined or tested their accounting records and other supporting evidence, by methods and to the extent we deemed appropriate, but we did not make a detailed audit of the transactions.

In our opinion, the accompanying consolidated balance sheet and related statement of income, together with the notes appended thereto, present fairly the position of Packard Motor Car Company and its subsidiary companies consolidated at December 31, 1940, and the results of their operations for the year, in conformity with accepted accounting principles applied on a basis consistent with that of the preceding year.

PRICE, WATERHOUSE & CO.

Packard Motor Car Company

(A MICHIGAN CORPORATION)

DIRECTORS AND OFFICERS

Directors

TRUMAN H. NEWBERRY   ALVAN MACAULEY   JAMES T. MCMILLAN
HENRY E. BODMAN   M. M. GILMAN   ROBERT B. PARKER

Officers

ALVAN MACAULEY
Chairman of the Board

M. M. GILMAN
President and General Manager

J. G. VINCENT
Vice-President of Engineering

HENRY E. BODMAN
Vice-President and General Counsel

G. T. CHRISTOPHER
Vice-President of Manufacturing

JAMES H. MARKS
Vice-President and Purchasing Manager

W. M. PACKER
Vice-President of Distribution

HUGH J. FERRY
Secretary and Treasurer

LEE J. EASTMAN
Vice-President

MILTON TIBBETTS
Vice-President and Patent Counsel

EUGENE C. HOELZLE
Comptroller

A. G. DENISON
Assistant Secretary and Assistant Treasurer

Active Subsidiary Companies

Packard Motor Car Company of New York   Packard Motor Car Company of Chicago
Atlanta Packard Motors, Inc.
Packard Motor Car Company of Canada, Limited
Packard Motors Export Corporation   Packard Motor Sales Company
Packard Limited, London, England

Transfer Offices

Packard Motor Car Company
Detroit, Michigan

Guaranty Trust Company of New York
New York City

Registrars of Stock

Detroit Trust Company
Detroit, Michigan

City Bank Farmers Trust Company
New York City

Auditors

Price, Waterhouse & Co.

ing grounds for the benefit of its dealers. A 1939 Twelve was easily defeated by the new 180. Today, the Packard Twelve is most interesting as an engineering exercise. Enzo Ferrari was inspired by the Twelve while he designed his diminutive V-12, which debuted in 1948. The Packard Twelve was the finest luxury automobile engine of all the multicylindered behemoths of the 1930s, but their day had clearly ended. In 1940, Lincoln offered the last of its big twelves (leftover '39s) while Cadillac offered a final V-16 until the parts bins were empty.

During the 1920's, even as his Royales were fait accompli, Ettore Bugatti preferred his Packard for long, fast business trips over any of his own, or competing, European products. The first Royale was fitted with a Packard body. When blue sky was tempered with reality, even the most gifted automotive visionaries selected Packard.

Although the Packard Eight of the 1920s was as refined as any auto in the world, and easily better than the Issota-Fraschini straight eight, there were reports of Cadillac V-8s turning in better service in certain rugged livery use.* By 1939, let alone 1935, the big Packard eights—with their five-inch strokes and two-piece blocks— were anachronisms, rather than exciting road cars. So there was little remorse over the departure of the old 320-cubic-inch Super-8 when the shorter-stroke, high-speed 356 cubic-inch Super-8 appeared for 1940.

Packard's engine designer, Howard Reed (a Buick alumnus) tried during the late 1930s to sell Packard management on not just overhead valves, but an overhead camshaft engine. He was told that the valve train's additional noise would be unseemly in a Packard.** That certainly could have been solved with Packard's even partial engineering attention, but at the time, except for Buick and Chevrolet, valve-in-block engines were the standard of the industry. Packard built the best.

During calendar year 1940, 76,927 Packards, several hundred more than in 1939, left the factory for a $774,147 profit. Extensive, single assembly-line tooling and war work both took a toll. Packard was as honored a name as any, and fiscally sound, as the annual report shows, but sophisticated marketing of often richly styled General Motors products called for new tactics.

---

*From a *Car Collector & Car Classics* article on a Rocky Mountain tourist charter service.

**Another gem from the gracious Marice D. Hendry, Auckland, New Zealand, observed in one of his rich *Car Collector & Car Classics* columns.

Packard
Ask the Man Who Owns One

16
Wartime

In 1940, the U.S. Army ranked seventeenth among all the world's armies. Even before the massive mobilization spurred by Pearl Harbor, Detroit had already become the arsenal of democracy. Calendar year 1942 saw 223,000 cars sold in America. In 1943 the sales figure dropped to only 139. American automakers produced a wartime total of 2,600,000 military trucks, 600,000 jeeps, and 49,000 tanks. The automobile industry was responsible for 10 percent of all American warplanes, 75 percent of all our aircraft engines, 47 percent of our machine guns, and 87 percent of all our aircraft bombs.

In 1939, Packard received a government contract to design a marine engine. Although originally planned as a redesign of the famed Gar Wood Miss America engine, which regularly beat the Rolls-Royce powered Miss England for the Harmsworth Trophy during the 1920s and 30s, some of that motor's features weren't suitable for Navy use. The engines first delivered in 1940 proved a great success, and they powered our entire torpedo boat fleet throughout the war.

But Packard is most remembered for its redesign and prolific production of the intricate Rolls-Royce Merlin, liquid-cooled supercharged V-12 aircraft engine. With the possible exception of the limited-production Napier Saber, the Merlin is perhaps the best piston-driven, liquid-cooled, high-performance aircraft engine ever built.

Ford hadn't thought it possible to produce the Merlin in the numbers and with the precision our allies needed. Packard not only improved and successfully produced the Merlin, but the company's legal counsel, Henry Bodman, rewrote the contract so that it became the basis for government contracts for years to come.

High-performance, liquid-cooled aircraft engines were the most exacting to produce. It was perhaps telling that Packard's most threatening rivals, Buick and Cadillac, built less demanding aircooled radial engines, tank parts, and bombshells.

The only other American firm to build high-performance, liquid-cooled aircraft engines was Allison, a separate General Motors division with GM's entire resources on tap: 250 parts, including crankshafts, connecting rods, and reduction gear from Cadillac; aluminum and magnesium castings as well as 75 additional machined parts from Delco-Remy; machined parts from Chevrolet, etc. Allison machined only 20 percent of its engine while 80 percent came from affiliated plants and subcontractors. Just as Packard's marine diesels of the 1950s outpowered GM diesels of equivalent weight, so did the Packard re-engineered-and-built Rolls-Royce Merlin outperform the Allison.

The only other automaker to build high-performance, liquid-cooled aircraft engines in any number was Daimler-Benz. In peacetime they had produced among the finest-quality autos and racing cars on the Continent. Although the Packard/Rolls-Royce Merlin displaced 1649 cubic inches to the Daimler-Benz D.B. 601's 2071, the Anglo-American engine produced more power. Messerschmitt Me-109s—including the Me-109R cooled by water that set the world record for absolute speed in 1939—used the D.B. 601.

The original Rolls-Royce Merlin was introduced in 1935, and the prewar British Merlin lacked the efficiency and simplicity of the Packard version. The engines can't really be considered the same unit, and the blowers are different.

Packard employees in the supercharger section worked with tolerances as close as 1/1,000,000 of an inch. The 14,000 parts in a Merlin engine doubled the number in an entire 1940 Packard automobile (and also doubled the number of parts of the Allison engine). It took five hours to cast a 1940 Packard automotive block, but 110 hours to cast the aluminum Merlin block. While the connecting rods in a 1940 Packard automobile engine needed 30 minutes of machining, those in the Merlin

A 1941 Darrin for sale for $450 in St. Louis, Missouri circa 1953. Photo courtesy William H. Friedrich.

A 1942 Darrin. Photo courtesy William H. Friedrich.

A 1942 Darrin. Photo courtesy William H. Friedrich.

required 31 hours. There were 70,000 inspections on 70 test stands for the Merlins. The Packard plant needed 30,000 gallons of fuel a day.

A special ceremony was held at the Packard factory, on August 2, 1941, when the first two Merlins were run on their test beds. By the war's end, Packard delivered 55,523 of the intricate powerhouses, and—as sole American producer—quintupled the Merlin output of Rolls-Royce and all subcontracted British manufacturers.

Packard's accomplishments might be better put in perspective by looking at the aircraft engine production of all the world's automakers. German aero engine roots in the automobile industry went as far back as the pre-World War I Daimler-Benz dirigible engines used by Count Zeppelin. Both Daimler-Benz and BMW built powerful aircraft motors during World War I. When the war ended, the Treaty of Versailles forced both firms to stop building aircraft engines of any kind. But Germany gained air superiority before World War II, and the United States suddenly had to develop a large and modern air force to replace its tiny, outmoded aircorps (mainly biplanes). "The Americans," said Goering, "cannot build airplanes. They are very good at refrigerators and razor blades."

Americans quickly proved Goering wrong. Buick opened a new plant at Melrose Park, Illinois for machining and engine assembly. Its Flint plants manufactured parts

A P-51 Mustang powered by Packard/Rolls-Royce Merlin. In the aircraft are World War II pilot and Korean ace Bob Love and his son. A pair of genteel authorities devoutly read this chapter, but I had to picture a veteran.

and assembled Pratt & Whitney Double Wasp aircooled radials. Chevrolet also manufactured "Double Wasps" as well as machined and assembled parts for Allison. Ford constructed its new aircraft engine plant at River Rouge, with a capacity of 40 Double Wasps (9043 contracted), for the United States War Department. Manufacturing employed 17,000 and covered 1,300,000 square feet. Packard Merlin production needed 14,000 employees and 1,000,000 square feet.

Packard developed the Liberty engine, and produced 6500 out of an industry total of 20,478 during World War I. In 1928, Packard developed the first aviation diesel, rated by the U.S. Dept. of Commerce at 225 hp at 1950 rpm. On May 25-28, 1931, this engine—in a Bellanca Pacemaker piloted by Walter Lees and Frederick Brossy—set a world nonrefueling endurance record of 84 hours, 33 minutes at Jacksonville, Florida. Packard was clearly no stranger to aircraft engine development.

Of the planes Packard powered, the most famous is the North American P-51 Mustang. The Mustang was originally designed for the British; it was accepted by the U.S. Army Air Corps only after it had proven itself. A U.S. Senate investigating committee rated the Mustang as "the most aerodynamically perfect pursuit plane in existence."

Unlike many aircraft, the P-51 was a fresh design. Early Mustangs, the P-51As, were first produced in October of 1940, and they were powered by Allison engines. Higher altitude, longer-range fighters were needed, and the famed Packard-powered Mustangs—beginning with the P-51Bs and Cs—arrived in early 1943. Although the 1120 P-51As used Allisons, all 14,556 P-51Bs through Hs had Merlin engines.

First the Nazis and later the Japanese learned to respect the Mustang at even the highest altitudes. And for the first time in the war, the Merlin-powered Mustang allowed fighter escort of long-range bombers deep into enemy territory. Ironically, an airframe meant for the British and powered by what had begun as a British engine became a wholly American effort. Although Packard stopped powering the flying gun platforms at the war's end, the P-51 was produced through 1952, and used in Korea. The National Guard used them until the early Sixties, the Spanish Air Force until 1967, and a turboprop version was proposed toward the end of the Vietnam War. Today, Packard-propelled Mustangs are still the ones to beat at the annual Reno air races.

In 1940, the Curtiss P-40 was the American fighter, and our mainstay until the P-51. The P-40 was an old design that had its roots in the radial-engined 1938 P-36 used in the Sino-Japanese War. About 15,000 P-40s were produced before being phased out during the war. There were 2000 of these fitted with Merlins and called Warhawks.

The Hawker Hurricane was an old design—the British P-40—perhaps best remembered for its part in the Battle of Britain. The Supermarine Spitfire was the "British P-51," and—with the Mustang and Focke-Wulf 190—among the best fighters of the war.

The Avro Lancaster heavy bomber was an old, vulnerable design, but none of the British heavy bombers were up to American standards. The De Havilland Mosquito fighter-bomber was another story. The twin-Merlin-powered Mosquito rivalled the Mustang as the world's fastest plane (discounting a handful of unreliable German jets toward the end of the war). The German Focke-Wulf 190 was the only other propeller-driven aircraft that could approach the two Merlin-powered planes, and it took a special model equipped with methanol tanks late in the war to do it.

There's an amazing and little-known, Packard-powered Mosquito story. During the war, De Havilland Mosquitos, wooden and therefore invisible to radar, were loaded to (and often beyond) their limit with Swedish ball bearings. Often there was only one pilot, though at times the cargo included some important government official. Stripped of all guns, the defenseless Mosquito left Stockholm with its vital cargo. Nearly every piece of war machinery imaginable used ball bearings.

Its twin Merlins emitting the distinctive crack, the sleek, wooden plane climbed quickly to 40,000 feet—spiralling upward to stay within Swedish air space. In one of the most tense and little-known air dramas of the war, the Mosquito would now go into nothing so much as a prolonged power dive all the way to England. The 900 miles were covered in nearly two hours.

The Mosquito's only defense was absolute speed. Even the dreaded Focke-Wulf 190 could manage but one interception of the streaking Mosquitos. Although a ghost to radar, many of the Mosquitos did actually streak. A special exhaust design, good for an extra 10 miles an hour, glowed fiery red in the night sky.

And to think that Geoffrey De Havilland, unaided by a skeptical Air Ministry, developed the advanced Mosquito at his own expense. He used wood both to conserve strategic war materiel and to save weight. Aside from its nonpareil standing among airplanes, the Mosquito seems an apt stablemate to another Packard-propelled wooden speed demon—the famed patrol torpedo boat or "Water Wasp."

Ask the Man Who Owns One

17

The Clipper

The 1941 models were introduced in September, 1940. These were again facelifted renditions of the familiar Packard themes. The 110 cost from $907 for the business coupe to $1291 for the Deluxe station wagon. The 120s ranged from $1112 for the business coupe, to $1496 for the Deluxe station wagon, and $1723 for the convertible sedan. The 160s cost from $1504 for a business coupe to $2405 for the De Luxe convertible sedan on the 127-inch wheelbase, $2009 for the five-passenger touring sedan on the 138-inch wheelbase, and $2161 and $2289 for the seven-passenger touring sedan and touring limousine. The 180s sold for $4550 for the 127-inch Darrin victoria, $3500 for a LeBaron sport brougham. $4650 for a seven-passenger, All-Weather cabriolet Rollson factory custom, $3405 for a six-passenger formal sedan, $2587 for a five-passenger touring sedan on the 138-inch chassis, from $2784 for a seven-passenger touring sedan to $4775 for a seven-passenger Rollson All-Weather town car, and $5550 for a LeBaron seven-passenger touring limousine on the 148-inch chassis.

Comparisons with Cadillac are understandable but generally unwarranted. Cadillac was one line of a huge manufacturer. At times of low ebb, they were supported by the parent corporation. On the other hand, Packard was the manufacturer, and the Six, 115-C, 110, Eight, Standard Eight, Super Eight, Twelve, 120, 160, 180 were separate lines. Cadillac 60, 60 Special, 62, 75, 90, etc., were models of but one line of a much larger organization. Packard's lines had to run from the lower-middle-price class six-cylinder 115-C of 1937 to the leading contenders in world class luxury—the Twelves and Super-8s.

That a firm which didn't exceed a twenty-fifth or so of GM's business could offer competitive products in all but the lowest-price levels (and there only because it was deemed unnecessary) bespeaks much. Hudson and Nash generally outsold Packard and employed more workers. Yet compare the number of engineering coups Packard garnered with those of both Hudson and Nash combined. Indeed, General Motors, with dozens the number of employees, was hard-pressed to outdo Packard in quantity, quality, or scope of engineering achievement.

The Buick Special model 40, with eight cylinders and overhead valves, put out scarcely more power than the same-displacement Packard 110, with six cylinders and valves in block. Yet a fair overhead valve straight eight (albeit with outmoded babbitt-rod bearings) was instantly grasped as the better buy over Packard's refined L-head six.

For years, along with the Chrysler and Gray Marine flathead units, the Packard 110 six appeared in numerous Chris-Craft speedboats. The engine was deemed rugged and powerful enough for taxi use even through the heavy 1949 bathtub models on the 141-inch taxi wheelbase.

In 1941, the Buick Century four-door touring sedan was actually $3 less (at $1288 versus $1291) than the Packard One-Twenty, four-door touring sedan. The Packard's facelifted tradition was becoming a little old, and especially against the Buick's relative sleekness supported by a strident ad campaign: "Better Buy Buick." Since 1936, Buick promoted flash, power, and youth with "Dynaflash" and "Fireball" engines, playing up overhead valves, and suggesting a blend of affordable luxury and performance that appealed to both young couples and their parents.

For $3 less, here was Buick's big 320-cubic-inch eight (165 horsepower) against Packard's L-head 282 cubic-inch eight with 45 fewer horsepower. To match the Buick's horsepower, and beat its torque, meant shelling out another $504 for the Super-8 160 that was otherwise the same car as the 120.

Model Comparison.
Chart Compiled From 1950 NADA Figures.

	Price (4-dr. sdn.)	Cylinders	Horsepower	Wheelbase	Transmission option
Buick 40 Special	$1021 ($1052*)	8	115	118" (121")	no
50 Super	*$1153 with Super 50 compound carburetors				
50 Super	$1185	8	125	121	
60 Century	$1288	8	165	126	
70 Roadmaster	$1364	8	165	126	
90 Limited	$2155	8	165	139	"
Cadillac Series 61	$1445	8	150	126	Hydramatic
Series 62	$1495	8	150	126	
Series 60S	$2195	8	150	126	
Series 67	$2595	8	150	139	
Series 75	$2995	8	150	136	
Chrysler Royal	$1091 ($1345)	6	112	121 1/2 (139 1/2)	Vacamatic trans.
Windsor	$1165 ($1410)	6	112	121 1/2 (139 1/2)	"
Saratoga	$1320	8	137	127 1/2	Fluid Drive std. Powermatic shift and Vacamatic trans. optional
New Yorker	$1389	8	137	127 1/2	Fluid Drive and Simplimatic trans.
DeSoto Custom	$1085 ($1310)	6	105	121 1/2 (139 1/2)	no
Dodge Luxury Liner	$ 954 ($1195)	6	91	119 1/2 (137 1/2)	
Hudson Super Six	$1007	6	102	121	Vacumotive Drive and overdrive
Commodore	$1087	6	102	121	" "
Big Boy	$1223	6	98	128	
Hudson Commodore	$1132	8	128	121	Vacumotive Drive and overdrive
" Custom	$1330	8	128	128	
Lincoln Zephyr	$1493	12	120	125	overdrive
	(Lincoln Continental: coupe $2727, cabriolet $2778. Stock Zephyr mechanics. Packard Darrin: convertible only. $4595. Stock Super-8 mechanics only for 1941-42)				
Lincoln Zephyr Custom	$2622	12	120	138	"
Mercury	$ 991	8	95	118	overdrive
Nash Ambassador	$ 970	6	105	121	overdrive
Ambassador	$1186	8	115	121	
Oldsmobile Special	$ 945	6	100	119	Hydramatic
Dynamic	$1010	6	100	125	
Custom	$1099	6	100	125	
Special	$ 987	8	110	119	
Dynamic	$1045	8	110	125	
Custom	$1135	8	110	125	
Packard One Ten	$1076	6	100	122	Electromatic Clutch overdrive
One Twenty	$1291	8	120	127	
Clipper	$1420	8	125	127	
One Sixty	$1795	8	165	127	
"	138 w.b. $2054	8	160		
"	148 w.b. $2206	8	160		
One Eighty (Darrin Victoria only on 127" wheelbase)					
" 138 w.b. $2632		8	165		
" 148 w.b. $2769		8	165		
Pontiac Deluxe Torpedo	$ 921	6	90	119	no
Streamliner Torpedo	$ 980	6	90	122	"
Deluxe Torpedo	$ 946	8	103	119	"
Streamliner Torpedo	$1005	8	103	122	"
Studebaker Commander Skyway	$1100	6	94	119 1/2	overdrive
President Skyway	$1230	8	117	124 1/2	"

A 1941 One-Twenty club coupe with 180 trim by the owner.

A 1941 One-Twenty with 180 trim by the owner.

The smooth lines of a 1941 One-Twenty. Photo by Susan Scott.

A 1940 180 (left) and a 1941 160. Photo courtesy William H. Friedrich.

A 1941 160 sport brougham. Photo courtesy William F. Friedrich.

The new car buyer was expected to pay $1795 (sedan prices) for a Packard with $1288 Buick power. And for $300 less ($1495) he or she could buy a new Cadillac model 62 four-door touring sedan with 346 cubic inches, and, with 150 horsepower, not much compromise in road-going muscle (although the carefully engineered Packards had equivalent and often better power-to-weight ratios than the GM contenders). Because Cadillac dropped the sale-robbing and redundant LaSalle, replacing it in 1941 with the base Cadillac model 61, Cadillac buyers weren't tarnished with a "lesser car" stigma as they might driving a LaSalle or as a One-Twenty buyer might face.

The Packard One Twenty was marketed as a Packard rather than a Macauley or Packardette (both of which had been suggested back in 1934) or in some way given a separate image. Packard couldn't drop the One-Twenty or the designation, because the car had been twice the seller the LaSalle had been, and it was still perceived as a sound buy. But the One-Twenty could be offered in a new guise.

Because Packard was, in the words of consultant designer Dutch Darrin, "so afraid of GM they couldn't see straight," the successful One-Twenty retained its traditional body as well as surfaced in an all-new shell. Mr. Darrin and Phil Wright (of Pierce-Arrow Silver Arrow fame) designed the Clipper. It was introduced in April of 1941. The Clipper took off; its promise was cut short only by Pearl Harbor and the curtailment of all passenger car production less than 10 months later.

Although on the One-Twenty's 127-inch wheelbase, the Clipper chassis was newly designed for a lower floor pan without sacrificing road clearance. The resulting car was a smooth, fleet design that was wider than it was tall. The Clipper was priced at $1420. That was $25 under the Cadillac model 61, and midway between the One-Twenty and One-Sixty.

Although offered late in the year, 16,600 Clippers were sold out of a total 1941 model run of 72,855 (including 34,700 110s, 17,100 120s, 3525 160s, and 930 180s. With sales appeal like that, it was obvious that the Clipper would become the basis for the entire 1942 line.

Largely because the Clipper name was revived during 1953 through 1957 for Packard's volume base line, many consider the 1941 Clipper an inexpensive Packard. It wasn't.

That Packard feared design obsolescence was obvious. In 1940, the grille—that had been scarcely changed in a decade—was narrowed and flanked with smaller side grilles in a nod to the narrower-prow noses sweeping the industry and typifying modernity to the consumer. The tall, narrow, and attractive LaSalle snout is a good example.

By 1941, GM had already finely honed the craft of giving only enough engineering for the dollar wrapped in the richest-looking steel and pot metal. No lesser manufacturer could quantum leap GM's styling status quo. Chrysler taught the industry that lesson with the 1934 Airflow debacle. At best, smaller makers, Packard included, could only anticipate GM and design accordingly.

Dutch Darrin was outraged to see his 1941 Clipper released without the front fenderline continuing through to the rear fenders (as Buick would have the follow-

A 1941 Clipper touring sedan parked under a Pan American Clipper. Photo John A. Conde Collection.

THE CLIPPER 151

A 1941 Super Eight, four-door touring sedan. Photo John A. Conde Collection.

A 1941 One-Twenty touring sedan. Photo John A. Conde Collection.

ing year). Darrin also did not like the production car's enclosed runningboards (that were) "hidden by ugly bulges below the doors." Though Packard management had been perhaps overly cautious, the production Clipper was nevertheless a sensation that was wholly unexpected by Packard. The Clipper had nearly the same profile as Darrin's 1940 sport sedan, a beautiful car that makes many wonder why the entire 1940 line hadn't been "Darrinized."

With its Hydramatic offered on 1940 Oldsmobile and 1941 Cadillacs, GM was first to market fully automatic transmissions. Chrysler touted its new Fluid Drive as the industry sought to make the act of driving as streamlined as its cars. Packard could only counter with its new Electromatic clutch, that eliminated clutch pedal operation in normal driving. The 1941 sales brochure even suggested that the Electromatic clutch be used with overdrive (appropriately for the times 1940's Econo-Drive had been renamed Aero-Drive for 1941) as a sort of semiautomatic transmission in city traffic. If the transmission was left in second gear, overdrive would kick in approximating conventional third gear; shifting and clutching would be done away with.

General Motors offered a wide array of shrewdly marketed cars. Each line blanketed just that field Sloan allowed. Packard could no longer afford to be synonomous with exclusively high-priced cars.

While Packard worried about company survival, one of GM's big dramas arose when Cadillac finally insisted on an end to Buick's one-upmanship. The last straw was a new line of Brunn-bodied Buick catalog customs (only several were actually built) that, coupled with Buick's equal torque and additional horsepower, would trump Cadillac with car buyers in the know.

Now that the UAW was grudgingly accepted, GM could concentrate on other concerns such as replacing trolley lines by offering entire fleets of busses at, or even below, cost. Similar offers of its diesel-electric locomotives were made to the superintendents of motive power at the nation's still mainly steam-powered railroads.

The going was getting tough; to survive meant countering GM's increasingly sophisticated products. Graham and Hupp were just two more companies that by 1941 could no longer take the pace. The car buyer was faced with many choices.

Let's shop the 1941 showrooms not as automotive historians but as new car buyers. I have purposely omitted the "low-priced three," Chevrolet, Ford, and Plymouth, as well as lower lines of Hudson, Nash, and Studebaker. These were not generally Packard competition. Crosley goes without saying.

Forget the details such as durability, engineering features, and performance flexibilities. As an ill-informed new car buyer, which would you have driven home?

That was Packard's problem.

18

Nothing New

There was really nothing new in 1942 from Packard, or any of the automakers for that matter. Baubles like DeSoto's disappearing headlights and Chrysler's weak—probably unnoticed by most passive viewers—copy of the Cord 810's front end stainless trim can be discounted.

The big problem was shortages of certain metals due to the war effort. Many cars, even expensive ones, were re-engineered to use cast-iron pistons. Aluminum was high on the war-demand list. Because of Packard's heavy defense contracting, East Grand Boulevard had aluminum pistons, though the company reported running exhaustive tests of cast-iron pistons with no loss of power.

Beginning in 1940, Packard built military engines—both torpedo-boat motors and greatly revamped Rolls-Royce aero engines—to the extent that, by 1942, 96 percent of the company's resources went toward defense work. Although car production was down 10,000 units from 1940, net earnings were several times 1940's thanks to defense work.

In 1934, George Christopher necessarily remodeled the Packard plant for volume production. This wasn't accomplished overnight, and it wasn't until the 1940 models, which shared so many components, that all Packards were finally built on one production line. The 1941 and 1942 models supported the remainder of this plant remodeling bill, but World War II meant that all of this efficient new assembly line—now the smoothest in the industry—had to be dismantled and stacked outside like cordwood to make room for, among other military concessions, 70 Merlin engine test stands. Nevertheless, 1942 earnings rose to $5 million. Packard was a healthy stock to hold.

While Packard coasted on its still-exalted reputation in 1941, competition from the substantial upper-echelon General Motors offerings trounced Packard and the industry. For 1942, having learned an expensive and soul-jarring lesson, Packard abandoned the traditional bodies for all models but the long-wheelbase livery cars, convertibles, and One-Eighty-only Darrin victorias. The conservative folk who felt they must travel in limousines, often as not festooned with sidemounts, were probably happy riding in stretch-out models that reminded them of the less egalitarian, more status-quo Thirties. Packard wouldn't, and couldn't—with all the defense work—bother tooling the new Clipper for long-wheelbase models. That came in 1946.

There also wasn't time, energy, or foreseeable financial returns to tool the new Clipper for convertible production; the traditional bodies were exiled here as well.

The 1941 and 42 Darrin convertibles were not as markedly different from the East Grand Boulevard production convertibles as the stunning 1940 Darrins had been. In the interest of lowering the radiator, the heavy-frame cross member under the radiator was removed in the 1940 Darrins. A thin strip of steel was substituted. This left the front fender braces without sufficient support, and so the Darrin's front fenders wiggled at speed (to the consternation of the buyer who'd just shelled out $3800 for a 120 Darrin or $4570 for a 180 Darrin).

Packard recalled all the 1940 Darrins through the selling dealers in order to install a reinforcing kit at factory expense. The 1941-42 Darrins used production radiators and hoods. Packard did not want anymore headaches, and especially not on cars generally sold to wealthy, visible, and vocal drivers. The Darrin victoria side notch was now merely formed into just the door. In 1940, this meant reworking both the door and body panels. Although the 1941-42 Darrins were no longer the pure, graceful, almost delicate design of the landmark 1940 models, they were still gorgeous automobiles. Rather than settle for a production convertible or even a Darrin factory-custom victoria, in 1942 Errol Flynn commissioned Dutch Darrin

A 1942 180 formal limousine. Photo courtesy William H. Friedrich.

to build a Clipper convertible. The resulting car was so beautiful that it's unfortunate that Packard didn't build any Clipper convertibles (though Derham offered a stretch out Clipper convertible sedan). There were to be no more convertibles until the 1948 bathtubs.

Because it would be hard to do any real harm to a 1948-50 Packard—short of disguising it as a giant melting blob of ice cream and placing it in the Museum of Modern Art—it's a wonder we don't have bogus Clipper convertibles. The 1948-50 pregnant elephant front clip can be removed and a Clipper nose can be substituted. There is a bit more work than that, but if you are to go through all the bother of rejuvenating an old automobile anyway . . . .Probably the reason we don't hear about such an undertaking is because of the "is it original?" mentality. Packard certainly didn't care if it was "original." The company just wanted to sell automobiles.

Many 1939 Packards were updated to 1940 models by the simple expediency of changing the front clip. Since the Twenties, Packard made newer bumpers, grilles, and fenders available to owners wanting to update their cars.

Prices for the traditionally bodied livery cars and convertible ran about the same as 1941. All other Packards for 1942 were based on the smooth, flowing Clipper. The 1942 model was a no-frills unit. Production of only "necessary" cars was made for buyers anticipating a long dry spell. Gone, too, were all convertible sedans, station wagons, and coupes. There was a three-passenger Clipper fastback available on both the six and eight (282-cubic-inch, 120-unit) chassis. The sixes and eights came on the previous year's 110 (122-inch) and 120 (127-inch) frames. All Super-8 160 and 180 Clippers came on the same 127-inch chassis as 1941's original Clipper. And all Clippers, whether six, eight, or Super-8, came only in two-door and four-door sedans. Anything longer than a 127-inch wheelbase was a traditional body.

Clipper four-door sedan prices ranged from $1250 for a six, $1305 for an eight, $1814 for the Super-8 160, and $2346 for the Custom Super-8 180. The 1942 Twentieth series model run totaled 33,776 cars. While calendar 1941 saw 66,906 Packards leave Detroit, only 6085 cars were built during 1942. Automobile production ceased on February 9 of that year.

156 PACKARD

A 1942 Packard-Henney. Photo by Susan Scott.

A 1942 Packard-Henney on a 160-inch wheelbase commercial chassis. Photo by Susan Scott.

Ask the Man Who Owns One

19

A Seller's Market

Packard claimed only a 1.2 percent profit on its 1941-45 business. The factory that had been only recently revamped for streamlined production of all models on a common assembly line was full of useless war tooling. The proving grounds had been leased to Chrysler for its tank testing, and the test track had to be rebuilt. Although 1945 earnings had been only 1.1 million dollars, Packard had no outstanding debt, a net worth of $109 million ($33 million of it in cash), and nearly 1800 dealers.

The sleek Clipper was now five years old, even though it had only a 10-month production run before the war, and its expensive tooling had not yet been amortized. In any event, Packard had given all its body business to Briggs. The 1941 traditional cars were the last to have Packard-built bodies. But after four years of nursing old cars, a car-hungry America made it a seller's market.

Beginning in October, 1945, Packard managed to produce cars again; all of them were Clipper Eight four-door sedans. Clipper Six production didn't begin until April of 1946 (with Super Clippers in May and Custom Super Clippers in June). Although lower-priced cars saved the company before the war, many think Packard might have survived longer had it again concentrated only on the carriage trade after the war. But Packard was now geared for volume production of lower-priced cars, even though the war's end would have been a fine time for a fresh total-luxury approach. The dramatic sales increases made possible by lower-priced cars were still fresh in management's mind, and Packard forged ahead never again to concentrate on strictly high-priced automobiles.

The Twenty-First series included the model years 1946 and 1947. Initially, the Clipper was available in only two body styles (two-and four-door sedan) and two wheelbases (120 and 127 inches), as it had before the war. Because Packard, like all other automakers, could now sell every car it could build, this wasn't a major problem. The company did quickly expand its lines. Taxi versions of the Clipper Six were offered, and 148-inch wheelbase models were again offered by contracting the Henney Motor Company. Henney had been building special bodies for Packard since 1935 by taking Clipper bodies from Briggs and reworking and trimming them as seven-passenger sedans and limousines. The 1946 Clipper Six prices ran $1461 to $1838 and the 1947 prices were from $1679 to $2465. As were the other Packard models, the Clipper Six was virtually the same car it had been in 1942. The 1946 Clipper Eight prices ranged from $1570 to $1869 and 1947 prices were from $1816 to $2149.

The 1946 Super Clippers cost from $1956 to $2290, and in 1947 from $2241 to $2772. The 1946 Custom Super Clippers listed from $2544 to $4496 and in 1947 from $2913 to $4668. The long wheelbase cars were offered only as Custom Super Clippers (which accounts for the latter high figures).

The 1946-1947 Twenty-First series totalled 80,660 cars: 2722 in 1945, 42,102 in 1946, and 35,836 in 1947. Of the total, three-fourths was evenly divided between Clipper Sixes and Eights; the remainder were Supers and Custom Supers.

In 1940, Briggs Body Company convinced Chairman Macauley that it could build bodies for less than Packard. Once Packard turned over its body business to them, Briggs began raising prices until the bodies became more expensive than if Packard had built them. In addition, steel was in fierce demand, as shortages plagued the industry, and Packard was particularly hurt. And, too, workers who would never have struck during the war effort were now doing so at suppliers throughout the country; organized labor was continuing inroads begun before the war.

It was little solace to Packard that its 1946 production had been 63 percent of

A 1946 Clipper Six touring sedan. Photo John A. Conde Collection.

its 1941 volume while the industry average was only 58 percent. Operating losses of $3.9 million in 1946 and $1.5 million in 1947 were turned into a mere $1.1 million profit in 1947, based on 1946 tax charge-offs.

In retrospect, many decry the abandonment of the traditional prewar bodies, not realizing or remembering how their sales appeal had been dwarfed by the Clipper. Also, the traditional body dies were not given to Russia during the war, but melted and used against the Axis. The Russian ZIS was a direct copy of the traditional-bodied Packards; it was not a duplicate. In any event, Packards were immensely popular with the Russians. Joseph Stalin's toy was his 1938 Super Eight convertible sedan.

The first of the 1948 Twenty-Second series was the convertible—Packards first postwar open car—introduced in the summer of 1947. Rather than keep the Clipper, let alone further refine it, Packard management felt pressured by the flurry of new postwar design activity throughout the industry. The result was a bloated creation that mirrored the slab bodies seen on most other cars. If Packard had forsaken the strictly luxury market, it had now lost its almost intangible grace as well.

The substantial look reflected a victorious nation's conspicuous consumption, and Packard rode with it. It was still a seller's market, and 95,495 of the new corpulent Packards found homes during the 1948 model run. Production picked up even if not to the 200,000-cars-a-year level President George Christopher had promised dealers. Despite (or perhaps because of) their appearance, the new Packards were

A 1946 Custom Super Clipper limousine. Photo by Susan Scott.

The Clipper version of the hallmark Packard grille. Photo by Susan Scott.

The front compartment of the 1946 Custom Super Clipper limousine. Photo by Susan Scott.

as solidly built as any in industry history.

Beneath the bulbous panels were new engines. The Six was consigned to export sedans and taxis. The lowest-priced line of Packards was now, and through the company's end, to be powered by eight cylinders. The new Eight and Eight DeLuxe rode on the 120-inch chassis, and were powered by a new 288 cubic-inch (3 1/2 × 3 3/4 bore × stroke; 130 hp at 3600 rpm, 226 ft. lbs. of torque at 2000 rpm) L-head that proved to be rugged and dependable. One of Packard's more underrated engines, it was used on the company's base line of cars through 1954. The venerable 282 cubic-inch engine was dropped. Prices ranged rom $2250 for the four-door club sedan to $2275 for the four-door sedan, and $3425 for the station sedan (wood trim and some special tooling reflected in this price) on the Eight model. A club sedan sold for $2517 and $2543 for a four-door sedan in DeLuxe Eight guise.

The next rung up was the Super Eight on the same chassis. It was powered by another new L-head displacing 327 cubic inches (3 1/2 × 4 1/4 bore × stroke, 145 hp at 3600 rpm). Prices were $2802 for the club sedan, $2827 for the four-door sedan, and $3250 for the convertible victoria. On a new, longer 141-inch wheelbase, Super Eights ran $3500 and $3650 for seven-passenger sedans and limousines, and $3850 and $4000 for DeLuxe versions.

Packard's top line was still powered by the 356 cubic-inch, nine-main-bearing engine—the biggest and most powerful in the industry. On the 127-inch wheelbase, the Custom Eight club sedan cost $3700, the four-door sedan sold for another $50, and the convertible victoria cost $4295. The 148-inch wheelbased Custom Eights sold at $4704 for a seven-passenger sedan and $4868 for a seven-passenger limousine. Packard was again offering commercial bodies. Henney waited until the new, bloated 1948 models to retool for ambulances and hearses; these were offered on a 156-inch Custom Eight wheelbase.

Although the Super and Custom Eight convertibles and Custom Eight commercial chassis were introduced early, the Clippers lacked these models, the rest of the company's cars were introduced two months later in September, 1947. Packard's new postwar production lines (controlled by Teletype) were running more smoothly, as shown by a 1948 calendar year run of 98,897 and a profit of $15 million.

Alvan Macauley retired as board chairman in April of 1948, and it was perhaps telling that that position would remain vacant until Packard's demise. George Christopher had complete control of the company, and—although one of the finest production men in the industry—some of his bad moves ranked with Macauley's subcontracting the company's body business. Christopher's predictions of 200,000 cars a year had led many dealers to expand. They were left high and dry when the factory turned out half that amount. While dealers still had six-month inventories of 1947 Clippers, Christopher advertised the new "bathtub." From 1947 to 1949, Packard lost 500 dealers.

The company's guiding lights were retiring. Men like Macauley and Henry Bodman, the board member and legal counsel who had urged Clipper production and who had rewritten the Merlin contract, could not be replaced because Packard had failed to groom new executives.

With the company still able to sell all the cars it could build and with plenty of cash on hand, not enough attention was paid to Packard's direction. The company was so complacent during a continuing seller's market that the 1949 models announced in November of 1948 were really the Twenty-Second series continued without change.

The first of the Twenty-Third series introduced in May of 1949 were also licensed

The rear compartment of a 1946 Custom Super Clipper limousine. Photo by Susan Scott.

A 1947 Custom Super Clipper. Photo by Susan Scott.

Custom Super Clippers: 1947 sedan (left) and 1946 limousine. Photo by Susan Scott.

In front are a pair of Custom Eight convertibles. At left rear is a 1947 Custom Super Clipper. Photo by Susan Scott.

as 1949 models. Cars and prices were little changed even though the Super Eight now shared the Custom's 127-inch wheelbase and sheet metal. The only long-wheelbase cars were the pair of seven-passenger Super Eights continued from the Twenty-Second series and the final offering of the six-cylinder engine as the 141-inch wheelbase New York taxi (the 120-inch sedan taxi and export sedan were dropped). Only two models of Custom Eights appeared, and both were on the 127-inch chassis: the four-door sedan at $3975, and the convertible at $4520.

The only real reason to bother with a new series at all was to herald Packard's fiftieth year in the automobile business. The Twenty-Third's noteworthy feature was Ultramatic (standard on the Customs and quickly made an option on Eights and Super Eights). Like Buick's Dynaflow, Packard's automatic transmission used a torque converter (not a simple fluid coupling, as did Hydramatic). There the resemblance ended.

Increased torque multiplication in the torque converter gave Ultramatic better acceleration than Dynaflow, and Packard's pioneer direct-drive clutch allowed the efficiency and engine compression braking of a conventional manual transmission once under way. In search of fuel economy, nonslip automatic transmissions are now common throughout the industry both here and abroad. Few realize that Packard was first.

Ultramatic was the smoothest and most refined automatic on the market. It garnered high ratings from *Consumer Reports* and all the day's automotive magazines. Nevertheless it lacked the performance possible with the four-speed geared

A 1949 Custom Eight, seven-passenger, four-door sedan. Photo John A. Conde Collection.

164 PACKARD

A Packard Eight by an Oldsmobile 88 (Chevrolet body, overhead-valve V-8) at a 1950 show. Photo courtesy John J. Weihl.

Hydramatic. Like Dynaflow, Ultramatic was a two-speed unit, though both transmissions had a manually selected low gear behind the torque converter for sandy roads or extreme hills. Ultramatic was the only automatic transmission developed by an independent automaker (most did without or would later buy from GM).

Packard was the only survivor from the first New York Automobile Show in 1900, and the only American automaker able to celebrate a golden anniversary. Studebaker had been in business since 1852 but it did not produce automobiles until 1902.

Beginning in November of 1949, the remainder of the Twenty-Third series were sold and licensed as 1950 models. Calendar 1949 production totaled 104,593 and the 1950 total was 72,138. Over 40,000 were the new 1951 Twenty-Fourth series cars, and 1950's $5.2 million profit was attributed to them.

Ask the Man Who Owns One

20

Against All Odds

For 1951, Packard offered what it called "contour styling." This was a vast improvement over the company's—and the industry's—earlier porcine look. The new shell would have to serve the company well because, with facelifting, it would be the basis for the last Packard-built cars in 1956.

The new Twenty-Fourth series styling was clean, smooth, and uncluttered. The Society of Motion Picture Art Directors gave its highest award to Packard for "embodying the most advanced concepts of automotive styling." Although generally attractive, the new Packard now looked as much a part of the field as many other cars. It also shared an "it crawled from the sea" grille opening with lesser products. Although a smooth and honest design, to some buyers it lacked a certain rich look of the upper echelon GM products. Not surprisingly, Europeans called the 1950 Buick's grille "the dollar grin."

The top of the 1951 line was called the 400, and the lower lines were christened the 200 and the 300. The 200 came on a new 122-inch wheelbase chassis; the 288 cubic-inch eight was standard, and the 327-inch engine was optional. With standard or overdrive transmission, the 288 came with a 7:1 compression ratio, 135 hp at 3600 rpm, and 230 ft. lbs. of torque at 2000 rpm. With Ultramatic, it came with a 7.5:1 compression ratio that gave another 3 horsepower and 5 more foot pounds of torque. Body styles began as low as $2195 for the business coupe (Packard's first since before the war). Two- and four-door sedans in both standard and deluxe trim were available.

Although the 200 line had originally encompassed a convertible and Mayfair hardtop, shortly into the Twenty-Fourth series production run these were upgraded into a separate 250 line using the busier 300/400 grille and 327 cubic-inch engine. The 250 Mayfair sold for $3166, and the 250 convertible cost $3200.

The 300 used the 327 cubic-inch engine as standard and came on a longer, 127-inch wheelbase. The extra length was in the body whereas before the war it was in the hood and front fenders. With standard or overdrive transmission, the 327 came with a 7:1 compression ratio: 150 hp. at 3600 rpm, 270 ft. lbs. of torque at 2000 rpm. With Ultramatic, it came with a 7.8:1 compression ratio (the highest in the industry). This gave 5 extra horsepower and 5 more foot pounds of torque. Packard fine tuned its inline L-heads to stay abreast of the horsepower race ushered in by the 1949 Oldsmobile and Cadillac Kettering overhead-valve V-8s. The 300 came only as a four-door sedan, opening at $2795, but a line of 156-inch wheelbase commercial cars was offered through Henney.

The 400 was the only line given another name, the Patrician, because the lone name of Packard no longer stood for as much car as it once had. The Packard 400 Patrician also came only as a four-door sedan. Ultramatic was standard, and the 155-horsepower 327 had nine-main bearings. The 400 opened at $3385.

During the Twenty-Third series, the 327 cubic-inch Super Eight could be ordered with the Custom Eight's grille and trim for an extra $286. The resulting car was called the Super Deluxe, and it was a thousand dollars less than the 356 cubic-inch-engined Custom Eight. The Custom Eight engine put out 160 horsepower, only 10 more than the Super/Super Deluxe engine, yet weighed an additional 300 pounds. With a boost in compression, the 327 now came within 5 horsepower of Packard's biggest engine, and the 356's additional production cost could no longer be justified. Excepting the 300's line of commercial chassis, all 1951 Packards could be built with only two engines and on two wheelbases.

Smooth new styling and lower prices than ever attracted those still drawn by Packard's reputation for quality, the company's lingering aura of elegance, or both.

A 1950 Super DeLuxe convertible. Photo John A. Conde Collection.

A 1951 convertible. Photo John A. Conde Collection.

The Twenty-Fourth series of 100,713 cars was the biggest single-year model run after the 1937 Fifteenth series high of 122,593 (the 1948-49 Twenty-Second and 1949-50 Twenty-Third series had been extended runs). This was a hollow victory in an industry increasingly geared to production runs in the hundreds of thousands.

George Christopher, the former GM production man responsible for Packard's flowing assembly lines, left the company in December of 1949 shortly after a grim board meeting over decreasing profits. Packard's treasurer, Hugh Ferry, replaced Christopher, and for the next two-and-a-half years Ferry's main priority was to find his own replacement. James Nance, a Hotpoint executive who had made his name in the postwar appliance business, was the choice.

Nance became president of Packard in May of 1952. His chief goal was to return Packard to its former luxury standard by acquiring Studebaker and merging with a combined Hudson and Nash for a major automotive corporation that could not just weather the Big Three but compete with them. The leverage of a big company was the key to successful purchasing. A full-line manufacturer capable of large production runs could support a large dealer network, and afford the more costly television advertising. To succeed in the automobile business it was becoming vital to use Big Three methods.

The 1952 Twenty-Fifth series was little changed other than upholstery trim and optional power brakes (Easamatic). Prices for the 200 began at $2424 for the two-door sedan, the business coupe dropped from the Packard lineup for good in a move to increase the remaining cars' status. The 250 Mayfair hardtop was $3224, and the 250 convertible cost $3476. The 300 four-door sedan could be had for $2795, and the plusher 400 version for $3689. While 62,951 1952 Packards were produced, an oversupply of 1951 models cut into the former's production run.

James Nance's first move to bring the Packard name back to a strictly upper-class standing was to segregate the lower-priced cars with a separate name. The 200 became the Clipper. This was a good choice because it had a ready association with Packard while lending the new medium-priced cars a glow of past success. The Clipper came in two- and four-door sedans beginning at $2544. The 288 now had a 7.7:1 compression ratio and horsepower was up to 150 at 4,000 rpm, with torque to 260; ft. lbs. at 2,200 rpm. The same car was also offered with the 327 cubic-inch engine as standard and called the Clipper Deluxe ($2691 for the two-door sedan, $2745 for the four-door). The 327 now had an 8.0:1 compression ratio giving 160 horsepower at 3600 rpm, and 295 ft. lbs. of torque at 2000 rpm.

The 250 designation was dropped, and the Mayfair hardtop and convertible were incorporated into the 300 or, as it was known now, the Cavalier line. Although the Mayfair and convertible kept their 122-inch wheelbase, they would be known as Packards—for the glamour that would bring—and not Clippers. Like all the 127-inch wheelbase Packard Cavalier line, they came with a four-barrel carburetor,

The 1951 200 was the last entirely new body shell offered by Packard.

The "it crawled from the sea" radiator opening introduced on 1951 models and shared with less illustrious makes.

The 1952 Packard Pan-American experimental sports car model. Photo John A. Conde Collection.

boosting the 327's horsepower to 180 at 4000 rpm and its torque to 300 ft. lbs. at 2000 rpm. Prices for the entire Cavalier line ranged much as they had for 1952 models. There was a new limited-production (750 built) convertible called the Caribbean. It was inspired by the 1952 Packard Pan American show car. Similarly, GM showcars led to the Oldsmobile Fiesta, and Cadillac Eldorado convertibles. For $5210, the Caribbean buyer got an otherwise factory convertible with a reworked hood, cutout wheel openings, wire wheels, a continental kit and the like. It was as close as Packard would come to offering a 1950s Darrin.

The Packard Patrician four-door sedan came with Ultramatic and many other features standard. With the 180-horsepower engine, it was the same basic car as the Cavalier. Packard's flagship sedan cost $3740.

In another attempt to either recapture old or garner new prestige, Nance commissioned Derham Body Company to build a handful of formal sedan versions of the Patrician (padded leather top, smaller rear window, etc.) for $6531. To further reinstate Packard's position in the luxury market, Nance had Henney build 100 "Executive sedans" and 50 limousines on a 149-inch wheelbase chassis for $6900 and $7100.

The 1953 Twenty-Sixth series proved Packard's last successful year with a model run of 90,277 (below Nance's 135,00 projection) and earnings of $5.4 million.

In a nod to both the past and logic, the 1954 models were called the Fifty-Fourth series. In December of 1953 Chrysler bought Briggs. This finally exploded a time bomb planted when Packard gave that company its body business in 1940. Although the remaining 1954 bodies were built in the Briggs plant under an agreement with Chrysler, the sudden loss of body-building facilities proved an enormous setback for Packard's new 1955 models, and the company itself.

Although inline engines had once been the dominant type in the industry, by 1954 only Packard and Pontiac were still powering their cars with straight eights. Packard's inline L-head eights were the most refined and powerful in the industry's

A 1953 Packard Panther Daytona, with Ed Macauley and Bill Graves. Photo John A. Conde Collection.

AGAINST ALL ODDS 171

A 1954 Packard Caribbean and the Sante Fe Super Chief. Photo John A. Conde Collection

history, but this was of little consequence when overhead valve V-8s were among the keys to sales success.

Ford and GM entered a frenetic sales race. They swamped dealers with cars that were necessarily offered at great discounts, and again proved the impotence of independent manufacturers.

George Mason of Nash-Kelvinator had already accomplished the first half of creating a fourth big automaker by combining his company with Hudson. Mason had urged Nance, in 1952, to accept the presidency of Packard in order to unite that company with Studebaker. Mason promised Nance the presidency of the completed four-line amalgamation, which was to be bigger than Chrysler. But by 1954, the six remaining independents—or the "Little Three" of Studebaker-Packard, Kaiser-Willys, and AMC (Nash-Hudson) had dropped from a combined market share of 10 to only 5 percent. Actually, there was only a "Big Two" as Chrysler's market share fell from 21 to 11 percent.

The combination of Studebaker-Packard was not a merger. Packard bought the South Bend, Indiana company in exchange solely for shares of Packard voting stock and the assumption by Packard of Studebaker liabilities. On October 1, 1954, Packard became the Studebaker-Packard Corporation, with Nance as president. If Packard had studied more carefully before buying, it would have found Studebaker's break-even point to be 282,000 cars (instead of the 165,00 given in the agreement papers). So saddled with a sick purchase, Packard continued to market its Fifty-Fourth series against all odds.

The price leader of the 1954 line was the Clipper Special. It came in a two-door sedan for $2544, and a four-door for $2594. These were the only models to use the 288 engine.

The Clipper Deluxe two- and four-door sedans, and a fancier version—the Clipper Super, including the new Panama hardtop—used the two-barrel carburetor version of the 327 engine (now up to 165 horsepower). The Panama sold for $3125, and the rest of the Deluxe/Super models ranged from $3590 to $3765.

Divorced from the lower-line cars, the Packard line opened with the Cavalier four-door sedan at $3344. This model used the four-barrel 327 (now up to 185 horsepower).

The rest of the 1954 Packard models used a bored and stroked version of the 327—the 359 (3 9/16 × 4 1/2). With an aluminum cylinder head and the highest compression ratio in the industry, 8.7:1, the four-barrel 359 put out 212 horsepower at 4000 rpm, and 330 ft. lbs. of torque at 2200 rpm. This was the most power Packard ever coaxed out of an L-head straight eight without supercharging. It was the last word in such engines.

There were three Packards on the 122-inch wheelbase: the Pacific hardtop (which replaced the Mayfair) at $3827, the convertible at $3935, and the Caribbean convertible at $6100. The Patrician, like the Cavalier, came on the 127-inch wheelbase, and was the plush flagship sedan it had always been. The final year of ambulances and hearses was 1954 when longtime builder Henney dropped Packard. The Packard straight eights lost favor as Cadillac took over the commercial car field for the exposure and resulting prestige this would bring its passenger cars. Because Henney also built the limousine and eight-passenger sedan, 1954 would also be the last year for those models.

Another setback came when a former GM executive, Charles Wilson, as President Eisenhower's Secretary of Defense, favored old GM compatriots with the dwindling defense work after the Korean War—but not Studebaker-Packard. Packard did build a trickle of PT boat engines after World War II, and the company had built marine diesels for the Navy since the early Fifties. In 1951, Packard contracted to build the J-47 turbojet engine developed by General Electric (for the F-86, XF-91, B-36, XB-51, B-45, and B-47), buying 55 acres next to the Proving Grounds in Utica for a factory. Studebaker had been assembling J-47 engines and building military trucks.

Another blow came in 1954 when George Mason died and his successor, George Romney, decided not to merge with Studebaker-Packard. Ironically, Romney turned down an offer from Alvan Macauley in 1948 to join Packard as an executive vice-president and board member. Macauley had been president of the Automobile Manufacturers Association and had worked with Romney during the war. George Mason replaced Macauley as president of the AMA and, hearing that his employee had been offered a job at Packard, quickly offered him one at Nash-Kelvinator—which Romney took. Romney went on not only to say no to the merger, but to market the compact Rambler just as Americans were becoming fed up with boulevard dreadnaughts. Romney also became governor of Michigan.

The 1954 Fifty-Fourth series numbered only 31,291 cars. Packard's 1955 Fifty-Fifth series was a significantly remade car, but there had been too many setbacks and it was too late in the game. After losing its body-building facilities when Chrysler bought Briggs, Packard had to tool for its own shells for the first time since the 1941 traditional-bodied models. Nance leased a former Briggs plant on Detroit's Conner Avenue to build Packard's bodies and as the site for the company's assembly lines. The modern one-level Conner plant was seen as potentially more efficient than the old multistory factory at East Grand Avenue. Nevertheless, it had only a quarter of the original Packard factory's 3,000,000 square feet. The cost of moving the entire assembly line to Conner Avenue, with the resulting production snags and diminished quality, would prove equal to any of Packard's other setbacks.

21

Conner Avenue

Ask the Man Who Owns One

From September to October, 1954, Packard moved its assembly line to the new Conner plant; there it built its first 1955 Packard on November 1. John Reinhart, Packard's chief stylist from 1947 through 1951—and among those who wanted to keep and refine the Darrin Clipper—was responsible for the 1951 contour styling. Richard Teague replaced Reinhart, and facelifted his efforts to the extent that many thought the 1955-56 Packard had a wholly new shell. After Packard's fall, Teague spent a year and a half as a styling consultant to Chrysler before joining American Motors.

The 1955 price leader was the Clipper Deluxe four-door sedan at $2586. The Clipper Super four-door followed at $2686, and the Panama hardtop sold for $2776. All models came on the 122-inch wheelbase, and were powered by Packard's new 327 cubic-inch V-8 (3 13/16 × 3 1/2 bore × stroke, 225 horsepower at 4600 rpm, 325 ft. lbs. of torque at 2400 rpm, 8.5:1 compression ratio, four-barrel carburetor).

The Clipper Customs were otherwise the same cars as above, although with Packard's full-length torsion bar (Torsion-Level) suspension optional and the new 352 cubic-inch V-8 standard (4 × 3 1/2 bore × stroke, 8.5:1 compression ratio, 245 horsepower at 4,600 rpm, 355 ft. lbs. of torque at 2400 rpm). The Custom four-door sedan cost $2926 and the Constellation hardtop sold for $3076.

The Packard models were all on the 127-inch wheelbase and came with Torsion-Level and Twin Ultramatic standard. Horsepower on the Patrician four-door sedan ($3890) and Four Hundred hardtop ($3930) was boosted to 260 and 275 in the Caribbean convertible ($5932) by using Rochester carburetors rather than the Custom's Carter unit.

In 1954, the Ultramatic transmission was modified to give snappier performance off the line as the horsepower race continued. Later it was redesigned for use behind the new V-8s by Packard's chief research engineer Forest McFarland. McFarland was the engineer largely responsible for Ultramatic in its original form in 1949. Assisting McFarland in the development of Twin Ultramatic was John Z. De Lorean, who had joined Packard as a transmission engineer after taking degrees in engineering and business under Chrysler's work-study program. When McFarland left in 1955, De Lorean became Packard's director of research until GM's Semon "Bunkie" Knudsen hired him to shape up Pontiac (which was suffering a reputation as an old man's car). The Twin Ultramatic proved more sensitive to hot rodding, owner negligence, and unfamiliar mechanics than most units, and it was never attuned to a V-8's torque curve.

Packard's last major engineering coup was its Torsion-Level suspension. A full-length torsion bar on either side of the chassis connected front and rear wheels and absorbed impacts fed directly to the frame/body with conventional springs. Torsion-Level's automatic load compensator was a heavy-duty electric motor that kept the car on an even keel by loading, or winding, the torsion bars one way or the other.

Torsion-Level was acclaimed by automotive magazines. It allowed the new Packards to roll sedately over roads that would cause other cars to bottom out or worse. GM brought out a troublesome air suspension a few years later, and Chrysler offered torsion bars in the front of its cars beginning in 1957, but Packard had surprised the industry almost, perhaps, as it had when it unveiled its Clipper in 1941.

The rush and expense to set up anew in the Conner Avenue plant had resulted in just enough bugs in the innovative and otherwise excellent new 1955 Packards to scare away many buyers in 1956. The V-8's original oil pump was improved as its vacuum booster pump, generally placed on the fuel pump, could suck air into the oil causing noisy or damaged hydraulic valve lifters. And the control boxes on the

A 1955 400, two-door hardtop. Photo John A. Conde Collection.

A 1956 Clipper Panama hardtop. Photo John A. Conde Collection.

The 1958 Packard Hawk. Photo John A. Conde Collection.

early Torsion-Level models were vulnerable to corrosion and road debris.

Only 55,247 1955 Packards were sold. That total was the lowest production run since the final "bathtubs" for 1950.

The 1956 Fifty-Sixth series was little changed other than some trim and mild price increases. The Clipper Deluxe sedan was priced to $2731, the Super sedan to $2866, the hardtop (the Panama name was dropped) to $2916, the Custom sedan to $3069 and the Constellation to $3164. The Deluxe and Super now used the 352 cubic-inch engine, which had a 9.5:1 compression ratio and a two-barrel carburetor for 240 horsepower at 4600 rpm and 350 ft. lbs. of torque at 2800. The Custom sedan and Constellation used the same engine but with four-barrel carburetion for 275 horsepower and 380 ft. lbs. of torque.

The 352 was bored one-eighth of an inch to 374 cubic-inches (4 1/8 × 3 1/2 bore × stroke, 10:1 compression ratio, 290 hp. at 4600 rpm with single four-barrel carburetor, 310 hp. with dual four barrels, 405 ft. lbs. of torque at 2800 rpm). The Patrician four-door sedan ($4160) and Four Hundred hardtop ($4190) used the 290 horsepower version. The Caribbean hardtop ($5495, new for 1956) and Caribbean convertible ($5995) used the 310-horsepower version. Twin Ultramatic was further improved to give better service than the previous year's unit and, in keeping with the tone of the Fifties and James Nance's past in the Hotpoint pushbutton kitchen, Packard offered "Touch-Button Ultramatic." Chrysler products also had pushbutton transmissions in 1956, and so too would other makes in the years to come.

Packard's new limited slip Twin-Traction differential produced by Dana Spicer proved less sturdy than hoped for. In Packard's heyday, such a new feature would never have been introduced without long and rigorous testing, but the company needed all the innovations it could muster to compete with the Big Three. Although Nance had worked to divorce the Clipper and Packard lines, in desperation a new model belying this tack was introduced in March of 1956. The Packard Executive was no more than a Clipper Custom with a Packard front end. Traditional lines of credit were drying up, and already Lincoln-Mercury began appealing to Packard dealers to change franchises.

Remember that Packard folded before it was fashionable for government to bail out big business—as Chrysler and Lockheed were saved in America, and Jaguar and Rolls-Royce in England.

There were many scenarios circulated but the reality was a management contract proposed by Curtiss-Wright in May, 1956. This provided more defense work and the Mercedes-Benz distribution rights. Because Studebaker sales nearly quintupled Packard's, future autobuilding was centered in South Bend, Indiana. There was always dim hope of bringing out more big Packards, even as 1957 and 1958 Studebakers were peddled under the Packard name.

As George Romney's earlier decision to bank American Motors' future on the compact Rambler had paid off, so had Studebaker-Packard's compact Lark generated profit in 1959. The "Packardbakers" and the Packard name were dropped in July of 1958. The Curtiss-Wright contract ended three months later. Such was the power of the Packard name, however, that Studebaker-Packard did not become the Studebaker Corporation until April of 1962, when it was decided that the proud name of Packard was anachronistic.

Studebaker limped along until 1966, fielding its compacts against Valiants, Corvairs, and Falcons of the Big Three. There were no 1967 Studebakers; now there was only a new money-making conglomerate, Studebaker Worthington, Inc.

One of the several attempted Packard revivals was a plan to import French Facel Vega Excellence sedans, adorn them with Packard grilles, and power them with leftover 374-cubic-inch Packard V-8s. But Daimler-Benz complained that this new "Packard" would be in direct competition with its Mercedes-Benz 300. The plan was shelved.

One of the names proposed for the Avanti was Pierce-Arrow because Studebaker had controlled that company from 1928 until 1933. The other name suggested was Packard.

In more innocent years, Packard stood for the best.

Ask the Man Who Owns One

22

Gothics

We've heard so many times that Packard was "the American Rolls-Royce," but Rolls-Royce has always been secretive about its power output and performance figures. One reason is that the company feels such information is too mainstream automotive, and that it is entirely too tacky to go on and on about sprockets and levers and torque figures. The company prefers instead to focus attention on the automobile proper.

For the most part, the only people who seem to get a kick out of such figures are "car people" and industry peers. Most of these people already know that Rolls-Royce—while making a wonderfully crafted automobile—does not make and has never made the "best automobile in the world."

In the first decades of our century, most engineers and mechanics on both sides of the pond agreed that a Rolls-Royce was a weak sister to a Lanchester and Simplex. The later "baby Rolls," the small horsepower 20/25, was an admitted copy of the American Buick. But in the words of one English road tester at the time it was, "... not quite so good." The Phantom I, produced through the first Cadillac Sixteens, was no more than a refined 1907 Silver Ghost engine. It was certainly a good thing then, but a little old by 1929. Also, six-cylinders, no matter how refined, were not enough against straight eights from Packard and Isotta-Fraschini—let alone a V-16 from Cadillac.

Other excellent sixes—Chrysler, 1929 L-80 Imperial, and Pierce-Arrow's 1928 Series "80"—had the same disadvantage. The more-cylinders-means-more-car nonsense culminated in ludicrousness like the 156-inch-wheelbase Cadillac V-16 two-passenger (plus rumble seat) roadster. Yet Rolls-Royce revamped the nearly quarter-century-old Silver Ghost engine for its Phantom II, which was produced alongside not just straight-eights and V-8s from every single luxury automobile producer, but V-12s as well from most of them: Cadillac, Lincoln, Hispano-Suiza, Pierce-Arrow and Packard. Most medium-priced American cars now had two more cylinders than the "best car in the world" Phantom II. When Rolls-Royce finally made an effort to stay in the luxury running with the V-12 Phantom III in 1936, most knowledgeable and car monied buyers were discovering a new crop of "pocket luxury cars" such as Buick Centuries, LaSalles, Cadillac 60s, and Packard One Twenties. These automobiles were clearly ending the days when mass meant power and long wheelbase and dead weight meant a smooth ride. Smaller fast-revving, more-efficient engines and independent front suspensions together meant nimbler, easier-handling packages that made monkeys out of even the most lead-footed Phantom III, Lincoln KB V-12, or Packard Twelve chauffeurs.

Even as Packard introduced a larger version of the One-Twenty's suspension on the senior cars in 1937, the old 385-inch Super Eight was quietly retired. The 320-inch Eight took its place and name. As Rolls-Royce proudly held up its long overdue V-12 Phantom III to an indifferent market, Cadillac dropped its V-12, and Packard began phasing out its heavy iron. Packard opted to "One-Twenty" its entire line to the extent that in 1939 the last separate crankcase/block Super-8 and One-Twenty were built on the same frame and shared the same sheet metal. Still the One-Twenty outperformed the Super-8.

Against quality car developments like these, regardless of the mid-Thirties economic conditions that had necessitated them, or even that those conditions were now gone, the Rolls-Royce Phantom III V-12 loomed an even larger millstone than respective V-12s at Lincoln and Packard. Lincoln, after making over 10,000 senior V-12s (not Zephyrs) since 1932, sold only a few dozen in 1940 (the final year of heavy iron from Ford Motor Company). Packard, producing about 6000 Twelves since 1932, sold only 446 in 1939. Like the final big Lincolns, the Twelves were leftovers from the previous year. Packard pieced the final Twelves together with little more than alternately painted grille bars and column shift to distinguish them from 1938 models.

Cadillac, backed with all of General Motors' wherewithal, sold only 212 V-16s in 1940. As late as 1938, General Motors decided to play it cautiously by trumping any final multicylinder efforts from the competition with an all-new V-16. Only General Motors could afford such a status write-off. Its final V-16 was actually an excellent engine that was far better than the earlier and, by comparison, anemic overhead-valve V-16. Even as GM pushed its Cadillac 60, 60 Special, LaSalle, and Buicks, it could afford to bring out a final, indomitable Sixteen (with its few hundred sales a year) solely for the panache that would filter down on the rank-and-file pocket luxury cars. Even if the Sixteen was ignored, it could hardly lessen the images carefully groomed for the smaller Cadillacs, LaSalles, and Buicks. Very shrewd marketing was why GM was on top and stayed on top.

This American review is important because, despite empty boasts by a handful of British and European automotive journalists, the Americans had long since bested the foreign makes in engineering excellence. It is hard to remain aloof in your Mercedes Grosser or Phantom III when an American Buick or Packard has just dusted your three-pronged star or "Spirit of Esctasy." Foreign autobuilders had long learned and copied from American development. Now American marketing was trumping them as well, and in the presumed stronghold of the highest-class luxury carriages. The Americans were trumping them with upper-medium-priced cars built on lookalike assembly lines by workers who, if frugal, could just manage on time to buy one of these new Centuries, Ambassador Eights, Commodore Eights, or One-Twenties.

If the 715 total Phantom IIIs had failed to make any impression in the world-class competition for luxury motoring dollars, how were they to endow the lesser Rolls-Royce, the six-cylinder 25/30, and its Bentley clone, the 4 1/4 litre, with market-assaulting class?

Although not as widespread as in the Twenties and early Thirties, wealthy daughters of new American money were still looking for (usually impoverished) British and European aristocracy, thus becoming instant Duchesses and Countesses. For many such Americans, and for a certain amount of extremely conservative old money, the Rolls-Royce mystique would continue to allow for a vital foot in the American door.

"Hmm, the Bryant girl married a duke."

And there was nothing any marketing genius at General Motors, let alone Packard, could do to match that.

As long as Rolls-Royce kept that vital, and highly visible, foot in both the wealthiest, and most prestige-conscious doors, it would never matter that its loftiest effort to date, the Phantom III, was the most troublesome V-12 of all. The Phantom III was easily bested in longevity, maintenance, and performance by Lincoln, Pierce-Arrow, or Packard. It seemed that every year an American playboy—who had made

his fortune designing such things as an hydraulic ram used to compact the load of garbage trucks—was leaving a Rolls-Royce-engined Miss England in the wake of his Packard-propelled Miss America. While the Rolls-Royce Phantom II capped the longest run of any automobile engine (longer even than the Model T Ford), Gar Wood's Packard-powered Miss America yearly took home the British International or Harmsworth Trophy for speedboats. That the Phantom III V-12 was terribly complicated and irksome did not, and would never matter, to those leading prestige families of Newport and Southampton who still looked to England, if not the Continent, for the last word in motoring elegance. Just as their daughters married impoverished dukes and counts.

To this day, "the elegance continues," even though there are signs that the most disinterested bystander realizes that the best car in the world is made by Mercedes-Benz. The clean, flowing Packard Clipper might have predated the Bentley Continental by a dozen years. Even General Motors offerings like the 1948 Cadillac sedanette and Chevrolet Aerosedan inspired the most rakish and sporting of Rolls-Royce Bentleys. No matter. No American offering could ever entirely replace Rolls-Royce among all of the status conscious.

The most exalted of all the 3048 Bentley-built Bentleys (before being bought and reduced to a badge and grille by Rolls-Royce) from 1922 to 1931 was the Eight litre. This automobile was a reflection of W. O. Bentley's open respect for Packard. The biggest and best of all real Bentleys used Packard's newly introduced hypoid rear axle and Bijur chassis lubrication.

Despite the perception by many (who should know better) of Rolls-Royce as a good-hearted, eccentric cottage industry building peerless automobiles, in reality the company was as devious and bottom-line oriented as any—including General Motors. Rolls-Royce quickly and skillfully sold a string of cobbled products that used the Bentley name and imagery to suggest performance that just wasn't there. The new Rolls-Royce Bentleys were slightly better road cars mainly due to higher-speed rear axles, and sometimes—but not always—slight suspension changes and increased carburetion.

The new Rolls-Royce Bentleys were an amalgram of American practice and components. They used Delco ignition, Stromberg carburetors, Packard ride control, front bumper weights to reduce axle tramp, and, just before World War II quelched auto development, Packard's Saf-T-Flex independent front suspension design used in the 1935 One-Twenty. After the war, of course, all Bentleys and Rolls-Royces used this suspension until the 1950s when it was replaced with a less costly General Motors knee action. Not only were Rolls-Royce and Bentley using the 1935 One Twenty's suspension, so was the postwar Daimler and, as a rear suspension, the postwar 2 1/2-litre Lagonda designed by W. O. Bentley.

After the war, Bentley settled into its role as an English One-Twenty or LaSalle. As at Packard before the war, when the Super-8 160/180 had thermostatic radiator shutters and the 120 fixed, Rolls-Royce kept its moveable shutters while the Bentley's were fixed. Also like Packard's 120 and 160/180, Rolls-Royce used the same frame and body for Bentleys and Rolls-Royce. Unlike Packards, the English cars did not share the same grille design.

Taking a clear look at the best cars of both England and America, it is hard to see where today's "classic" hysteria comes from (unless only a car with moveable grille bars and unborn calf hide upholstery can so qualify).

This point, viewing both the pinnacle of American and English motordom, it seems long overdue to once and for all exorcise a word that has become—if it has not always been—meaningless: classic.

The Parthenon—a celebrated Doric-columned temple of Athena built on the acropolis at Athens—is classic. The Rolls-Royce grille is an unabashed "copy." Is it classic? Athena was—perhaps still is—the goddess of wisdom and women's crafts in Greek mythology. Yet the automobile that 1500 years later paid tribute to a tribute was considered a weak sister to a Lanchester or Simplex, and later, even a Buick—among others.

The radiator ornament adorning every Rolls-Royce is a statuette of a mere mortal, a then-young English Lady who, at least recently, was still among the living. Introduced to counter French vulgarity, Rolls-Royce's "Spirit of Ecstasy" was ever after called the Flying Lady, as was Packard's "Winged Goddess of Speed."

Perhaps we could be inventive, like decent automotive engineers, and come up with more thoughtful and apt words than the meaningless cliche, classic. Because Packard grilles are pure Gothic cathedral (somehow fitting on those many ambulances and hearses), it makes perfectly good sense to call Packards Gothic cars. For those students, and even drivers, of superior American automobiles who still genuflect to the pagan Parthenon grille, the reflection of the noble and lofty intent of the great Gothic cathedrals should be more than ample aesthetic replacement.

To this day, members of the motoring press—road testing the latest model from Rolls-Royce—describe it as either a 1938 Packard or 1956 Chrysler with digital display instrumentation. The engineer responsible for Rolls-Royce's first V-8, introduced in 1960, was asked at its debut what he thought of the best car in the world's new powerplant. His reply: "It's bloody near as good as the Chrysler."*

In 1951, Rolls-Royce offered a manual transmission only for all three of its lines: the Silver Wraith, Silver Dawn, and Bentley Mark VI. Yet Buick had the Dynaflow on its Roadmaster since 1948 and as an option on its lower-line Special and Super since 1949. Cadillac had Hydramatic since 1941 (and Oldsmobile since 1940), and Packard introduced its Ultramatic on its 1949 models (the 23rd series, standard on the Custom and optional on the Eight, Eight Deluxe, and Super).

At 120-inches, the Silver Dawn/Bentley Mark VI wheelbase is the same as lower-line Packards from 1942-1950. At 127-inches, the Silver Wraith's wheelbase is the same as the prewar Packard One-Twenty, Super-8 160/180 and postwar Super and Custom Clippers. Yet even with aluminum bodies, the Rolls-Royce products are far heavier than the respectively wheelbased Packards (and with no more or fewer horsepower). Not only did the Rolls-Royce products not offer an automatic transmission, they didn't even offer an overdrive. For economy and high-speed cruising, the Rolls-Royce 3.73 axle ratio used in all its 1951 offerings was not as advantageous as the overdrive Packard's effective 2.95 and even 2.8 ratios.

In 1952, Rolls-Royce finally offered what seems a prerequisite of a modern postwar luxury car: an automatic transmission. This was the General Motors Hydramatic, offering neither the turbine smoothness or the economy and road performance of Packard's direct-drive, lock-up Ultramatic that offered as much compression braking as a straight manual transmission.

Perhaps then, it is Packard, more than any other automobile (Rolls-Royce included), that rightfully deserves the appelation, "the best car in the world." Qualities so often a knee-jerk reaction to Rolls-Royce, panache and elegance, (those "wraithlike" attributes) can be better served by superior engineering as well as patiently fitted veneer. Packard bested Rolls-Royce on engineering and performance. Beyond this, Packard's greatest coup was offering packages of superior engineering and an almost "classless" panache and elegance affordable by nearly any of the workers in its factory.

The whole idea of unaffordable automotive excellence—or unaffordable quality clothing, housing, or nutrition—by the workers whose labors produce them is abhorent to the American character. Equally, the finest and noblest art and music have survived the centuries because they could be appreciated by anyone with the spirit to enjoy sincerity and quality of thought and deed. While the Parthenon owed much to slave labor, the great Gothic cathedrals of Europe were both built and frequented by the free men who erected them. Of course, Packard's entry into the middle and even lower-middle-price tiers was hardly a grandiose gesture of magnanimity. Like Rolls-Royce's 20/25hp cars and lower-line Bentleys, it was an act of survival.

Ironically, Henry Ford—the man whose boundless egalitarian spirit and hatred of class oppression led to the first wide-spread "everyman's car" (half of all automobiles on American roads in 1920 were Model Ts)—became in later years a flagrant bigot and tyrant who would not hire blacks or Jews.

Packard began as a high-quality automobile and kept both quality and price as high as possible for a production automobile. Realizing, as did Rolls-Royce and many other formerly exclusive products, that such continued tack meant corporate demise, Packard built popularly priced cars with as much of the previous care and attention as possible. That Packard did this with content workers who might themselves purchase many of their products showed, thorough quality and durability, the truest class.

Surely there is no better measure of the best car than the amount of engineering goodness and honesty of construction at an affordable price. Packard owners can take heart that they are driving automobiles beyond the constraints of class.

---

*Thanks to New Zealand automotive historian extraordinaire Maurice D. Hendry for this pearl.

Packard

Ask the Man Who Owns One

23

Original Aura

Some things are better left unknown. With such a saying before me, I blithely go off in search of my 1940 Packard's first owner.

I hate the expression "original owner." Why does everything have to be "original?" Original miles. What other kind are there? Authentic's not a bad word. Remember genuine? Lionel trains and Daisy air rifles were always "genuine."

"You mean, you've owned this creation eight years and just decided to investigate?" Oh, I tried. How I tried those first months. Detailed letters to harried DMV clerks who could care less. Deadend phone calls.

I know where the parts came from. I dug, or arranged the digging up, of nearly all of them. Ugh! A horrifying tale in itself.

"He needed bodies, and he wasn't too particular where they came from . . .." Like a windshield dividing strip off a '41 ambulance. The things that windshield dividing strip's seen. Lopatcong Township Ambulance. Cream. In a Jersey junkyard just a few miles east of the Delaware River/Pennsylvania border.

I can hear someone saying, "So that's what happened to the old beast." Or worse, "I wondered what happened to that windshield divider strip."

Hey, wait a minute . . . I had to replace my "original" windshield divider strip because it was too badly pitted to bother replating. Then why was the ambulance's in perfect shape? Here it sat with saplings (actually pubescent trees) growing all around it. Well, it's stainless steel.

Why, I'm surprised no keeneyed judge has spotted the infraction. Nay, the bastardization: "1940 used chrome-plated steel, not stainless. Half-a-point . . ."

I know where the right rear fender came from. North Carolina. Did I see the car it came from? Well, no. How do I know it's "original?" How do I know someone didn't just let it age slightly in their tool shed for 35 years? Because a fellow Packardite told me over the phone that it came off a sedan in Sanford, North Carolina. How do we know the car was from Sanford? I was in Pennsylvania when I bought it. Someone could've planted the fender down in the tarheel state to fool me.

"Ha, ha. You bought an unoriginal fender. The donor was sold new in Norfolk, Virginia and got clipped on an icy road in 1946. And the fender was replaced with one from the Packard Dealer's *parts department*." Not original/factory-installed, maybe. Maybe a field-replacement rear fender adorns my rolling paean to the best and the brightest of 1940. How do I know? How does the fellow who sold it to me know? Wasn't his car. He didn't buy it new.

Didn't see the car in Texas one of the splash panels came from, either. Looked original. Had light surface rust. No pitting. Could've sat on a parts shelf for 35 years. Know how I know it hadn't? Because it had a score mark where someone—some living creature, probably an original inhabitant of Earth—tightened the nut against the washer. How do I know someone didn't reproduce it? And put a score mark on it, and left it in his, her, its backyard for a month?

How, indeed?! How *do* you know?

Because the car was virtually intact when I bought it, we should concentrate on the car proper. I don't think it was faked. It looked like an "original" 1940 Packard One-Twenty, four-door sedan someone left in a suburban garage for many moons. All right. How could I tell?

Because it had That Smell.

That distinctive, "I've been forsaken in this garage for many, many years" smell. There is no mistaking it. I don't think you can fake That Smell. I don't think any chemist at Reichhold Chemicals or Diamond Shamrock has synthesized That Smell. Yet. I know Pep Boys had Nu-Car Smell, because as kids we used to marvel that anyone would buy such a thing.

As kids. How do you know I'm not an original adult? I could be a highly evolved kid writing this. It is conceivable that a kid could grasp all this.

Lord help him.

Also, there was that Patina of Neglect. Dow and Du Pont are racing to create an instant spray-on Patina of Neglect, but they will have to pay me for the copyright to use that name: Patina of Neglect. Remember it.

Can you imagine what will happen when Patina of Neglect hurdles 47 government agencies and hits the market? Folks will spray it on *everything*. Late-model lawn furniture. "Classic" Cougars and Montegos. Pets. Dozing in-laws.

No, I'm not going to lampoon "Classic." That's the most embarrassing word ever. The Parthenon, okay. Everything else, no. No more instant Classic. No more mental autopilot. You know how junior high girls say "Ooo, gross . . . ?" Well, there's that voice you're always hearing whenever cars barely out of the *Blue Book* are discussed. It wafts through conversations like a chirping sparrow. "Classic."

Vintage. How can it be a "Vintage" car show? Or a collection of "Vintage" cars? They're not *all* of "recognized and enduring interest, importance, and quality." Can't *all* be the "best and most characteristic."

So, it had That Smell. And Patina of Neglect.

It also had Disarray. Cylinder heads are not found lying on the floor of the backseat. Pistons might be in the trunk, but not just three of them.

Original Disarray. Fake Disarray is easy to spot: the cylinder head is laying on the garage floor, along one of the walls, a light coating of dust has been patiently applied; maybe even a cobweb has been arranged.

Esoteric Items. Won't get involved with 'em. Every car has them: the last inspection sticker; faded tickets, receipts, and violations are on the floor, left in the glove compartment, clipped to the sunvisors, or resting on the rear seat window ledge. Withered scraps of scribbling in the trunk. Dead Sea Scroll confetti. Pistons become Esoteric Items when they're in the trunk and there are only three of them.

Unless it is a Saab. Then the pistons would become Esoteric Items if there were eight of them. In the trunk.

AmbiEnce is handled by That Smell and Patina of Neglect. AmbiAnce is taken care of by Disarray and Esoteric Items. Together they round out Aura. This is the glow, the Big Picture when you first swing open the garage door. If there is one.

Damage; nicks, scratches, dings, dents. Damage is joint property of Disarray and Patina of Neglect. So Damage does not rate a kingdom of its own.

This is why there are so many Classic Cougars and Montegos. They have not survived so long. They might more easily have Original Undamaged Bodies.

We can include Esoteric Items under Disarray, for without Disarray there would be no Esoteric Items. Some would reverse these. But items—be they Classic, Vintage, or Esoteric—are but items. Disarray is a force.

So, no Classic, Vintage, or Esoteric without Disarray. What's a 1940 Packard doing in a suburban garage nearly four decades later? Isn't that the height of Disarray?!

Now that you've established Originality with your old friends That Smell, Patina of Neglect, Aura, and Disarray, you're ready. For what?

Why, to find out if your wheeled time traveler is a bastard. Or famous . . . Possessor of Super-Aura. By following up the vaguest of leads. By writing DMV. And making more deadend phone calls.

---

*This chapter originally appeared in *Packard Cormorant,* quarterly magazine of the Packard Club.

Ask the Man Who Owns One

24

Rebuilding Tips

Although there are a number of excellent books on the subject, I will contribute a few words on "restoration." Most of my tips are little more than applied common sense. First, and sadly, the very word "restoration" means dear little these days. New seat covers and an overhauled motor do not a restoration make.

Too many of the glistening high-point cars seen at shows and auctions are actually mechanically unsound and offer little true driving pleasure. When it comes to Packards, this can be especially treacherous. Nearly any big L-head straight eight will idle smoothly with anything short of a thrown rod. Also, most heavy, long wheelbased automobiles will seem to ride smoothly enough.

Many people who have been in the hobby and who have even owned Packards and the like for years have never ridden in a truly sound car. To drive a Packard that has been methodically and systematically rebuilt is a treat unknown to all but a few in the hobby.

Nearly any Packard capable of motion will idle and ride better than a Model A Ford or other such popular machines. The difference between a carefully rebuilt Packard and the tired Packard with new rings, kingpins, and thousands of dollars of new paint is as dramatic as the contrast in performance between the Model A and the "paint overhauled" Packard.

If you are lucky enough to find a straight, rust-free, and sound low-mileage Packard that has been sitting for a while, you might get by with but a little work—relatively speaking. Standard procedure calls for dropping and boiling the gas tank, blowing out the gaslines with compressed air, and overhauling the fuel pump and carburetor.

Failure to do this with either a full rebuilding job or a low-mileage "original" will lead to trouble. Gasoline gums and leaves varnish. In a car to be stored or driven only occasionally, low-octane aviation gasoline will sit indefinitely without going bad.

When rebuilding the brake system, don't forget to switch to silicone brake fluid; it has been commercially available for many years. The military has used it for some time in vehicles at arctic stations. Silicone brake fluid does not draw moisture into the brake system. Moisture leads to rust, and rust leads to the pitting of wheel cylinders. Barring replacement of brake lining, rust is the main reason brakes need rebuilding. You can use silicone brake fluid in any brake system, but the system should be dismantled and carefully cleaned with alcohol first.

Because silicone brake fluid does not deteriorate or harm painted surfaces, many rebuilders use it in power window lifts and power top cylinders, too.

The older cellular type radiator worked fine, and theoretically, does as well or better than the modern tubed type of radiator. After many years, however, some of the cells might have been clogged or purposely pinched off (leading to a cooling system operating under capacity). Later Packards with tube type radiators might suffer undercapacity because many radiator shops "fix" leaks by simply blocking off the offending tube. The owner drives away, and the problem is "solved" until—caught in traffic on a hot day—the car runs hotter than ever. Regardless of which type of radiator your Packard has, it should go only to a reliable radiator shop.

Substituting a custom modern radiator core is fine, but it should be neither under capacity nor too much over capacity. Under-capacity problems are obvious, but vastly over-capacity problems are a little more insidious.

Most prewar automobiles had, by modern standards, marginal cooling systems. Overheating was not uncommon but neither were water bags hung from the front bumper. Overheating is murder on any engine, but it is especially hard on L-heads (with their valve-in-block arrangement). An engine that never reaches operating temperature because of too large a cooling system will never work as efficiently as intended. Also, an engine that doesn't reach operating temperature will create additional condensation that ultimately winds up in the crankcase as carbonic acid, lowering the effectiveness and life of the engine oil.

Engines are designed to turn in their best performance at operating temperature and internal clearances that are so specified. Problems can be avoided if the engine block is free and clear of deposits in the water jacketing, and if the radiator is clean and healthy.

I use distilled water and Prestone—as do Harrah's and Cunningham's collections of cars—that, although displayed, are also likely to be driven in the real world at any time. Cunningham's mechanics also add half a pint of a cooling-system preservative originally developed for marine diesels and sold by diesel engine dealers. Water is still the best coolant, and the car will run cooler with just water.

To prevent rust formation, a good-quality antifreeze, like Prestone, which contains a water pump lubricant, provides excellent peace of mind. Antifreeze, however, will seep where even water does not. In an original car that has been sitting for years or decades, it might be a good idea to install a fresh head gasket before using antifreeze.

Some cars seem to get along fine with just water and a pint of soluble oil, (which inhibits rust). If you are starting out with a fresh engine and all new gaskets, and want protection as well as continued cleanliness, a blend of about 60 percent distilled water and 40 percent Prestone seems to be the solution.

Engine oil is tricky. Climate, engine health, and type of driving are all factors. In an engine that has never been torn down—and which hasn't been regularly run since before the advent of detergent oils—you'd be safest with a nondetergent motor oil. In an engine that has been carefully rebuilt, it seems a waste not to use the best, most modern lubricant possible.

As far as multigrade versus single grade, the discussion continues. Harrah's Collection uses 10W-40 in its cars after a nondetergent break-in of 500 miles. They feel the multiweight oil clings more tenaciously to the cylinder walls and bearing surfaces to prevent start-up scoring. Other experts claim the use of nondetergent break-in oil is an outmoded and even dangerous practice. Harrah's Collection is in Nevada, where it can get quite cold, and the 10W-40 no doubt helps cold, dormant engines spin readily.

After much talk with oil-company engineers and polymer chemists, I'd lean toward a high-quality 20W-50, like the Kendall GT-1 I use, even in cars that could just as readily use straight 30W year round. Many owners and rebuilders who spurn multiweights still remember the first such products that often quickly broke down to the lighter weight of the base oil. Polymer chemistry has made advances in the last three decades. Unfortunately, there still seems to be a contingent who feel "those old engines weren't meant for multiweight . . . detergent . . . antifreeze, etc.''

After the expense and time spent rebuilding old machinery, it only seems sensible to use the best of modern technology to both preserve it and keep it running.

Not enough has been heard, at this writing, on the new synthetic oils, although I have heard nothing against them.

One horror story I should pass on to you follows. Wishing to improve on old technology, an owner rebuilt his 1937 Packard engine—reducing each internal clearance by a thousandth—thinking that his approach allied with modern lubricants would ensure a long life of healthy running. Of course, just the opposite happened as the unfortunate fellow wound up with a very expensive seized engine.

The crucial step in rebuilding your Packard, or any other car, is finding a good machine shop. After the expense and time spent machining and rounding up parts, the relatively minor cost of balancing the engine will pay vast dividends in driving pleasure. Consider that even such a small amount as 1 once only 1 inch from the axis of a rotating part becomes 2 pounds, 10 ounces at 1200 rpm, and 11 pounds, 6 ounces at 2500 rpm. Packard engines, as they left the factory, didn't just idle smoothly. They drove smoothly, and at all speeds up to top end. That is something evidently forgotten by most hobbyists today.

Balancing is important even in cars with overdrive. Overdrive reduces engine rpm at a given road speed, but not driveshaft speed. The driveshaft in my 1940 One-Twenty was balanced in addition to the engine; in overdrive or out there are no irritating vibrations. Decades of use and ham-handed mechanics take their toll on all parts of a car. When rebuilding your Packard, overlook nothing. As surely as Murphy lives, the part you overlook will one day embarrass you.

Perhaps one reason that the "concours d' elegance" has become so popular with neophyte collectors is because it is always much easier to find journeyman painters than professional machinists. After all, there has always been a demand for shiny automobiles, but the changes and developments in automotive technology have not demanded an army of knowledgeable engine men. Packards ran as well as they looked. Rebuild yours accordingly.

Another place corners are cut on both bush-league and 100-point restorations is the suspension. New shocks and kingpins are not panacea. Every bushing, every connection, every bolt must be tight and within specs. Failure to rebuild a Packard to specifications will give you a shiny old car that rides better than a new econobox and that garners trophies, but it won't give you a Packard. For example, the Saf-T-Flex front suspension introduced on the One-Twenty in 1935 and on all Packards in 1937 was the most sophisticated suspension anywhere short of a race car or limited exotic.

Saf-T-Flex was replaced in the Clippers with a less-costly knee action a la General Motors products. Rolls-Royce, Bentley, and Daimler copied Packard's Saf-T-Flex suspension, and riding in a car so equipped you'll see why. Saf-T-Flex is one of the features that makes a prewar Packard a better road car than comparable General Motors and Rolls-Royce products. Decades later, British sports cars such as Austin-Healey 3000s and the like still echo 1935 engineering from Packard.

If you are on a limited budget, do only what you can as thoroughly as you can. Don't race through the entire rejuvenation, cutting corners in a mad rush to get on the road. Care and time on the underpinnings always pays off. Sloth and indifference will show. Entire businesses are devoted to making high-point restorations run like the cars they once were. To lightly go over the engine, transmission, front end, etc., hoping to "get by" is planting a time bomb in your glittering carriage. It is always much easier to do it right the first time than to disassemble highly polished hoods and fenders later.

On a low-mileage, always-garaged car, you can often rewire only the bad wires (generally in the engine compartment or to the taillights). The wires under the dash on such a car often will still look new. If you are rebuilding a car completely, it is well worth it to replace the entire wiring harness. The modern replacements, like those of Harnesses Unlimited, match the factory wires while offering all the benefits of modern materials.

On the subject of wiring, too much has been written about six-volt systems and hard starting. Packards, and other six-volt cars, didn't give owners trouble starting or they wouldn't have left the showroom floor. If you use a good-quality battery with the correct number of plates, the heaviest and shortest battery cables to and from good connections, and have otherwise a sound, rebuilt electric system, your car will start.

Because my 1940 One-Twenty sits for weeks between runs, I use a Group IV battery, of the type that was original equipment in Packard Twelves (rather than the Group II called for). This is only for the benefit of extra capacity in a car that sits for extended periods. With a Group II battery, I had no trouble, while all around were hobbyists spending small fortunes on 12-volt conversions and the like.

A battery disconnect switch is a great idea as an antitheft device as well as a convenience when working on the car. Take care that the switch is rated higher than the number of amps your starter draws.

I have had excellent service from Denman tires, and there are many good brands on the market. Nevertheless, the best tires will not make up for driver error. As today, auto manufacturers were in business to sell cars—not tires. The low inflation pressures given in the owner's manual were to ensure a soft, luxurious ride. Such tire pressures can be dangerous in a Packard on tour with several couples, their accouterments, and at today's sustained high speeds.

For all the lombasting of the 55 mile-an-hour limit, modern traffic still averages much higher speed than was usual in the 1930s and 1940s. A half ton of human cargo in an already heavy car on the Interstate riding on 22 pounds of tire pressure will lead to wasted gas and suspension and tire wear (if nothing else). Bathtub Packards in particular were marginally tired; inflation pressure is crucial. In the interest of safety, fuel economy, handling, and wear and tear, keep inflation pressures up.

As far as authenticity goes, only 1 car in 20 had whitewalls during the 1930s. Although most prewar cars today feature wide whitewalls, these actually were in greatest vogue around 1950; just check the ads.

To have a Packard that rides and drives the way it was intended, there are dozens of things which should be rebuilt. One often overlooked is the accelerator linkage. Half the travel can be lost motion if this linkage hasn't been rebuilt. Adding this with a sloppy column shift and worn clutch linkage can make for a tiring drive.

There is just no way to give "the best that hearts and minds can produce," a "trade restoration," or a used car lot overhaul and detail, and wind up with a Packard. Why is all this important? For one thing sheer economics. If you do something right the first time, you won't have to do it again. Secondly, for all this mind-numbing talk you hear at shows and meets, "Is it original?" and "Is it authentic?" there seems to be very little interest in that most important Packard attribute: performance. People who will worry about the presence or lack of a pinstripe in the upholstery material will never worry about a tired drivetrain. Thirdly, and perhaps most importantly, you've picked this particular year and model of Packard because it says something to you. Living in the frenzied, technocratic twentieth century, perhaps it's reassuring to have a study on wheels—where it's always the Best of 1927, 1936, 1948, or 1956. Your wheeled retreat, this hallowed time machine, is a mockery, a crude illusion, if the engine rattles or the gears clash.

Only a couple of tips remain. On engines with mechanical valve lifters, always increase the clearances given in the shop manual. This is one time when it is smart to deviate from Packard practice. When Packard suggested setting intake valves at .007 and exhaust valves at .010, labor rates were lower than they are today, parts were readily available, and Packard was interested in not just smooth running, but quiet running. But a long, hard pull up a hill and closely set valves could burn in an instant. All for the sake of an inaudible idle—a Packard hallmark. Far safer, and far less costly, is to set the intake valves at .009 and the exhaust at .012. A trace of valve noise is always preferred over the loping of a burned valve(s).

Consider the idea of starting the car up every now and then. A fire department used to fast idle its trucks for 15 to 20 minutes periodically while they sat for weeks between calls. After a while they found this practice was leading to ring jobs—not preventing them. Often you'll hear someone say how he or she drives around the block a few times every week or runs the engine until the temperature gauge is warm. A few blocks or even a few miles does nothing but draw condensation into the crankcase. The condensation combines with carbon dioxide to form carbonic acid, which assaults the oil and internal engine surfaces. And the temperature gauge only indicates water—not oil—temperature at only one spot in the engine.

Starting the engine just for 10 seconds to drive out of the garage to polish the car is murder if the car, then polished, is driven back into the garage to sit. If the engine starts, the car should be driven the equivalent of 20 miles on the highway to equalize the temperature of the cylinder block, head, and manifold. An old mechanic's test was to place a hand on the bottom of the oil pan. If the pan was hot, the car had been driven enough.

The only thing worse than the practice of "warming up" the engine now and then is the one, usually seen at shows involving the early brass-age models, of slowing the idle until the participants are able to count off the engine's revolutions. At this point, the cylinder walls are certainly starving for oil and the bearings are being galled.

If the patience and perserevance of other honest endeavors are applied to the rebuilding and maintenance of your Packard, all will end well.

Ask the Man Who Owns One

25

Sources

On the following pages are listed businesses that have supplied parts and services for my giant pandas. Many people either not involved with or new to the resurrection of old automobiles might question the soundness of mailing often substantial checks to strangers on the other side of the continent (or pond, remembering our foreign Packard fanciers). Yet I have found these suppliers of parts and services, on the whole, a fine and decent bunch. Many could only be described as "gentlemen and scholars." Perhaps that is understandable from those serving fellow aficionados of the car "built for gentlemen by gentlemen."

Considering the number of women Packard enthusiasts—lasting quality knows no bounds—that famous phrase from the company perhaps should be amended. But I think that is surely understood. Even the slightest modification of phrases of antiquity is revisionist history. An abundance of revisionist history and myth are among the reasons that I am most eager to ground this tome in fact. Let the only revisionist history be that of improvements of our Packards made possible by modern chemistry and technology.

There are great and vast parts sources, private hobbyists, swap meets, salvage yards, and junkyards. The first two can be readily found listed within the pages of *Hemmings Motor News, Old Cars Weekly,* and the Packard Club's *Cormorant News Bulletin.* Salvage yards and junkyards are generally best found by looking through your local telephone directory, or even by just driving off into the sticks. There are of course, great well-organized enclaves of recycled automobilia, generally calling themselves "Classic Parts" or "Restorers and Dismantlers," and pricing their wares accordingly. Junkyards, large and small alike—the most elegant of which might be referred to as wrecking yards—just might have a hulk ready, willing, and able to donate an organ needed to keep your favorite car alive or bring it back to life.

Roger Abbott
1199 South El Molino
Pasadena, CA 91106
(213) 795-6113

Mr. Abbott sells engine compartment decals, rubber parts, rear view mirrors for 1941-47 Clippers, and all manner of odds and ends; many unavailable elsewhere.

John A. Conde
1340 Fieldway Drive
Bloomfield Hills, MI 48013
(313) 338-4478

John Conde supplies original automotive literature amassed through the years as historian of American Motors, and from collecting material since 1945.

Denman Rubber Manufacturing Company
Warren, OH 44482
(216) 898-2711

Denman makes quality tires. After thousands of miles, the 6.50 × 16s on my 1940 One Twenty still have nearly new tread. Denman is an old, established tire maker, yet its prices are no more than and often are lower than many of the newer firms appearing like toadstools overnight, attracted by the growing vintage automobile marketplace's lure of lucre. For further savings, consider buying "blems" (seconds) with almost imperceptible cosmetic defects (never structural). You'll save 20 percent on such tires. One such "blem" was that the 3 in the "32 lbs. maximum (tire pressure)" was reversed. Because those raised black characters on the black section of the tire are little larger than this type, the car will likely roll indefinitely with its "blem" undiscovered. And of course, there's something nice about buying tires from a tire company in Packard's hometown.

Bill Hirsch
396 Littleton Avenue
Newark, NJ 07103
(201) 642-2404

A supplier of quality upholstery, paint, and trim pieces, Mr. Hirsch has nearly all the Packard paint charts. He can match, as nearly as is possible to do so, the factory colors. It should be remembered, however, that Packards are not Fords. For a few dollars extra, Packard would, to quote Mr. Hirsch, "match your wife's lipstick." Yet too often we've seen brigades of "is that an original color?" clipboard wielders assaulting an authentic Packard with their ignorance. Obviously you wouldn't paint a carefully rebuilt 1937 Packard a Sixties' tangerine metal-flake or Fifties' candy-apple red, but a "period" color other than one of the dozen or so "factory" colors is fine. It also shows a certain strength of character, probably why many of the best Packards—and cars in general—stay away from the stifling atmosphere of the show circuit.

There is no such thing as a "correct" color for a Packard; there are only factory and special-order colors. If you insist on the factory-mandated approach, buy a Model A Ford. This same holds true for upholstery fabric. You would want to use the sort of material available from the mills during your Packard's era (not polyester), but any shade of period fabric is correct in a Packard. Many of the Custom Super-8 One-Eighties are, as the name suggests, "customs." There were only a handful of factory fabrics. My One-Twenty was painted factory Packard Blue because I like the color and wanted as "thoroughly a Packard" Packard as possible. But it was a tough decision. There were many other tempting colors, both factory and period.

Egge Machine Company
8403 Allport Avenue
Sante Fe Springs, CA 90670
(213) 945-3419

Egge's slogan is "The parts house for old cars." They serve all makes (Packard included) engine and chassis parts. The parts have either been acquired or produced by Egge.

Five Points Classic Auto Shocks
17121 Palmdale
Huntington Beach, CA 92647
(714) 842-0707

Five Points rebuilds all types of ancient shock absorbers, including Lovejoy and Houdaille, for all makes of cars. Five Points has the tooling required for this specialist work. They quickly rebuilt my One-Twenty's fifth rear shock without a hitch, and for a fair price.

Harnesses Unlimited
Box 435
Wayne, PA 19087
(215) 688-3998

Makers of top-quality wiring harnesses for many makes, Harnesses Unlimited specializes in Packards. My 1940 Packard uses one of their harnesses; everything was complete and as promised. Replacing an automobile's complete wiring system is no single afternoon's chore, but once installed, a great source of likely problems is neatly ended. Harnesses Unlimited workers are sticklers for authenticity. Each wire is surrounded by durable PVC. Offering advice and tips, Leighton Bates of Harnesses Unlimited went far beyond the call of duty. Excellent firm.

Kanter Auto Products
76 Monroe Street
Boonton, NJ 07005
(201) 334-9575

Kanter handles new old stock (NOS) and reproduction Packard pieces. Fred and Dan Kanter's father was a Packard-driving, liquor-company executive. Through the years, the Kanter brothers have bought out many entire Packard dealer inventories. They sell parts for other cars, including Facel-Vegas, but Packards are their favorite. The Kanters can hardly be accused of giving things away, but then they know their parts. Appropriately, their business is in an old silk factory built in the early 1800s.

John A. Kepich
8231 Orchard Road
Concord-Painesville OH 44077
(216) 352-7990

John Kepich sells Packard parts from parts cars, dealer inventories, and buying trips. Like many suppliers, he's always unearthing new caches. We wonder when it's going to end. Fortunately, new reproduction parts are coming onstream. John works hard to see that parts go out when promised.

>Metro Moulded Parts
>P.O. Box 33098
>Minneapolis, MN 55433
>(612) 521-0123
>(Shop)
>3031-2nd Street North
>Minneapolis, MN 55411

Metro produces quality reproduction rubber parts for many old cars, Packard included. Their prices are reasonable, and availability and shipping are excellent. In the case of an unusual Packard (or other) model, Metro will even strike a mold from the original piece. Again, a thoroughly helpful and enthusiastic bunch. Metro's catalog is one of the most helpful dollars you'll spend.

>Packard Farm
>R.R. 9, Box 514
>Greenfield, IN 46140
>(317) 462-3124

I can't say enough good things about this Packard Farm. It might be a disservice to the others listed here, but if I had to pick a single "best" supplier, the nod would go to Packard Farm. Their honesty and openness is refreshing. Several times they went far beyond the call of duty in their readiness to help a fellow automobile rejuvenator. Packard Farm sells parts from dealer stocks, parts cars, and quality reproduction items.

>Packard Parts Unlimited
>Box 823
>Groveland, MA 01834
>(617) 372-9912

This listing is stictly a sentimental memorial. Mr. Roland M. Crawford died several years ago, and his survivors sold off his business. I never met Mr. Crawford. Maybe it's just as well. I did hear his marvelous, often irascible, voice, and envision the archtype Packard man on the other end of the wire. He was honest and as good as his word. He wanted no misunderstandings. Rather than sell me some sheet-metal item, he explained that he preferred to sell such pieces to those customers who dropped by in order to avoid any misunderstanding (i.e., one person's "good, used," is another's "junk;" one person's "slight surface rust" is another's "pitted").

Once, early in my first Packard's rejuvenation, I asked him to send a particular item as soon as possible. The reply was typical Roland Crawford: "Mr. Scott, it's cold. It's windy. The part you want is under 3 to 4 feet of snow and ice. Now if you can wait until April, when it thaws, I'll go out and dig it out."

A knowledgeable and enthusiastic Packard man, Doug Judy, told me that Mr. Crawford had worked in a lumberyard for most of his life. When he retired, his boss gave him his cared-for, though tired, 1941 One-Eighty. Mr. Crawford immediately fell under its spell, and he began the search for replacement parts. In those years after the demise of Packard, yet before any real and widespread interest in old cars other than bonafide "horselesses" and brass and Edwardian era antiques (and of course ponderous heavy classics like Duesenberg Js and Packard Twelves of the early Thirties), finding parts was much more difficult than today. Mr. Crawford not only found the parts he needed, but enough to set up a full-scale business. (A similar scenario in 1960 led the Kanter brothers from parts for their first Packard to a large, full-time concern.)

Dealing with Mr. Crawford somehow enhanced the Packard experience. On several occasions, smaller parts from Packard Parts Unlimited came to me in cigar boxes: Thompson & Company Palmas "Fine Quality Cigars," and EW "The Masterpiece of Fine Cigars" Top Stone Bouquet. But somehow you already knew that Mr. Roland Crawford enjoyed good cigars. He had to; he was an old-line Packard man. So I wasn't surprised when some of the parts arrived so crated. Indeed, I still have those cigar boxes.

Mr. Crawford's stationery was the best of any—including Packard's—that I've ever seen. In the upper left-hand corner was PACKARD, in script. Below that was the finest slogan of any manufacturing concern: Ask the Man Who Owns One. Below that was the Packard family crest. Example of his correspondence reminds us what inflation, growing interest, scarcity, and time have done to the prices of old automobiles. Just a few days later, I bought my 1940 One-Twenty, and just several blocks from home.

People like Mr. Crawford have been the real boon of all my dabbling in wheeled relics. I think that, wherever Mr. Crawford is now, he is driving a suitable chariot, Top Stone Bouquet or Thompson & Company Palma clenched firmly between his teeth.

>Lynn Steele
>Route 1
>Denver, NC 28037
>(704) 483-9343

Like Metro Moulded Parts, Lynn Steele produces an array of rubber items for nearly all American automobiles (except Fords). Mr. Steele originally did much the same thing in Michigan in the automobile industry that he does for old car renovaters today. His thorough knowledge of the exact part for each model of every make, in addition to Packard, is remarkable. Everything said of Metro applies to Mr. Steele.

Tel. 617-372-9912

PACKARD PARTS UNLIMITED
Box 823
GROVELAND, MASSACHUSETTS 01834

Ask the Man Who Owns One

6/13/75

Name — MICHAEL SCOTT
Address — 123-B REEDER ST.
EASTON, PA. 18042

ITEM	YEAR 1940	MODEL 120	BODY NO.	PRICE
Pair Horns, 1938-40 (Same)				22.50 P. Pd.
Credit, returned (1) Ex. Pipe				15.00
Bal. Due				7.50
Post & Ins.				1.95
				9.45 DUE

Mr. Scott:-

    I cannot understand the problem with Ex. Pipe. I have sold many of these with no problem. ALL 120 Models use 2-1/4" pipe and there is no reason it would not fit in Manifold. Of course you have to use the original mounting flange, which you may not have.

Thank you for your inquiry regarding Packard parts. Shipping charges are not included in the following price list. All items of size and weight not accepted by Parcel Post will be shipped Express, shipping charges, collect. Estimated postage + handling

No parts accepted after 30 days.
No parts returned without written permission. Shipping expenses, plus a 20% handling charge on all returned goods.

Packard

Ask the Man Who Owns One

PACKARD PARTS UNLIMITED

Box 823

GROVELAND, MASSACHUSETTS 01834

Tel. 617-372-9912

7/13/74

Name: Mike Scott
Address: 121 East Wayne Ave.
Easton, Pa. 18042

ITEM	YEAR	MODEL	BODY NO.	PRICE

Sir:-

Reference your letter, Packard wanted.
I have the following:

1940-120 Packard sedan, sidemounted, trunkrack, excellent interior, presently registered, running, and with current Massachusetts Inspection. Needs work on Running Boards, and fenders. Engine, good.

$2500.00

Thank you for your inquiry regarding Packard parts. Shipping charges are not included in the following price list. All items of size and weight not accepted by Parcel Post will be shipped Express, shipping charges, collect. Estimated postage + handling

No parts accepted after 30 days.

No parts returned without written permission. Shipping expenses, plus a 10% handling charge on all returned goods.

Steve's Studebaker-Packard
South Second Street
Napa, CA 94559
(707) 255-8945

The injustice of singling out a "best" Packard source is too apparent when I recall my dealings with Steve's S-P. Steve is honest and direct, and runs his business accordingly. A degreed industrial engineer, Steve's knowledge of Packards and automobilia in general is astounding and goes far beyond that of an intelligent, well-educated mechanic. Earlier in his career Steve was the service manager for a Cadillac dealer. His business is mostly, but for a few mechanical items, postwar Packards: NOS, NORS, rebuilt and used parts. If like me and many Packard fans, you have also fallen under the spell of the quality products of Lionel, you have all the more reason to deal with Steve. Also, no one knows more about Ultramatics than he. His prices are reasonable, and his savvy priceless.

Terrill Machine Company
Route 2, Box 61
DeLeon, TX 76444
(817) 893-2610

Terrill Machine Company sells mostly engine and tune-up components. Reasonable prices and good service.

Jim Hill
P.O. Box 547
Goodwell, OK 73939
(405) 349-2763

Jim advertises as "still trying to be your cheapest source of parts: timing chains for most 1935-54; rod inserts for 110s, 120s, 1948-54 8s; mains for 110s and 120s; gasket sets for 1940-1950 '356' and the 1948-54 '288' and '327'."

Robert Zimmerman
365 St. Leger Avenue
Akron, OH 44305
(216) 784-7155

Mr. Zimmerman sells what is called "literature" by those embroiled in raising wheeled Lazaruses: Ancient magazine full-page color ads, sales brochures, and owner's manuals. Mr. Zimmerman knows his stuff, which he prices reasonably, and is a pleasure to deal with.

The Packard Club (Packard Automobile Classics)
Box 2808
Oakland, CA 94618

The Club publishes a beautiful and professional color quarterly called *The Packard Magazine*. Mr. Richard M. Langworth is the capable editor, bringing a unique blend of information, humor, and esoterica to each issue. After seeing so many of the various club (Packard and other marque) publications, my vote for the one automobile magazine air-dropped to my desert island to remind me of some of industrialized civilization's more interesting achievements from the first half of the twentieth century would be the Packard Club's quarterly. Each month the club sends *The Cormorant News Bulletin*: cars for sale, parts, services, personal glimpses, members' cars, etc., all enjoyably presented by editor Linda Seebach. Before you do anything, even if you haven't found your Packard as yet, I recommend that you write the club regarding the current subscription price.

Armand's Auto Upholstery
2660 North Main Street
Walnut Creek, CA 94596
(415) 934-4373

Armand is a third-generation auto upholsterer in car-crazed California. At one time or another, Armand has owned a brace of Kaiser Darrins, a 1948 Packard convertible, a 1938 Eight (120) convertible, and a 1940 One-Eighty 1807 (138" wheelbase) limousine, and others I can't even recall. So car oriented a native Californian is he, that Armand even relaxes at his vacation cabin in the Sierras, out in the garage, upholstering cars. His shop and employees reflect this single-mindedness to a craft, and it appears before long that his son will make it four generations of auto upholsterers. I suspect that in a few short decades from now, our methanol-powered steam and electric/magnetic cars will be upholstered by a fifth-generation of this family. Armand's friends at nearby Classic Auto Body & Paint, 1401 Stradella Court, Walnut Creek, California 94596 (415) 938-3131, can offer a befitting exterior for Armand's upholstery.

W.B. Transmission
2780 Cloverdale Avenue
Concord, CA
(415) 932-1234

Owner/operator Wayne Ballerstein is a friend and a first-class mechanic of long standing. Wayne worked and headed the motor pool on island after island in the Pacific theater of World War II. After the war, he worked for a large Packard agency (then a Hudson outlet). When Hudson was dying, Wayne still ran a franchised Hudson garage, and set up winning Hudsons for racing in the later Forties and early Fifties. He also has worked in a number of General Motors' dealers' shops, and is the one the nationally advertised chain transmission shops turn to for help with a difficult mechanism. But don't call on a professional—whether Wayne or someone else—and expect them to scout all the pieces you need and do the intricate and hard work. It is better to have parts sources lined up well before turning over the job to skilled hands. You'll free a highly trained professional like Wayne to devote his time to the actual task of rebuilding, and certainly save time and expense. Wayne does not run a "restoration shop." Not to disparage the work of many an honest and capable "ground-up" rebuilder, Wayne is the sort who usually winds up correcting the glossed but shoddy mechanical shortcomings of "high-point" restorations. He is most in his element when the customer drops off just the engine, transmission, or rear axle requiring attention.

If this isn't enough, Wayne's brother, Bud, can offer nonpareil painting. And John Williams, master of the welding torch and the astute observation, will solve anything.

Hemmings Motor News
Box 100
Bennington, VT 05201

Hemmings brings you twelve issues of ads, many pictures, cars for sale, parts, literature, services, tools, products—everything you could possibly need or imagine needing to revitalize an old automobile. Write for current subscription rates. If you subscribe to no other publications, get Hemmings and join the Packard Club. Even if you are just interested in cars in general—whether half-century-old Auburns or Triumphs of the Sixties—the pictured car-for-sale ads are unrivalled in the automotive press for entertainment value. Hemmings Motors News also publishes *The Vintage Auto Almanac* for the owners and rebuilders of all brands of automobiles: Vintage Auto Almanac, Box 945, Bennington, VT 05201.

Old Cars Weekly
700 East State Street
Iola, WI 54990

Old Cars Weekly is a tabloid with classified cars for sale, parts, services, hobby news, auction hysteria, and occasionally, dreadful downhome politik. Interesting auto history footnotes and do-it-yourself counseling offer balance, though.

Steve Messenger
1340 Warren Street
Martinez, CA 94553
(415) 228-2763

A patient, systematical, and relentless repairman of our favorite automobiles, ancient radios, and houses, seemingly no aspect of static or moving electro-mechanical device is beyond Steve's ken. Steve needs no further advertising beyond word of mouth. This listing is a thank you for much first-class craftsmanship over the years. Steve's favorite Packards are, like those of many knowledgeable owners and mechanics alike, the eminently driveable prewar models, especially the nimble six and well-balanced One-Twenty. An associate, Henry DeVries, brings an equally long and adroit career as machinist par excellence to our shores, epitomizing Dutch finesse with every piece of metal touched. Though backlogged with contracts for the dreaded military-industrial complex, Henry seems happiest when machining some bit of Packard quality. He drives an equally amazing 1941 One-Sixty club coupe.

Packard Parts West
1810 Monterey Drive
San Bruno, CA 94066
(415) 589-8992

A ceramic engineer for a manufacturer of electronic audio and visual power tubes, Don Figone's sideline is that of supplier of Packard parts and esoterica, predominately for the 1940-42 models. Don knows as much about these premiere road cars as possible. He has owned at one time or another nearly every chassis and body style, at present including a 1940 One-Twenty Darrin victoria with less original sin than even Packard and Dutch Darrin envisioned.

Hibernia Auto Restorations
Hibernia, NJ

Robert Turnquist and his staff freely offered their advice over the phone and through the mail in the early days of my 1940 Packard's exploratory surgery.

Strahle's Garage
Lehigh Drive
Easton, PA 18042
(215)253-3758

Bill Strahle is the zenith of that school known as shade-tree mechanics. His bucolic owner/operator garage across the lane from the over 150-year-old* Delaware Canal is a mid-twentieth century version of Longfellow's Village Blacksmith. Although a workday garage and not a high-toned restoration shop, Bill has access to a top-notch machine shop and can work miracles (for which I'll vouch).

---

*Linda Rogers, reference staff member—precisely, young adult specialist of the Contra Costa (California) Library System—was of considerable aid in determining the age of this landmark.

Ask the Man Who Owns One

Epilogue

Scarcely had I broken in my newly rebuilt 1940 One-Twenty when, in February, 1976, I ran Pennsylvania to New York to North Carolina to Northern California in five days, without overdrive (which was added on the West Coast). The trip was entirely without mechanical mishap. The only incident was a warning for slight weaving as I attempted to retrieve my camera from the back seat while pacing a fast freight train for an action shot as we raced over the desert outside Phoenix.

Many times during the cross-continent drive was I to thank equally Packard engineering and Bill Strahle's mechanical ability as the $300 in traveler's checks to my name went solely for gasoline, food, and curios.

Stopping for gas on the Tennessee side of the Blue Ridge summit on I-40 (formerly the more poetic if less smooth Route 66), the pump lady, who must've noticed my Pennsylvania plate, asked where I was headed. "California," I answered. And in that automatic tone of so many who deal with the public day in and day out, she bade me farewell with a "We'll see you." Through the years I've wondered what on earth she meant.

I could never help noticing the juxtaposition of the Strahles' picturesque Easton, Pennsylvania establishment, like one of the small, evocative sketches seen in autumn issues of *The New Yorker,* with the dormant yet surprisingly well-preserved Delaware Canal. Considering that the power of a single horse moved the weight of a loaded modern tractor-trailer truck over its placid waters, it might not be a bad idea to awaken the simple, graceful canal (though substituting electric, methane, or hydrogen power for Dobbin).

In the opening pages of my 1940 Packard's owner's manual, it is suggested that Packard owners were looked to by other motorists as "the better class of drivers," and expected, as such, to set an example of safe and considerate driving. Equally, many among us would like to see our industry again lead international competition by quiet, quality example—as Packard did. This is not vulgar nationalism, but a civilizing neighborhood pride in the world city. This pride goes beyond the quality of technology, and into its very nature.

Fossil-fuel burning is a dead-end road by any definition in anyone's book. Methanol-powered automobiles* are already performing smoothly and cleanly. Proponents include Bank of America, the State of California, Ford Nissan, and Volkswagen—among others. An ongoing search for socially and environmentally acceptable wheels seems never ending as the pragmatists among us realize that cars must be fool-resistant, if not foolproof.

Methanol combustion yielding aldehydes must be treated for a wholly clean power source, electric cars to date lack range, asbestos in brakes, clutches, and schoolroom insulation—the refinement continues. By 1980, Daimler-Benz had already built prototypes of a hydrogen-powered car, which seems one of the best steps in the right direction yet. This heartening news holds promise for concerned motorists everywhere.

It's just that some of us would rather have benign Packards.

---

*The irrepressible Justin Roberts of the Contra Costa *Times* (Walnut Creek, California) must be thanked for his campaign to see more alcohol go into cars than drivers.

The Edward Benson Family's partially reassembled 1940 One-Twenty. Photo by Kay Gill.

Ask the Man Who Owns One

Further Reading

Boulton, David *The Grease Machine: The Inside Story of Lockheed's Dollar Diplomacy.* New York: Harper & Row, 1978.

Cooke, Alistair *Alistair Cooke's America.* New York: Alfred A. Knopf, 1973.

Douglas, William O. *Towards a Global Federalism.* New York: New York University Press, 1968.

Forbes. Various issues. New York: Forbes Inc.

Fortune. Various issues. Chicago: Time, Inc.

Gray, Robert *Rolls on the Rocks: the History of Rolls-Royce.* Salisbury, England: Compton Press Ltd., 1971.

Jerome, John *The Death of the Automobile: the Fatal Effect of the Golden Era 1955-1970.* New York: W.W. Norton & Company, Inc., 1972.

Jane's All the World's Aircraft. London, England: Sampson Low, Marston & Co., Ltd., 1942-45.

Kimes, Beverly Rae, ed. *Packard, A History of the Motor Car and the Company.* Princeton, New Jersey: Princeton Publishing, Inc., 1978.

Langworth, Richard, ed. *The Packard Cormorant.* Various issues. Contoocook, New Hampshire: Dragonwyck Publishing Inc.

Madsen, Axel *Private Power: Multinational Corporations for the Survival of Our Planet.* New York: William Morrow and Company, Inc., 1980.

Moritz, Michael and Seaman, Barrett *Going For Broke: The Chrysler Story.* Garden City, New York: Doubleday & Co., Inc., 1981.

Mostert, Noel *Supership.* New York: Alfred A. Knopf, 1974.

Rothschild, Emma *Paradise Lost: the Decline of the Auto-Industrial Age.* New York: Random House, 1973.

Sandstrom, Gösta E. *Man the Builder.* New York: McGraw-Hill Book Company, 1970.

Stein, Ralph *The American Automobile.* New York: Random House.

Stern, Michael and Jane *Auto Ads.* New York: Random House, 1978.

Yates, Brock *The Decline and Fall of the American Automobile Industry.* New York: Empire Books, 1983.

Index

Index

A
air-conditioning, first automotive, 125
American Motors, 176
Anthony, Earl C., 17, 42-44
automatic spark advance, 2
Avanti, 176

B
Bentley, 26, 102, 183
Benz, 1, 6
Bijur chassis lubrication, 82, 108
Blackmore, George, 8
Bodman, Henry, 142
brougham, 1941 160 sport, 149
Brunn All-Weather Cabriolet, 111
Brunn Touring Cabriolet, 111, 115
Brunn touring cabriolet, 1938, 114
Brunn touring cabriolet, 1939, 118
Bugatti, Ettore, 141
Buick Skylark, 169
Buick, 10, 33, 37, 39, 41, 78, 102, 125, 141-42, 153, 166.

C
cabriolet, 1939 Twelve Brunn, 117
Cadillac Eldorado, 169
Cadillac, 10, 12, 16-17, 33, 36, 37, 125, 142, 146, 166, 177
convertible, 105, 109-111, 120, 162
convertible, 1950 Super Deluxe Packard, 167
convertible, 1951 Packard, 167
Cord, Lycoming, 82
coupe, 1927 Twelve convertible, 111
Crosley, 153
Curtiss-Wright, 176

D
Dagmar, 37
Daimler, 1, 102, 183
Daimler-Benz, 142-43, 176
Darracq, 15
Darrin victoria, 125, 146, 154
Darrin, 1938 One-Twenty, 122
Darrin, Dutch, 121, 124, 149
Darrin, Kaiser, 124
Darrin, the Packard, 121
De Dion-Bouton gasoline tricycle, 1
De Dion-Bouton, 7
De Lorean, John Z., 173
De Palma, Ralph, 6, 32
Decauville, 15
Delco-Remy, 142
Depression, weathering the, 82
Derham, 69
Dietrich, 69
Dietz oil auto lamp, 7
Doble Steamers, 6
Dodge, 12
Doud, William, 12
du Pont, Pierre, 37
Duesenberg Model A, 39
Duesenberg, 7
Durant, William Crapo, 10, 33, 37
Dynaflow, 165
Dyryea brothers, 3

E
Easamatic, 168
electric cars, 6
electromatic clutch, 153
electronic clutch, 153

F
Ferrari, Enzo, 141
Ferry, Hugh, 41, 168
Fiat, 15
Fleetwood town car, 1920 Twin Six, 31
Fluid Drive, 153
Ford Thunderbirds, 8
Ford, 12, 17, 33, 153
Ford, Henry, 10, 35, 69
Ford, Model T, 6
Franklin, 17
Fuller, Alvan T., 18

G
Gar Wood Miss America, 142
gearshift pattern, H
General Electric, 12
General Motors, 1-2, 10, 12, 33, 37, 41, 69, 82, 102, 129, 142, 154, 172, 178, 183
Gilman, Max, 41
Graves, Bill, 170
Gray Wolf, 3, 6, 15-17,

H
H gearshift pattern, 2
H transmission, 8
Hall, Elbert, 33
Henney-Packard, 1942, 156
Hispano-Suiza, 33, 177
Holbrook, 69
Honeywell, 8
Hudson, 12, 33, 146, 153, 168
Hupp, 153
Hydramatic, 165

I
Indianapolis Speedway, 32
Isotta Fraschini, 39, 141, 177

J
Joy, Henry Bourne, 10, 12, 22, 32, 41
Judkins, 69

K
Kahn, Albert, 10, 12, 41
Kahn, Julius, 10
Kettering, Charles, 33
Knudsen, Semon, 173

L
Lagonda, 102
landaulet, 1907 Model 30, 4
landaulet, 1918 Twin Six, 34
LaSalle, 74
LeBaron, 69
Leland, Henry M., 10, 33
Liberty aircraft engine, 26
Liberty engine, 32, 36, 144
limousine, 1910 Model 18, 14
limousine, 1912 Model, 48
limousine, 1914 Model 235, 24
limousine, 1937 Twelve formal, 112-13
limousine, 1940 formal, 130
limousine, 1942 180 formal, 155
limousine, 1946 Custom Super Clipper, 159
limousine, 1946 Custom Super Clipper, 160
limousine, 1946 Custom Super Clipper, 161
Locomobile, 35

M
Macauley, Alvan, 17, 22, 26, 32, 36, 41, 121, 161, 170
Mack, 35
Marriot, Fred, 6
Mason, George, 172
Maxwell, 17
McFarland, Forest, 173
Mercedes Grosser, 178
Mercedes, 15, 33
Model T Ford, 36
Morgan and Williams, 2
Mors, 7, 15
Murdoch, Jacob, 17
Murphy, 69
Mustang aircraft, 144

N
Nance, James, 41, 168, 176
Napier Saber, 142
Nash, 102, 146, 153, 168
Nash, Charles W., 37, 41
Nash-Kelvinator, 172
National Electric Lamp Company, 12
New York and Ohio Company, 1-2, 8, 12
Newberry, Truman, 12

O
Ohio Automobile Company, 2, 8, 10
Oldfield, Barney, 6
Oldsmobile Fiesta, 169
Oldsmobile, 10, 166
Oldsmobile, Ransom E., 10
Otis, Charles C., 9

P
Packard & Weiss, 2
Packard advertisements, 46-68
Packard airplane engines, 144
Packard annual report for 1934, 97-101
Packard Canadian plants, 120
Packard Caribbean, 1954, 171
Packard Cavalier, 168
Packard Clipper, the, 149, 154
Packard convertible, 105, 109-111, 120
Packard Darrin, 1941, 143
Packard Darrin, 1942, 143
Packard Deluxe Eight, 78
Packard Eight, 42, 69
Packard Electric Company, 1, 12, 120
Packard Engineering Building, Lehigh University, 2
Packard family history, 1
Packard hardtop, 1955 400, 174
Packard hardtop, 1956 Panama Clipper, 174
Packard Hawk, 1958, 175
Packard Light Eight, 81-82
Packard Model A, 1-2, 10
Packard Model B, 2
Packard Model C, 7-9
Packard model comparision table, 147
Packard Model F, 7, 12, 15
Packard Model G, 12
Packard Model K, 12
Packard Model L, 15-16
Packard Model N, 17
Packard Motor Car Company, 10
Packard Motor Company, 1940 annual report for the, 131-140
Packard One-Twenty, 1941, 148
Packard Panther Daytona, 1953, 170
Packard quality, 38
Packard Single Eight, 39
Packard Single Six, 39
Packard Six, 108
Packard Six, 22-42
Packard slogan, origin of the, 9
Packard Standard Eight, 81
Packard stockholder's booklet, Depression-era, 92-101
Packard stockholders, message to, 107
Packard Super-8, 125
Packard Thirty prototype, 17
Packard Twelve, 141
Packard Twin Six, advertisement for, 27
Packard Wire and Cable Division of General Motors, 2
Packard, finding parts for a, 180
Packard, James Ward, 1-2, 6-8, 12, 15-16, 41
Packard, rebuilding tips for a, 182

INDEX

Packard, sources of parts for a, 186
Packard, Warren, 1
Packard, William Doud, 1, 48
Packard-Henney, 1942, 157
Packard-powered airplanes, 145
Packard/Rolls-Royce Merlin, 144
Packard-Weiss, 8
Packardbakers, 120
Panhard et Levessor, 7
Panhard, 15
Patrician, 166
Peerless, 16-19, 36
phaeton, 1911 Model 30, 15
phaeton, 1929, 41
phaeton, 1931, 76-78
phaeton, 1933, 83
phaeton, 1936 sport Twelve, 103
phaeton, 1936 Twelve sport, 106
phaeton, 1939 Twelve, 115
Pierce-Arrow, 17, 19, 35-36, 108, 120, 124, 149, 176, 178
Pontiac, 41, 102, 169
Powell, Dick, 121

R

Rambler, 17
Reed, Howard, 141
Reinhart, John, 173
Reo, 17
roadster, 1928, 71
roadster, 1930, 73
roadster, 1938, 80
roadster-coupe, 1933 Twelve, 84
roadster-coupe, 1934 Super Eighty, 84
Rockefeller, John D., 8
Rockefeller, William, 8
Rolls-Royce Merlin, 142
Rolls-Royce, 2, 26, 32-33, 102, 129, 143, 154, 176-79, 183

Rollson cabriolet, 146
Rollson Town Car, 111, 125
Rollson, 69
Romney, George, 176
Royce, Henry, 2, 6
runabout, 1913 MOdel 48, 23
runabout, 1929, 72

S

Sacco and Vanzetti, 18
Schmidt, Charles, 6, 12, 15, 17
Scott, Mrs. Lawrence N., 19
sedan, 1924 Model 226 Second Series, 35
sedan, 1925, 37
sedan, 1928, 70
sedan, 1934 Twelve Dietrich convertible, 84
sedan, 1936 Super Eight convertible, 109
sedan, 1936 Super Eight Dietrich convertible, 105
sedan, 1936, 104
sedan, 1937 One-Twenty, 110
sedan, 1938, 80
sedan, 1939 Super Eight, 119
sedan, 1940 One-Twenty touring, 127
sedan, 1941 One-Twenty, 152
sedan, 1941 Super Eight, 151
sedan, 1946 Custom Super Clipper, 162
sedan, 1949 Custom Eight, 1963
Simplex, 15
Sloan, Alfred P., 37, 153
spark advance, automatic, 2
Stanley Steamer, 6
steam cars, 6
Stoessel, Rudi, 121
Storrow, James J., 41
Stanley Steamer, 6
Stoessel, Rudi, 121
Storrow, James J., 41
Studebaker, 153, 168, 172, 176
Studebaker-Packard Corporation, 172

T

Teague, Richard, 173
Torsion-Level, 176
touring car, 1906 Model 24, 11
touring car, 1909 Model 30, 5
touring car, 1913, 25
touring car, 1916 Twin Six, 26
touring car, 1917, 33
touring car, 1925, 37
touring car, 1926, 40
town car, 1920 Twin Six, 30-31
Toyota Corolla, 7
transmission, automatic, 165
transmission, three-speed sliding gear, 2
Twin Six touring car, 26
Twin Six, 1920, 28-30

U

Ultramatic transmission, 166, 173

V

victoria, 1933, 83
victoria, 1939 Super Eight, 120
victoria, 1940 Darrin, 123
Vincent, Charles, 32
Vincent, Jesse, 26, 32-33

W

Weiss, George, 2, 9
White, 35
Wilcox-Rich, 125
Winton, 9, 15-16
Winton, Alexander, 7
Wright, Phil, 149

Y

Yates, Brock, 3

Other Bestsellers From TAB

☐ **INSTALLING SUNROOFS AND T-TOPS**

Here's the complete illustrated guide to customizing almost any vehicle with a sunroof or T-top! Written by an automotive customizing expert, it covers everything from factory-installed units to luxury aftermarket conversions to do-it-yourself techniques. Packed with practical advice and professional tips, it includes a complete listing of sunroof and T-top models and manufacturers for dual and electric sunroofs! 176 pp., 154 illus.
Paper $14.95   Book No. 2132

☐ **UNDERSTANDING AUTOMOTIVE SPECIFICATIONS AND DATA—Flammang**

This invaluable guide includes explanations of all the common figures and numerical concepts pertaining to automotive operation—specs, sizes, ratings, and more—you need to do tune-ups, overhauls, or adjustments, plus those dealing with engine size, power, economy, and body measurements. Hobbyists, amateur mechanics, and automobile enthusiasts will all find this guide indispensable. 208 pp., 123 illus. 7" × 10".
Paper $12.95   Book No. 2116

☐ **BASIC BODY REPAIR & REFINISHING FOR THE WEEKEND MECHANIC—Caiati**

With this illustrated, step-by-step repair and refinishing guide at your side, you can take on almost any basic bodywork and come out with professional-looking results! Using only a minimum number of hand or power tools you can keep your car in like-new condition... or refurbish and restore that old car to an almost-new appearance! There's even a list of sources for materials, tools, and parts. 192 pp., 230 illus.
Paper $11.95   Book No. 2122

☐ **CONVERTIBLES: THE COMPLETE STORY—Gunnell**

The first all-inclusive guide to convertibles that combines both technical and historical data, this is a volume that will be appreciated by automotive historians, collectors, restorers, and convertible enthusiasts alike. The author covers just about every convertible ever produced from the first open cars to be referred to as "convertibles" in 1928 to snappy new models from Ford, Buick, Chevrolet, and Pontiac. You'll get an expert's advice on how to buy, sell, and restore convertibles, find up-to-date ragtop values, even find out about homebuilt convertibles, how to join a car club, and more! 224 pp., 224 illus. 7" × 10".
Paper $20.50   Book No. 2110

☐ **THE 1960s SUPERCARS: A REPAIR AND RESTORATION GUIDE—Hossain**

This authoritative new handbook provides all the information that every '60s car enthusiast needs to choose, repair, restore, and drive or show his vehicle to best advantage. It's filled with professional tips, tricks, and techniques and gives a step-by-step guide to planning the restoration of your '60s car including listings of sources and suppliers for parts, tools, manuals, and more! 224 pp., 112 illus.
Paper $13.50   Book No. 2077

☐ **STUDEBAKER: THE COMPLETE STORY—William A. Cannon and Fred K. Fox**

Here is the most complete study ever undertaken on the Studebaker family, the company they founded, and the extraordinary vehicles they made... all in one beautifully bound, lavishly illustrated volume for collectors, car enthusiasts, automotive historians, and anyone who appreciates a true American success story! Filled with fascinating and little-known details, this book captures the tempo of the times and the personalities of the people who influenced the company throughout its operation. 352 pp., 354 illus. 11" × 8 1/2".
Hard $39.95   Book No. 2064

☐ **REBUILDING THE FAMOUS FORD FLATHEAD—Bishop**

Step-by-step, easy-to-follow instruction for restoring the Ford V-8 flathead engine. Covers every model made from 1932 right through 1953, including the Mercury version. Includes all the tables, data, schematics anyone needs to tear down, overhaul, and put the flathead back into like-new running condition... plus, it incorporates all the newest techniques and diagnostic testing available. 140 pp., 101 illus.
Paper $7.95   Hard $9.95
Book No. 2066

☐ **THE AUTOMOTIVE SECURITY SYSTEM DESIGN HANDBOOK—Daniel J. Gifford**

With the expert guidance provided by this state-of-the-art security handbook, you can not only protect your vehicles, but do it at a fraction of the cost of commercially made and installed security units! Absolutely nothing is left out from selecting the type of device needed to step-by-step construction installation procedures. You can rest assured that your vehicles are safe from thieves and vandals! 240 pp., 206 illus.
Paper $12.95   Hard $18.95
Book No. 1734

---

*Prices subject to change without notice.

Look for these and other TAB books at your local bookstore.

TAB BOOKS Inc.
P.O. Box 40
Blue Ridge Summit, PA 17214

Send for FREE TAB catalog describing over 1200 current titles in print.
Or Call For Immediate Service   1-800-233-1128